D1246903

ABOUT THE AUTHORS

DeWitt Copp is a novelist and documentary film writer and teaches history at St. Luke's School in New Canaan, Conn. His film "The Day Before Tomorrow," documenting the work of the Ballistic Research Laboratories in Aberdeen, Maryland, won a Film Media Award for 1960 and was produced by Warner Brothers. He attended Syracuse University, where he met his wife-to-be, Susan, and during World War II he flew with the Army Air Corps. He lives in Lewisboro, N. Y., with Susan and their two children, Peter and Wendy.

Marshall Peck, formerly a reporter and editor with the European edition of the New York *Herald Tribune*, now is cable editor of the New York edition. A graduate of Northeastern University and a veteran of World War II, he lives in Lewisboro with his wife, Huguette, whom he met and married in France, and two children, Marshall and Anne.

BETRAYAL AT THE UN

BETRAYAL AT THE UN

the story of Paul Bang-Jensen

by DeWitt Copp and Marshall Peck

THE DEVIN-ADAIR COMPANY,
NEW YORK 1963

Canadian Agents: Thomas Nelson & Sons, Toronto

Library of Congress Catalog Card Number: 61-6796

Manufactured in the United States of America
by H. Wolff

First printing, December 1960
Second printing, February 1961
Third printing, March 1963

This book is dedicated to the friends of Paul Bang-Jensen: Danes, Hungarians, Americans, and with particular gratitude to his friends in the U.N. whose names unfortunately must remain anonymous.

And let me speak to the yet unknowing world
How these things came about: so shall you hear
Of carnal, bloody and unnatural acts,
Of accidental judgements, casual slaughters,
Of deaths put on by cunning and forced cause,
And, in this upshot, purposes mistook
Fall'n on the inventors' heads: all this can I
Truly deliver.

HAMLET

CONTENTS

Introduction xi

To the Reader 2

Part One : Inquiry 3

Part Two : Betrayal 77

Part Three : Accusation 141

Part Four : Judgment 197

Part Five : Execution 237

Appendices

    1. Bang-Jensen's Memo to His Wife 277

    2. Letter of Recommendation from Niels Bohr 280

    3. Memo: Alleged Duties of the Deputy Secretary 282

    4. Memo Naming Bang-Jensen Keeper of Secret Register 283

    5. Telegram Sent to Prospective Witnesses 284

    6. Memo from William Jordan to Bang-Jensen 285

    7. Bang-Jensen's Letter to His Superior 285

    8. Report on Bang-Jensen from Jordan to Andrew Cordier 288

9. *Memo to Cordier from T. G. Narayanan, Who Passes* **289**

10. *Memos: Bang-Jensen Appeals to Cordier and Dag Hammarskjold* **290**

11. *Bang-Jensen Reports Sabotage to Hammarskjold* **293**

12. *Exchange of Memos Between Bang-Jensen and Ralph Bunche* **295**

13. *Memo: Hammarskjold Appeals to Alsing Andersen* **302**

14. *Memo: Dragoslav Protitch Orders Bang-Jensen to Surrender the List* **304**

15. *Letter Appointing Investigating Group* **305**

16. *Bang-Jensen's Letter to Tribunal Secretary* **306**

17. *Comments in Danish Press* **307**

18. *Arthur McDowell Replies to Eleanor Roosevelt* **309**

Notes **325**

Index **329**

INTRODUCTION

NOVEMBER, 1956, was a momentous and crucial month in the swiftly ebbing tide of the Western cause. The Hungarian nation, which had risen in courageous and inspiring revolt against its Soviet captors, was, for the fatal lack of action on the part of the United Nations, blasted into submission.

For a few golden moments the Hungarians had torn a gaping hole in the Iron Curtain. They faced the new day with surging hope. They faced it with a clear call for help. The call went unanswered. The hope withered and died. The hole was sealed up in blood, and the November winds fanned the smoldering rubble in the ruins of Budapest.

In that time of lost opportunity, few people in this country knew Paul Bang-Jensen. Yet, because of Hungary and its terrible significance, a little more than a year after the uprising was crushed, Paul Bang-Jensen's name would be known round the world.

Like the Hungarian Revolution, his fame and hour were brief; all too eagerly swept aside. As the inevitable machinery of events ground on, there were in this country sporadic press reports and infrequent magazine editorials concerning his ordeal. But in the passage of another year, the

American public had forgotten him. Like the revolution, too, his end was sudden and ruthless. His disappearance three days before Thanksgiving, 1959, again brought him to the front pages of the Western world, sharing equal space with the futile United Nations debate on the subject of Hungary and its wretched fate.

The finding of Paul Bang-Jensen's body on Thanksgiving Day morning, to all indications a suicide, gave the newspapers their final headline fling at him; the bitter story ended, the irony complete.

But not quite, not quite. There are places Paul Bang-Jensen will be remembered. There are those who cannot forget.

To the Hungarians, he was a martyr.

"When I saw the picture of his body lying in that path, he looked to me just like a Freedom Fighter I had seen killed . . . only on that man someone had placed a handful of flowers."

To his friends, he was someone apart.

"I tell you, Paul was all the things most of us wish we could be and never are."

To those who sat on the fringes of the matter, to those whose objectivity was influenced by stronger voices against him, he was a figure more pathetic than heroic.

"He was very romantic, you know . . . he exaggerated things all out of proportion. He was terribly vain, and his judgment was never good."

And to the towering forces of opposition, he was worse than a fool.

"He was a psychotic . . . a crackpot! He went off his rocker . . . an alcoholic . . . it's a tragedy."

On that one point, all seem to agree . . . "a tragedy!" But whose, mankind's, or simply Paul Bang-Jensen's?

BETRAYAL AT THE UN

TO THE READER

THE Danish given name of Povl Bang-Jensen has been rendered in this book as "Paul," excepting in the transcription of documents.

"Peter Marshall," as a character in the book, is a composite of the authors, DeWitt "Pete" Copp and Marshall Peck.

All characters in the book are real, and all names used are their real names. Anonymity has been preserved in certain cases; characters so protected are identified by initials or by a nameless reference such as "the FBI man."

Part One: Inquiry

CHAPTER 1

WHEN THE PLANE began its descent toward the cloud layer, Peter Marshall turned and pressed his face against the window, looking back toward the tail. He saw the lovely grace of the vertical fin against the yellowish December sky. Out of the corner of his eye, he could see the purple-black surface of the cloud-layer moving upward. There was beauty in the geometric angle of their approach to it.

Now in the insistent hiss of the slipstream and the heavy beat of the engines there came a name . . . a name from out of the cosmos . . . catching the swift rhythm of descent, a name that would not fade.

"Paul Bang-Jensen . . . Paul Bang-Jensen . . . Paul Bang-Jensen!"

Paul Bang-Jensen, may your tribe increase. No, that wasn't right. He had a tribe, a wife and five kids, but Paul Bang-Jensen was no more.

"Paul Bang-Jensen. . . . Paul Bang-Jensen . . . Paul Bang-Jensen."

The plane sank down toward the roiled cloud crest, and

now, looking back, he could see the slashing rays of the setting sun, casting great shafts of red and orange and yellow, reaching out in farewell, touching the tail fin . . . turning it for an instant to gold.

Downward . . . down, sucked into the restless incubus. The scene was gone, but the name stayed.

"Paul Bang-Jensen!"

A modern Hamlet? No, Hamlet was a man who could not make up his mind, but this Dane made up his mind . . . he made up his mind to kill himself. Had he? Did he? Peter Marshall didn't know, but that's what the papers said. That's what the police said . . . they should know.

The evil gray mass of the clouds spat its moisture on the window. He hoped they would be breaking out soon. There would be the first hint of lights through the torn underbelly of this mess, then they'd break free, throwing off the last tatters of the shroud. Then the long approach, and finally down . . . down upon the earth, and the December rain cold and clammy. Thank God, it wasn't ice. It was mild for December.

"Paul Bang-Jensen." Would the name stay in his head after he had left the plane? It had not been there when he left Chicago, but during the flight he had read the article in the magazine. Then he had read it over again.

How could a man who'd been dead for twenty-four to forty-eight hours be clean shaven?

That was a good question. It came back fiercely, triggered by the article . . . triggered by something out there . . . triggered by the ghost of Paul Bang-Jensen . . . the pitiful ghost . . . of a tortured man, who walked alone . . . the empty, wind-wracked, November streets . . . walked alone and his torture like the frenzied dance of autumn-driven leaves. Peace, to find peace! . . . to lie down!

"I think Bang-Jensen's story would make a terrific yarn . . . a good book."

"*Who is Bang-Jensen?*"

"*Danish fellow . . . worked at the U.N. He was the one who wouldn't turn over the names of the eighty-one Hungarians who wanted to keep their identities secret. Wouldn't give them to Hammarskjold or anyone at the U.N.*"

"*Good for him.*"

"*They canned him for it.*"

"*Dirty poker?*"

"*I dunno. Sounds dirty to me. I'd like to look into it.*"

Peter Marshall gave a great sigh of relief as the plane emerged suddenly from the overcast. He could see lights through the rain, even the shadowy shape of the earth.

He took the magazine from his lap and put it in the seat envelope in front of him. This magazine and its small article . . . it raised doubts . . . serious doubts. A man, a fighter . . . left home Monday . . . to go to work at CARE . . . no show . . . alive Monday. Tuesday? . . . Forty-eight hours at the outside, that means alive till Tuesday afternoon. Where? . . . clean shaven. But note . . . and gun in hand . . . and gun his own.

What are you trying to do, make a murder out of a "perfect suicide"? This is what the police called it. You're not a policeman.

But with a wife and five kids!

Marshall heard and felt the pleasant "thump" of the landing gear locking into place.

"Paul Bang-Jensen." The slipstream's cry was more moderate. But the name was still there.

Look, you're a writer. Is this something to write about? The death, that's the tragic climax, but what about the life?

Okay, it's worth looking into, but where do you start?

The plane's wheels scuffed the runway, then held solidly, the speed dissipating rapidly, the blue lights winking by.

I start right here . . . back on earth.

After greetings with wife and children had subsided to a normal sinking back into the pleasant routine of home, he called his editor friend, Tom. He did most of the talking, and Tom said, "It sounds good, I'll call you back."

Less than a half hour later the return call came.

"I've talked to Devin. Come in for lunch Monday. We'll have Clifford Forster there."

"Who's he?"

"He was Bang-Jensen's lawyer. Devin knows him well."

"Wonderful!"

He slept little that night. The name in the plane would not leave him. Even when he slept, it intruded. By morning he'd come to the definite conclusion, he was haunted by Paul Bang-Jensen.

CHAPTER 2

THEY SAT at a round table in a corner of the restaurant at the Prince George Hotel where they could talk in privacy, and Clifford Forster had no hesitation in talking.

A slightly built man with a large head, an expansive forehead and quite bald, he was, Marshall judged, in his middle forties. The lawyer tapped a cigarette gently against the table, before plunking it between his lips.

Marshall thought to himself, he's straight, he's smart, and he's on the right side of the fence. Legal counsel for the "League for the International Rights of Man," mighty high sounding.

Forster said, "Even though I have no doubt it was suicide, to me it was murder—murder in the political sense. When Helen Bang-Jensen called me that Tuesday morning to tell me he was missing, I told her to prepare for the worst." The voice was lightly pitched, coming in swift though quiet bursts.

"He was terribly depressed . . . I went abroad this last

summer, and before I left, I recommended that he see a psychiatrist."

"Why was that?"

"Well, twice he talked about killing himself. I said, 'Look, Paul, what can you solve by that? You've got Helen and those five wonderful kids. They depend on you. Never mind whether you're making a lot of money or not, they depend on you!' Well, he was beyond that. After his final dismissal from the U.N., he had a kind of breakdown. He'd stay in his room over week ends . . . he couldn't sign his own checks. He was crushed by the fact that after the U.N. had gotten rid of him, he couldn't find a good job."

"Why not?"

"Well, let's put it this way. He was unusually gifted and brilliant, but he was fifty years old, he was not an American, and the U.N. had put the kiss of death on him. Those are three pretty good strikes against a man in this day and age."

"And you have no doubt he killed himself?"

"None."

"What about this defector story that was in *Newsweek?*"

"Defector story? What's that?"

"As I understand it, back in November of '56, either during or right after the Hungarian uprising, Bang-Jensen was approached by a Soviet at the U.N. who wanted to defect to our side."

"I never heard that. What was his name?"

"I don't know. The idea was that Bang-Jensen would act as a go-between. The defector had information about Soviet infiltration at the U.N. Bang-Jensen talked to an American on the U.S. delegation. He in turn passed on the word to Washington. Somehow the whole scheme got back to the Secretariat, and the Soviet official got the bum's rush. Also I read later that Bang-Jensen tried to see Allen Dulles of C.I.A."

Forster put out his cigarette and with a quizzical shrug

declared, "He never said anything to me about it . . . I think I'd take it all with a large grain of salt. I'm not saying it's not so, but it's just something he never related to me."

"When did you see him last?"

"About two weeks before his death. I came back from Europe in September. I found him somewhat improved. He had been going to see a psychiatrist, but he was still gravely worried about the future. The CARE job, you know, was on a consultant basis, and it wouldn't last."

"And nothing came through for him?"

"Nothing. Our American system of hiring is not very enlightened."

"But his friends, he had lots of friends, didn't he?"

"Not lots, a few. We did what we could. He was offered a teaching position in Denmark, but he didn't feel qualified. More than that, here he had an American wife and five children being brought up as Americans. I don't think either he or Helen wanted to change that."

"It seems incredible that nothing turned up."

"It's sad . . . tragic. He was an unusually talented man, but his talents were quite selective and specialized. Do you know about his career in Washington before he came to the U.N.?"

"No."

"You should go talk to Henrik Kauffmann and Adolf Berle about that. Paul was an extremely dedicated civil servant. Neither he nor Helen were ever what you'd consider right-wing conservatives. He was a liberal in the European sense; an anti-Nazi and an anti-Communist. You know, even after they threw him out, he believed in the purposes of the U.N. Helen still does. I think of all the names they called him—and I assure you they tried to pin everything on him from alcoholic to homosexual—the one that hurt the most was 'McCarthyite.' "

"Who called him these names?"

"They came out of the U.N."

"And they fired him because he wouldn't hand over the names of the Hungarians who wanted their identities kept secret."

"Well, there's a lot more to it than that." Clifford Forster smiled. "There's a tremendous mass of documentation that you'll have to read. You should have a copy of the Gross Report . . . even though it's marked confidential."

"Do you have a copy?"

"I did have, but I turned all my files over to the Senate Investigator."

"What! What Senate Investigator? Why does the Senate want to know about Bang-Jensen!"

"I don't know," Forster replied mildly. "I think they're probably going to look into the whole U.N. aspect of the case."

"What's the investigator's name?"

"David Martin."

"Martin . . ." Peter Marshall stared at the table cloth and made a mark on it with his spoon, then he looked up at the lawyer. "Let's be frank about this . . . do you think there should be a book on Bang-Jensen?"

The attorney nodded, "Yes, I do, but it's not an easy story." He smiled. "You'll have to do a great deal of work to begin to understand it. When you've read all the documents, we can talk again."

"How do I get them, if you've handed them over to the Senate?"

"I can give you the names of people who will have most of them. The Gross Report, I'm not sure. I think there were only about twenty-five copies all told, and as far as the U.N. is concerned, it's still confidential."

"I have a few contacts. Maybe I can do a little nosing around."

"Good."

"You see this, then, as a story of injustice on a high level?"

"Thirty-eight stories high," the attorney quipped. "I only represented Paul before the Administrative Tribunal. That's analogous to our Supreme Court. That was his last appeal. I knew it was hopeless right from the start."

Peter Marshall walked with his head canted against a chill north wind toward the rising mass of Grand Central Station. Even though Clifford Forster had said a book was a good idea, that he would assist if he could, Marshall felt let down and disappointed.

What had he expected, anyway . . . a spy story?

Of course, just because Forster wasn't familiar with the defector side of the case didn't mean it had never happened. It wasn't likely a reputable magazine would print such a thing if there weren't some truth in it.

The big question: do we go on with it? And if we go on with it, to whom do we go next? Henrik Kauffmann, former Danish Ambassador to the United States? . . . Adolf A. Berle, Jr., former Assistant Secretary of State, long-time friend of Bang-Jensen's and his short-time lawyer? No, that's a part of the complication. You've got to read some of the documentation before you see them.

Forster had given him the names of two people who could supply him with some of the papers involved. He had a third source of his own that he was sure would be valuable. When he reached Grand Central, he would call all three. If he was lucky, he would take it as a sign and go on a bit further.

He would also call the Reverend Haskins of Great Neck, Long Island.

At the time of Bang-Jensen's death, Marshall had saved all the stories on the case that had appeared in the New York newspapers. On studying each account, he had reached the conclusion that one of the few consistencies found throughout was the name of the Bang-Jensens' pastor —the Reverend Stuart C. Haskins.

If he was going to pursue his investigation into the realm of documents, he was also going to pursue it into the area of human interest. To get to know a man he'd never met, he'd have to get to know the people who had been close to him.

CHAPTER 3

AT TEN O'CLOCK in the morning, Peter Marshall parked his car in front of a two-story, sepia-colored, modern colonial house. Its size made him wonder if he'd gotten the right place. He'd never met a parson who lived in a home quite as imposing and quite as upper-middle class as this. It appeared the Community Church of Great Neck was very much a going concern.

The front door was opened almost instantly to his ring. He saw before him a tall, slightly ministerial gentleman with a crop of sandy hair, gray at the temples. The eyes that held him with a steady appraising gaze toed down slightly toward a strong Roman nose.

The Reverend Haskins was dressed in comfortable tweeds, and Marshall judged him to be a man in his mid-fifties. His expression was on the severe side, but his words immediately reversed the feeling.

In a friendly, direct manner, Peter Marshall was ushered in, moving from central foyer to expansive living room. The decorations were conservative and modest. From the paintings on the walls, he gathered the family liked the out-of-doors. He noticed a big stack of records and a humorous photo of two grandsons.

They sat down and exchanged small talk for a moment, and then Stuart Haskins got down to business.

"Of course, you probably know that the U.N. started in Lake Success, at the Sperry Gyroscope location. This means that even today Great Neck is a U.N. community.

"Andrew Cordier, who is the Executive Assistant to Dag Hammarskjold, lives here and is a member of our Community Church. He's the number two man in the U.N.—David Vaughan, manager of the buildings, and Glenn Bennett, who is in charge of Visitors' Service, they live in the community and are also members.

"Bang-Jensen was never a member of the Church, nor is his wife Helen." Marshall wondered if he detected just a hint of pique in this last.

"I believe she had a Catholic background but managed to grow away from it. Their children all attend our church school, and they're a bright, adorable bunch.

"Of course Paul's background in Denmark undoubtedly had some influence on his attitude. The intelligentsia there are outside the church for the most part. That's pretty general—except for Baptism, Confirmation, Marriage, and Death. I would have described Paul as a nonconformist . . . a freethinker would be closer."

Peter Marshall wondered whether he should offer the counter opinion, expressed in the press by Helen Bang-Jensen and by two of the people he had seen the previous day, to wit—that the Dane had very strong religious convictions, that he was indeed a God-fearing man. He let it go, not wanting to interrupt.

"I suppose you know that Paul came to the U.N. after ten years with the Danish Embassy in Washington? He joined it with the same spirit that a minister feels when he gets the call. I know that from the things he said."

"When did you first meet him?"

"I came here in 1955, and of course, one of my first duties was to go around and visit everyone connected with the Church. I found the Bang-Jensens cordial although quite uninterested in church themselves. They did, however, want the training for their children, and whenever there was some kind of activity in which one or more of the children appeared, both parents would attend.

"I'm ashamed to say it, but I became aware of Paul's trouble at the U.N. through an editorial in the *Saturday Evening Post*. I must have been asleep at the switch.

"I went out and called on him. He told me he was awaiting a review of his case. He was not hopeful that it would be favorable, and in the meantime he was quietly looking for work of a temporary sort. He was nervous, but I wouldn't say highly so. He felt there was a possibility that the review would turn out well and that he could go back to the U.N. That was what he wanted more than anything.

"I asked him if he had any written material about himself. I said I'd pass it around to people who would be willing to go to bat for him. He gave me a résumé with some excellent endorsements. Do you have that?"

"No, I don't."

"Well, I'll give you a copy. We handled the whole thing very quietly . . . as you would in a men's club. We'd say, here's a deserving man. He has five children and wife, and he needs an income.

"There was no success, and presently, because of his strained economic situation, I began to look on my own. I thought of the Church World Service. It's a large organization that is set up to help refugees all over the globe. It maintains a large staff and its activities are extensive. I thought this would be a natural for Bang-Jensen. I went to the Reverend Norris Wilson who's its chief and told him all about Paul. Another influential layman here in town put in a good word and the situation looked promising.

"Then suddenly the whole matter was dropped—like that." Reverend Haskins lifted his hands, then let them fall.

"Apparently one of the members of the U.N. group that was reviewing the Bang-Jensen case was on the Board of the Church World Service. It was thought this member would be embarrassed by having to pass on Bang-Jensen's employment."

How compassionate, Peter Marshall sighed to himself, how divinely Christian.

"By that time Paul's morale was pretty well shattered," Haskins continued with a note of sadness. "He told me he could not take any type of demanding work that called for concentration and thought. The job he finally got at CARE was not demanding . . . but of course it paid less than half his former salary.

"Paul never sought me out for help, it was always I who went to him. Near the end he began coming to church. I would see him there . . . alone . . . weeping.

"On my own I appealed to Glenn Bennett for information on Paul's case. I was going on the premise that the U.N. would not dismiss him without cause.

"Bennett did not get any information, but he told me that Bang-Jensen was guilty of insubordination and that he was mentally unstable, not in his right mind . . . to some extent, psychotic. While this sort of report was continually being put out by U.N. people, I still saw nothing in writing.

"I had no reason to believe that Paul was unstable. He'd become unnerved, yes, but being unnerved by economic conditions and being mentally unbalanced are as different as night and day.

"This past summer I went to England and I didn't re-

turn until the first of September. I had no further contact
with the family until the tragedy."

"And how is Mrs. Bang-Jensen taking it?"

"Very well, I'd say. She's a very strong woman, and the
children are quite unusual. I think, financially, they're all
right for the time being. He left some life insurance, and
there's whatever he had from his severance pay. Their
friends have rallied around to help both morally and financially. College, of course, is a coming problem. I believe
some of the Hungarian organizations are planning to assist.
They see him as a martyr." [1]

Reverend Haskins picked up the two documents[2] beside
him on the couch. "The U.N. put these out after his death.
Glenn Bennett got them for me, and I'm sorry, but I can't
give them to you without his permission. They tell the U.N.
side of the story, and as I suspected, there really are two
sides to it. I only wish I'd known what I know now."

"Is there a Department seal on them so I'll know where
to apply for a set?"

"No, just the U.N. seal."

"That's rather odd."

"I'm not sure this is for the public."

"Then why put them out?"

"I don't know. Perhaps for people in the U.N. They're
dated December 22, 1959, and January 1, 1960."

Peter Marshall made a notation amongst the rapid scrib-
ble of notes he'd been taking. This is one post mortem I'll
damn well get, he said silently.

Waving the documents gently, the Reverend continued,
"Understand, this doesn't change my opinion of Paul Bang-
Jensen as a man. He desired to the last degree to be careful,
cautious, to save Hungarian refugees. However, it does
modify my opinion of his good judgment with regard to
human relations. I think he turned on people with whom
he disagreed . . . he gave me the feeling that he thought

he was always right . . . that his superiors were always wrong. He said there were Communist saboteurs in the Secretariat. That was his belief. In carrying the torch of the free world against Communism, he was a selfless man . . . some people have wanted to make a martyr out of him. True martyrdom, however, comes out of great sacrifice against forces over which the individual has no control. I don't believe Paul Bang-Jensen quite fits that description."

Peter Marshall sat in the rear of a delicatessen on Great Neck's main street, eating a hot pastrami sandwich, cooling his mouth with ale, and reflecting on his morning's work. The proprietor of the establishment, a happy, ebullient Greek, had ushered him to the rear of the store where there were several tables and accompanying wicker chairs. He was the only eating customer and he was pleased with the privacy.

The Reverend had certainly been open and candid. He, of course, like Forster had no doubt that it had been suicide. Both these men had identified the body.

"Mrs. Bang-Jensen told me that her husband had discussed suicide with her this last fall," the tall clergyman had said at the door. "He had told her he realized it was not the solution to anything. But I think anyone who could discuss it in that light would not put it out of his mind."

Peter Marshall opened his pad to a page where he had pasted Paul Bang-Jensen's photograph. He could describe the looks without trouble, the combination of sensitivity and stubborn resolve showing through eyes, and mouth, and chin. It was a handsome face, a distinguished face, a warm face; somewhat introspective, reserved. The wide mouth was touched by an enigmatic smile. His children must have seen that smile a lot, until near the end.

"They were a very close-knit family. He was crazy about his children and they returned his love."

All right, so he could describe the Dane's looks, but he had to admit, the character of this man was still more shadow than substance. At this early date, there were already contradictions, doubts. It would take a lot more searching before he would know his man for what he really was.

He was going to take a deep breath and telephone Helen Bang-Jensen. Her home couldn't be more than a mile or two from where he sat this minute.

Her voice was beautifully modulated, soft but wonderfully clear. He felt he wanted to reach out and touch it. He wanted to help, and knew he was helpless, knew he was calling not to comfort but to pry, to ask, to get his foot in the door.

"You must understand . . . I'm really exhausted, and the whole thing is extraordinarily complicated."

"I realize that, Mrs. Bang-Jensen, and I want to try and sort it out."

"Offers have been made to me to write a book about my husband. I don't want to, but I may change my mind. The libel laws in this country are very strong."

"I'm willing to buck that, so is my publisher."

"It's an ambitious project . . . I'm really the only person who knows the whole picture."

"Yes, and that's why it's so necessary for us to meet." The words were so much hash in his mouth.

"People are calling me all the time." It wasn't a complaint, just a statement of fact, with the weariness and strain showing through only a little. "I've just been on the phone for a half hour with a Danish correspondent. My mother-in-law in Denmark was so upset over a story that appeared in the Danish press saying that myself and the children were on relief. She was very distressed. The Danish correspondent told me this was a misunderstanding, but it's typical . . . I—I do wish you well. Why don't you call me again? . . . If a conflict arises, I'll try to help."

"I'm afraid several have already."

"In what regard?"

"This story of a Soviet defector—" it was the first thing he could blurt out.

"Where did you find that out!" There was surprise and a note of concern in her voice.

"It came out publicly in *Newsweek* magazine. I believe Robert Morris, the judge from New Jersey who was your husband's lawyer—"

"No, that's not right. Mr. Morris was never my husband's lawyer, as such. He did one or two things for him. The lawyers were Mr. Berle, Joseph Panuch, and Clifford Forster."

"I see, but the defector story is true, isn't it?" He tried to make it sound as though he knew it was true.

It worked. "My husband did not want it known," she answered quietly. "He said there was too much at stake. Even as late as this past fall, I asked him to write it down. He said he'd told the F.B.I. and he didn't want to put anything down. That was the end of his responsibility, which, of course, was right.

"I—I worked hard with my husband. I just couldn't meet you now. I know how difficult your work must be, and I'm fully appreciative. I'm not being coy . . . I have to protect myself physically and emotionally." Her voice faded away, and he distinctly heard a choked-off sob. "I can't go into this. . . ." She said it in a whisper.

When he came out of the phone booth, which was one in a line that stood above the railroad tracks of the Great Neck railroad station, a mixture of emotions churned his stomach. He felt like a heel for having bulled ahead, but one thing was checked out, and he was excited by it, buoyed up. The defector story was no pipe dream! Behind it might lie the motive for the "perfect suicide."

Whistling in the dark, sure. But right now he was going to whistle his way to Alley Pond Park. That's where they'd found Paul Bang-Jensen fallen cold and dead . . . on Thanksgiving, 1959. He'd find the spot, look over the neighborhood, ask some questions maybe. It wasn't far. He had a map, and brother, when your luck is running good . . . play it!

CHAPTER **4**

DESPITE THE MAP, it took Peter Marshall a good half
hour to reach his destination. It was little more than two
miles from Great Neck, but he got lost several times. Once,
when asking for directions, the Samaritan he questioned
shook his head in defeat and said, "I don't believe you can
make it from here by car."

He finally made it, more by luck than navigation. It was
Alley Pond Nursery on the corner of 233rd street that
zeroed him in. He turned and drove slowly up the short
length of the street. There was woodland to his left, a close-
set row of houses to his right, and the wire-fenced play yard
of Cloverdale School capping the drive.

In those woods was the spot he sought, but first he would
have a look at the neighborhood.

When he finally parked the car next to a large sand pile
across from the Nursery, he knew why this place had been
so difficult to find. It was an isolated little community right
in the middle of suburbia; a cul-de-sac, hemmed in by highways and woodland.

The neighborhood proper consisted of a grid of seven

streets running north and south, bordered on the north by West Alley Road, which roughly paralleled Horace Harding Expressway, and on the south by 67th Avenue. Cloverdale Boulevard rimmed the neighborhood to the west. The eastern periphery, 233rd Street, was fronted by an arrowlike spur of woodland, jutting out to form the northern extremity of Alley Pond Park.

Horace Harding Expressway and the Belt Parkway made their intersection at a lower level several hundred yards farther to the east, and the gently snaking Belt marked the woodland's outer edge.

On the seven streets, intersected by 64th Avenue, there were close-set rows of neatly landscaped and well-kept homes. They stood back to back; modest, modern, and, for the most part, attractive. There seemed to be a lot of children. A nice neighborhood, with the large white-faced school, built in 1955, blocking any further enlargement of the community.

But what a spot to find! How would one ever come to this place if one didn't know where it was beforehand? The bus from New York stopped by the Nursery. But going toward New York, it made its stop on the far side of the Expressway. More than that, the bus Bang-Jensen usually rode would have stopped more than a mile away on Northern Boulevard. The only other way a stranger could find this part of Douglaston, Queens, would be to stumble on it by mistake . . . or to be brought here.

Peter Marshall got out of the car and followed a small path into the woods. Just in driving around the small rectangular-shaped community, he'd had the feeling he was being observed. It was probably imagination, but this undoubtedly was the sort of place strangers were noted quickly . . . a small-town quality of observation. He didn't want to make himself conspicuous.

The day was raw and gusty. The wind huffed through

elm and ash, making the branches groan and crack. He was looking for the bridle path he'd read about, and suddenly the little trail he walked debouched onto it. He was at its northern end, at the edge of a rather steep bank that sloped down to meet the rising curve of West Alley Road. He looked off toward the intersection of the two arterial highways. The sound of the swift flow of traffic was a muted hum, unceasing . . . in a way, ominous.

A tiny piece of country in a wilderness of homes, highways and shopping centers. Great place for small boys, dog walkers and their hounds. Great place for suicide . . . or for murder.

The bridle path was wide enough to drive a car down. He followed its gently curving course in a southerly direction. Through the thin screen of trees and underbrush he could see the homes on 233rd Street. He estimated they were no more than several hundred feet distant.

Two small boys passed him, going in the opposite direction. They gave him a curious stare and muttered shy "hello's" to his greeting.

He came to a place where the path branched, the left fork curving downhill toward the Parkway. He continued on the main route, looking for an oddly forked tree. From a photograph, he had picked it as a definite point of identification.

The police had said the path was little used, but he saw all kinds of evidence to belie the statement; beer cans, newspapers, a library book, footprints, a rusted toy . . . and through the underbrush, a glimpse of movement as others walked neighboring paths.

He heard a child's voice shouting, "You're dead!", and then he saw the tree, and stopped. The path was heavily rutted, the frozen earth showing the imprint of tire marks and water drainage. There was a profusion of oak leaves cluttering the rigid earth. Paul Bang-Jensen had lain here.

Looking around, Peter Marshall wondered how a man

could have found his way to this place in the night. It was possible, of course, and he could see that the route ahead would have been an easier approach. But oh, how dark it would be in these woods at night. The street lights over there would offer nothing. How did he know Paul Bang-Jensen had come here in the night anyway?

Well, he had come here at some time by some means or other, that much was certain. He was dead here, that too was certain. Marshall could feel no horror at the thought, only a growing sense of surprise.

How did Paul Bang-Jensen reach this neighborhood in the first place? There was no indication or any reason to believe that the Dane had ever visited this community, or its wooded environs, prior to his last hour.

Clifford Forster had said he thought his client had spent those missing hours walking . . . walking. He was a great one for walking.

Well, it was possible he could have stumbled onto this path . . . followed it . . . tripped, fallen . . . up . . . on. On to where? Get it over with now! It was possible, but it didn't seem an adequate explanation.

He saw a piece of white paper caught in a bush and picked it up. He opened it and read the heading "Police Department" and, underneath, "City of New York—New York 13, New York." There was a city seal at the top and what looked like blood spotches all over the page. His blood!

He pocketed the paper and moved on up the path, sure that he had been seen . . . caught in the act! Caught in the act of what?

The path became a wide clearing, centered by a large elm. It spilled out onto the corner of 233rd Street and 67th Avenue. To his left was the edge of the school playground; to his right, houses and a man in his front yard, watching him.

The man was standing by a small power boat overturned on sawhorses, the hefty outboard muffled in a canvas cocoon. He pretended to be fiddling with something on it, but as Peter Marshall came across the street toward him, he gave up the pretense and waited, hands in wind-breaker pockets.

The man's name was Gannon; he was a short, stubby citizen with the look of the Emerald Isle all over his face. Gannon had a shrewd gaze and a garrulous, knowing manner.

"I thought it must be something like that," he confessed as Marshall explained his visit. "I saw you go by . . . saw you in the woods."

Marshall smiled. "Strangers are noticed."

"Yeah. You want to come in?"

He turned toward the house and Marshall saw the dog on the front steps eyeing him.

"Oh, that's not necessary, Mr. Gannon. I just wondered if you could tell me anything about the case."

"Have you seen Abe Cohen yet? He found the body, along with a man named Galka."

"Yes, I know. I'm planning to visit them."

"Well, Abe lives over on the next block," Gannon gestured, "and Galka is a few streets down. Most people around here think it was murder, not suicide."

Peter Marshall tried to hide the impact the casually spoken words made. "Oh? Why's that?"

"It's just a feeling. Man like that wouldn't have known about a place like this. I have some police friends right here in the neighborhood . . . they don't buy it. Of course, they don't want to get mixed up in it either."

"You were here Thanksgiving?"

"Oh, sure. The police made a command post of my house. Leggett, he's the chief of detectives, he was sore as hell when he arrived and found the body had been turned over before the proper examination. When it was realized who the dead man was, a lot of big police brass showed up.

Most of them stayed right here, talking to those television interviewers, giving their verdicts." Gannon gave a droll chuckle. "All the brass."

"I suppose the police questioned a lot of people?"

"Everyone on this street, I guess. But what the hell, who could hear a twenty-five-caliber from over in those woods with the windows shut? It would be a muffled sound anyway."

"Maybe they wanted to see if anyone had noticed him in the area."

"No one noticed him . . . cause he wasn't here." Gannon gave a knowing smile. "Look, I don't think this has anything to do with it, but it is a kind of a coincidence. There was an old Buick that had been parked sometime Wednesday night right there on the corner of this street and Sixty-seventh. I walked by it and noticed that it had an extra set of license plates in the back seat. I thought it might have been a stolen car, so I called the hundred thirteenth precinct at Cunningham Park Station and reported it. That was before the big excitement."

"And what did the police do?"

"Well, before they came to investigate, another car drove up with two men in it. One hopped out and got in the Buick, and they both drove off."

"Kinda peculiar, isn't it?"

"Well, we've had stolen cars around here before. We are kind of out of the way, if you know what I mean."

Number 61-26 Cloverdale Boulevard was a small one-story dwelling, with brick facing and a walk running to a step-up side entrance. It looked much the same as the houses all along the street. But he saw that, like the others, it had its own characteristics.

He'd felt a little let down in failing to find Mr. Abraham

Cohen at home. Now, he took a deep breath as he rang the bell of the Galka household.

A pretty blonde girl came to the door and opened it a few inches. There was a combination of suspicion and curiosity in her look. Before he'd half explained his purpose, the girl was joined by a tall dark-haired young man of about twenty-five. Marshall judged the two to be husband and wife.

"Come in," the young man said, opening the door wider. "My father doesn't speak English very well."

Peter Marshall was ushered by the two into a good-sized living room. A large, partially curtained picture window fronted on the street. Next to it, a small man with Slavic features rose from his chair, a section of *The New York Times* in his hand, the rest of the paper on the floor. He wore a red-checked shirt, buttoned at the collar.

His son spoke swiftly in Polish, and the father nodded and replied in a husky voice.

"What would you like to know?" the son asked.

"I'd like to hear about that morning . . . Thanksgiving morning when your father went for his walk . . . with the dog, Peppy." He grinned, looking around for the Boxer in question.

Largely through the interpreting of the son, the story came out. Joseph Galka and Peppy had left for their walk about 7:45 A.M. that crisp Thanksgiving Day morning. They had walked up 64th Avenue and entered the woodland. Dog and master then proceeded along the muddy bridle path, heading south. Peppy in the lead started barking and Galka thought the dog was excited by Abraham Cohen's mongrel, Fluffy, who was also barking frantically. It was Fluffy, approaching from the opposite direction, who had discovered the body. Cohen saw the body too, and called to Galka.

"You didn't know who he was, of course?" Marshall asked.

"No . . . he was face down . . . his legs straight out in the path. We didn't know he was dead. I thought he might be a bum . . . asleep . . . his arms crossed above his head."

"I'm not sure I understood that. You say his arms were above his head?"

"Yes, folded like so." The son translated, and the father demonstrated, extending his arms upward and crossing them so that they haloed the top of his head.

"He's sure?"

"Positive. My father is observant."

"Was there anything else he noticed? What about the condition of the clothes?"

"He wore a coat . . . it was pulled up at the back. The clothes did not seem too muddy."

"How close did he stand?"

"As close as we are," came the translation.

Joseph Galka put down his paper and spoke rapidly to his son.

"He said when he heard the man was dead, he thought the position of the body was peculiar—placed as if it had been put there. When a man is hit by a bullet, his body goes sprawling." The son threw out his arms. "He doesn't fall neatly."

Marshall didn't know if this was so or not, but it would seem so. "What about footprints?"

Joseph Galka had seen none. While Abraham Cohen had gone to call the police, he had walked out of the woods and stood on the sidewalk with the dogs. Neither man had touched the body.

"Right away a black pick-up truck drove up with two men in it. They asked my father what happened. My father thinks it was a wrecking car and they had heard the police call."

"Did he notice a garage sign on the truck?"

"No . . . just the two men. Mr. Cohen came back then and the pick-up drove into the woods and down the path. When they came back, the driver called out to my father and said, 'He's dead.' Then they drove away."

"How long was it before the police arrived?"

"My father says it was about half an hour before a patrolman showed up."

"I suppose your father was questioned?"

"Oh, sure . . . they had his picture in the paper."

"Did he see the gun?"

"No . . . but my father can't get over how the body looked, like it had been placed. No one around here thinks he killed himself."

There it was again. "That's just a feeling, hey?"

"Yeah, but when they say he'd been in those woods since Tuesday, nobody believes it."

"Why?"

"There's talk around the neighborhood that some woman walked her dogs there Wednesday. I don't know who she is, but that's the talk I've heard."

"Would anyone know who she is?"

"No, it's just talk. But people are in those woods all the time. Kids, hikers, you know."

Peter Marshall thought he was beginning to know, but he cautioned himself not to get carried away with it all. Impressions were no substitute for facts.

Driving past the Cohens' two-story house in a final check, he saw a car had pulled into the garage beneath. He came to a quick stop.

"Abraham," he said aloud, "if you've come home, I'll kiss you."

Abraham Cohen had come home, but Peter Marshall didn't carry out his threat. Instead he sat in the Cohens' living room and listened to his articulate host relate his experience.

Cohen, he gathered, was a well-to-do man, up on world affairs. He was straightforward, with a dry humor showing through his brown eyes. His accent was pure Queensborough, and he did not find it necessary to seek for words. Fluffy, the brown-and-white mongrel, sat nervously by his side, but obeyed his commands to keep still and lie down.

Much of Abraham Cohen's story paralleled and corroborated what Marshall had already heard from Joseph Galka. Some of it in a way that shook him.

"I thought he was a tramp who might have been frozen. It seemed he had on a short top coat like yours. The pants I took for dungarees, wet, muddy, unpressed.

". . . When I heard later it was Bang-Jensen, I thought the body was in a funny position for a man who had shot himself."

"Did you say that to anyone else?"

"No . . . just to my wife." Cohen grinned.

"What was so strange about the position of the body?"

Cohen got up with a sigh from his easy chair and lay face down on the floor. He extended his arms and crossed them in front of his head. Marshall saw that the only difference between his graphic description and Galka's was the distance the arms were stretched out. In Cohen's judgment, they were out all the way.

"Did you see the gun in his hand?"

"No, I did not see a gun. There were a lot of leaves. His face was in the leaves." Cohen got up stiffly and with a grunt. He chuckled at himself. "I'm no detective, although I like to read detective stories, but I just can't get over the unusual position . . . the way he lay there. You shoot yourself in the head—" He shook his own. "I don't know."

And then with a sly grin, "The police were mighty slow to arrive at first. Of course, they didn't know who he was, and when they found out, I think they were happy to call it suicide.

"I promised I'd take my two grandsons bowling that morning, and when we came back around noon, the place was jumping with police brass, those television fellows Gabe Pressman and John Tilghman, you know?

" 'Nuther funny thing, there's a man named Kubiack who works for the U.N. who lives in a house right across from where they found Bang-Jensen."

Cohen read Peter Marshall's reaction correctly. He shook his head. "No, it's only a coincidence. The police didn't find any connection between the two. They called me on it. I guess they called a lot of people, but they weren't acquainted."

Cohen could add nothing to help in tracing the pick-up truck. Black, two men, one in his teens.

Marshall thought he had gotten all there was, and he thanked the youthful grandfather for his help and stood up.

It was then Cohen casually commented, "I know the police say the woods aren't used much, but a neighbor of mine up the street, he walked in there on that Wednesday, and he didn't see a body. His name is Hageman. He lives in the corner house. Drop by if you want, but no need to tell him I sent you."

He walked the short distance to the corner of 67th Avenue and 232nd Street, trying to weed the exuberance out of his reasoning. All the news accounts had described Bang-Jensen as lying with his hands tucked under his chest, the gun in his right hand. The two men first on the scene were independently sure Bang-Jensen's arms were above his head. If they were, did it mean anything?

Perhaps the change had occurred when the police had turned him over, but—

Both men independently referred to the position in which he lay. Well, who was to say how a man might fall after he'd shot himself? Actually he could lie down and shoot himself.

Sure, and then stick his arms out over his head.

He knew one thing, whatever the position of the arms, he was going to get further corroboration from those characters in the pick-up truck. All he had to do was find them.

As to what Hageman was going to tell him now, he could only hold his breath again. Maybe somebody's estimate of when Bang-Jensen died was going to get knocked full of holes.

The Cape Cod-type house sat on a landscaped rise above the street level, facing the school. It was painted gray and had a wide stone porch. Peter Marshall noted that its roof was a little higher than that of any other house in the area.

A short, grizzled man of about sixty answered the ring. He was in shirt sleeves and came out onto the porch despite the cold. "Nancy, the dog," he said, with a heavy German accent and an apologetic smile. "She might make a fuss."

With his fine beak of nose, his strong square face, his blocky physique, George Hageman put Peter Marshall in mind of a sea captain. His hair was white, but under beetling brows his eyes were sharp and clear.

He listened, nodding his head, as the visit was explained. The door opened and an attractive young lady handed out a jacket, giving Marshall a cold look.

George Hageman chuckled as he was helped into the garment. "A little chilly," he said, and then with a twinkle, "Are you from the F.B.I?"

"No . . . I'm just a writer."

"Well, it's all right. I'm glad you came to talk to me. No one else has ever come to ask me about it. You see, when

I heard them say on the radio he had been lying there since maybe Monday, I said, that's not right. I know that's not right. He was not there late Wednesday afternoon. I passed the spot twice. Nancy misses nothing, and I don't miss much . . . even though I am an old fellow." He chuckled.

"Tuesday we did not walk because it rained." Marshall underlined the mental note already in his mind to check out the weather for the days in question.

"Wednesday my wife and I went shopping in Long Island City, and when we returned in the afternoon, Nancy and I went for our walk.

"Usually we walk twice a day. In the morning we go to the right," he faced the direction of the woods and gestured, "and in the afternoon, to the left. That Wednesday, about four o'clock, we went to the left." He indicated again, and then with a wag of his head, "I don't walk that way any more. . . . It gives me a funny feeling . . . to know."

"What was the weather like that afternoon, Mr. Hageman?"

"Windy. Very windy. It was clearing up after the rain."

"And you followed the bridle path?"

"Oh, yes . . . If he had been lying there, I could not have missed him . . . poor fellow . . . Besides, my wife and I heard the shot that night."

"What!"

"Yes," Hageman nodded. "We heard it. We were in bed about eleven. It wasn't a backfire. It was a shot, all right, I'm sure. My wife said, 'Someone is shooting,' and I said, 'Probably boys.' They sometimes go in the woods to shoot."

"Now, wait a minute. Your window—was it opened?"

"Oh, of course. Our bedroom is at the top. Here." Hageman walked to the end of the porch and leaned out, pointing up.

Peter Marshall saw the window that faced toward the woodland.

"And no one came to question you?"

"No one . . . just you." George Hageman peered at him with a foxy grin and said, "It's all right if you are from the F.B.I."

Before Peter Marshall left the community for the day, he went back to the spot where Paul Bang-Jensen's body had been found. Through the trees, in the fast-fading light he could see George Hageman's bedroom window, overlooking the other housetops that lay between.

He drove away, heading for the Whitestone Bridge, knowing he was coming back the next day. It was all very well for Clifford Forster to advance the theory that Paul Bang-Jensen had spent the hours between his disappearance and death walking . . . or sitting on a park bench, but it just didn't jell.

No man was going to walk around for three days and two and one half nights and not be noticed by someone. He wasn't going to amble around for that long and be found beardless.

The police had been looking for him as early as Tuesday noon.

The news had hit the early editions of the Wednesday afternoon papers.

He was a distinctive-looking person, and he had a most noticeable accent.

No sir, it just didn't hold water. Paul Bang-Jensen had been somewhere in those lost hours, which now numbered a pretty definite fifty-seven and a possible sixty-five . . . autopsy reports notwithstanding. He had been somewhere other than on the by-ways and the highways of this endless suburbia. And there was on this night, nearly two months after his death, a person, or persons unknown, who knew a part of the answer, or all of the answer, to where he had been.

The question was, why had they kept silent?

CHAPTER 5

PETER MARSHALL learned that the weather on Monday, November 23, 1959, had been on the mild side, overcast and with a trace of rain in the evening from 7:45 P.M. to 9:10 P.M.

The next morning, Tuesday, the rain really began to fall. It started at 7:20 A.M. and continued on through the day and the night. It was a mild day and night, with the temperature reaching 60 degrees and the wind strong out of the south.

On Wednesday, the rain stopped at 9:15 A.M., but it remained overcast and windy; the wind veering to blow from the west and the temperature dropping fast. From 3:40 to 4:10 P.M. there was a trace of rain, followed by fast clearing. By 5:00 o'clock in the evening, the sky was totally clear, the sun setting at 4:37 P.M.

Marshall deduced that George Hageman and his dog must have had their walk that day sometime after 4:10 P.M.

The wind continued to blow hard from out of the west. At 10:00 P.M. it was clocked at the Battery weather station in

New York City at 46 mph. At 11:00 it was down to 43 mph, and at midnight, 33 mph. With it, the temperature hit its low of 33 degrees.

The question was: would the sound of a .25-caliber shot carry against a wind, blowing at approximately 43 miles per hour, so that George Hageman and his wife could hear it through their open bedroom window?

There were a lot of variables involved, and it was not until several months later, after considerable experimentation, that he could answer "Yes, they could" with enough authority so that he was willing to let it stand.

He spent the better part of that Sunday morning exploring Alley Pond Woods and Park. The bridle path ambled on past the edge of the school property. It followed a slight uphill course through a thin stand of hemlock and then dropped rather sharply to skirt a circular pond's edge. The pond was thinly iced, but he could see that it was shallow. There were tall reeds growing around most of it. Several teenagers were being unnecessarily raucous around its far edge. They stopped their shouting long enough to mutter something among themselves as he passed.

The trail, which sprouted numerous tributaries right and left, rose again, leveled, and in a few hundred feet spilled out onto the large, grassy park area. On its northerly side, he could see a closely set group of administration buildings. They were set low and had a rustic look. There was a gate house and a considerable area set aside for parking. Even on this cold morning, there were a dozen or so cars using the facilities.

He went down across the fields, thinking a man might take refuge in such a place. But even during the week, rain or shine, there would be a caretaker on the premises. In daylight a man could walk the bridle path and its attendant side trails without any trouble. After sundown, it would be one helluva go, and to prove it, he was going to stay here until dark and give it a try. He'd probably fall into that pond.

At the administration building, he learned that the entrance to the park was off Grand Central Parkway and that no regular bus from Great Neck or New York City traveled it.

That afternoon he conducted his house-to-house campaign. He began on 67th Avenue, across the intersecting street from George Hageman's residence.

At the first house, no one was home.

At the second, Mrs. Delancy knew nothing.

At the next, a frighteningly pregnant woman with a butch haircut and a very loose kimono invited him in. "I'm waiting for a baby" she explained, and then, to make up for it, she told him that Mrs. Jacobs who lived around the corner had heard the shot. He was grateful for the information, but anxious to leave, not wanting to assume the duties of a midwife.

Outside the corner house, a man was putting license plates on a Ford. He had nothing to add.

Mrs. Jacobs, a beefy woman with thick glasses, would not open the door to him. She talked through the glass partition. "I don't know anything . . . I don't know anything!" she repeated, shaking her head. There was fear and suspicion in look, gesture, and voice. If she knew anything, she was not going to admit it.

The lady next door had not been home Thanksgiving week.

He skipped Gannon's house and paid a call on Allison Kubiack, who worked for the U.N. There was a sailboat hull, a Woodpussy, beached on the front lawn. It looked as if Gannon and Kubiack shared an interest in the sea.

Peter Marshall took an instant liking to the tall, dark-haired, mustached man who opened the door. There was geniality and warmth in his eyes, intelligence in his face.

"I'm going to bowl you over," Marshall said in greeting.

Allison Kubiack gave a quick, knowing grin as he heard the purpose of the visit. "Won't you all come in?" he said, his accent revealing a Southern background.

Kubiack and family had been away Thanksgiving, partaking in a yearly celebration with Chinese and British friends.

"Did you know Bang-Jensen?"

"I had met him, but I didn't really know him. I'm in the Education Department, films and that sort of thing."

"What's the feeling at the U.N. . . . or is there any?"

Kubiack smiled. "Yes, there is. . . . People are quite divided on it."

Marshall wanted to ask Kubiack how he felt, but he didn't. Outside once more, he said, "I see you like to sail."

"Love it . . . She's not very big, but she's a lot of fun."

"I know. I had an old clinker-built sloop once."

"Last summer I sailed up to the Newport races on a forty-five-foot ketch. That was a real ship . . . gives a man a feeling of being on top. It's the closest thing to gliding I know. Have you ever done any gliding?"

"No. I've done a lot of flying."

Kubiack smiled. "I guess I feel about motorized planes the same way I do about stinkpots." He nodded toward Gannon's power boat. "When you glide, there's just you and God up there."

By the time Peter Marshall reached the end of the block, he realized that though the houses might seem all very much alike, the people living in them were dissimilar and amazingly heterogeneous. Whether it was the pretty Irish wife, or the Jewish family still in their pajamas with papa at his easel painting a country scene, they were for the most part a highly vocal and intelligent group.

Those who offered their opinions shared a common belief: despite note, and gun, and evidence to the contrary, it was murder, not suicide.

More important than opinion, however, were the odd bits of information he gathered.

Buses from the city, making a stop at the Nursery, ran at half-hour intervals around the clock.

A little lady with horn-rimmed glasses walked her dog on Thanksgiving eve about 11:30 P.M. It was a nasty night. She had walked on the sidewalk bordering the woods. She had heard and seen nothing out of the ordinary.

The twelve-year-old son of a nurse with a French accent had been in the woods on Wednesday in the early afternoon. He had been on the bridle path, but did not pass the spot where the body was found. He saw no one.

A man named Andrew Mulholland, who did not invite him in, and kept his hands on his unfriendly Boxer, was cold and uncommunicative. He had a fixed sneer beneath his black, pencil mustache. He had not heard or seen anything. He did not walk his dog in the Park.

This was the man Gannon had told him the police had chased away from the scene several times. Later Marshall saw Mulholland and the Boxer walking toward the Park. Still later, he saw Mulholland get in his two-tone DeSoto and speed away.

The Carahalios house was the last one on the street. Mrs. Carahalios was anxious to talk.

"My son Paul always takes Blackie—he's a terrier—for a walk on a leash every morning. We have to walk him on a leash because he's not too friendly. We got him as an older dog. Well, on Thanksgiving they went out at just about eight. They went up the street beside the woods, toward the school. I heard barking and I went to the window. I saw Paul trying to hold Blackie, and Blackie was trying to run into the woods. I wondered what the matter was. He was halfway up the block and right opposite the place they found the body. Paul came back and said, 'I just can't take care of him today. Something in the woods excited him.' "

Mrs. Carahalios took a deep breath and made her point. "Paul and Blackie went the same way at the same time every day that week—Monday, Tuesday, Wednesday—even in the rain, and Blackie behaved—he never acted up until that morning."

"You say it was eight o'clock? I thought the body was discovered before eight."

"No, it was a little after eight when they found him."

"Do Paul and Blackie ever walk in the woods?"

"No, I never allow Paul and my younger boy to go in there without an older person."

"Why is that?"

"I've heard my neighbors say there are funny people walking around in those woods. Some people come a long way to walk their dogs. I'll tell you something." Mrs. Carahalios gave a knowing nod and lowered her voice to a conspiratorial level. "Everyone around here thinks there's something fishy about the whole thing . . . that the body was put there. Either that, or he was led in there, and then killed."

After dark, he tried to walk the bridle path. It was as difficult as he'd expected. He didn't go far, and he went very carefully. It wasn't only fear of falling that made the experiment a short one. Even though he could see the street lights and the lights in the windows of the houses, he felt terribly alone. Vulnerable. It was bitter cold and the wind stirred through the underbrush and made the trees creak. It was bleakly dark. Every sound about him bore its own particular tone of malevolence . . . even the murmuring monotone of the highway traffic.

God, what a cold and empty place to die!

It took him a full day of searching to find the black pick-up truck and its driver. He did it by the slow process of elimination, inquiring at garages on Northern Boulevard. He knew it was a matter of finding a garage that had road-service facilities and a short-wave radio capable of receiving police calls. He thought, too, the driver might have talked about his experience and the word would get around.

The latter supposition led him to Don & Joe's Auto-body just as he was about to give up the hunt as a bad job.

Larry Gallo he found to be a short, heftily built, quite good-looking man of about thirty-five. He had no reluctance in talking.

"Yeah, I heard the call on the police band." He grinned. "We're not supposed to have one. I thought it was a 10-32, that's an accident report. It took me about three minutes to drive over there." He grinned again and explained. "We're all psychos in this business, we drive like crazy."

"Did you have someone with you?"

"Yeah, the kid. His name is Don Bruce. He came along for the ride. He's a high school kid. When we got there, I saw this man standing on the sidewalk with a couple of dogs. I asked him where the accident was. He didn't speak English so good, but I got the idea somebody was in the woods. I thought maybe I could help. Maybe a guy was sick or somethin' . . . I like to help when I can. I drove down that trail to have a look. Boy, did the police give me hell about that later! Said if there had been any other tire marks, I covered 'em. Well, he was lyin' there with leaves all around him. The legs of his pants were hiked up, you know. They looked soaked, but his coat seemed dry."

"Did you touch him?"

"I knew he was dead. I was in the Army . . . I've seen bodies before. His face was white as chalk. I knew."

"Did you touch him?" he asked again.

"Just his leg with my foot."

"Did you notice the position in which he lay?"

"Oh, on his stomach, flat, his legs in the path."

"How about his arms?"

"Arms? I didn't really notice." Gallo laughed. "Frankly, I wanted to get the hell out of there."

"You didn't see his arms over his head?"

"No . . . If they had been, I doubt if I'd have seen them anyway. He was in a big pile of leaves."

Marshall didn't ask him how he could see Bang-Jensen's face if he were lying head down and the leaves were so thick. Instead, he listened as Larry Gallo told him about returning to the scene after he had learned the dead man's identity on the radio. It was then Larry got his first dressing down from the Law. Later they had questioned him at the garage.

A telephone directory and a dime got him Donald Bruce. And the teenager unknowingly lined himself up with Joseph Galka and Abraham Cohen.

"Yes, it seemed like his head was resting on his arms . . . like he was asleep."

"You mean his arms were extended?"

"Yeah . . . and folded like."

"His forehead resting on them?"

"I couldn't tell for sure, but I think so . . . that, or they were just in front of his head."

He thanked Donald Bruce, and when the boy asked him if he was going to get his name in a book, he replied he wouldn't be a bit surprised.

He hung up and spoke to the telephone. "The time has come, the Walrus said, to go and have a talk with the boys in blue."

CHAPTER 6

THE SNOW CAME DOWN in a heavy, windless fall, and Peter Marshall, rising up into it from the subway, growled at himself for not having worn rubbers. He hoped 240 Centre Street was not far distant.

He asked directions and picked his way gingerly along the unshoveled sidewalk. Centre Street was an old street, and Police Headquarters, at 240, was an old building. He arrived, feet wet, with a coating of virgin flakes on shoulders and hat. As he stamped his feet and shook off the snow, he took in the drafty foyer. An elevator shaft rose from the center of the floor. It was coldly embraced on either side by marble stairways, elbowing up to the second floor. On the walls were numerous bronze and wooden plaques naming patrolmen who had died in the line of duty and in war.

Walter Arm, Deputy Commissioner of Police, had his office on the second floor. Like the building, it had a drab, 1890 quality. One stark window looked out on the winter scene. Hanging on the walls was an interesting assortment of old-time police photographs. The furniture was sparse, adequate.

He had known Walter Arm in the days when the latter had been a police reporter for the *Herald Tribune*. He thought Arm must know his job uniquely well, having worked on both sides of the fence.

A short man, with a good poker-playing face, Arm gave him a curling grin as they shook hands and made small talk. On the Deputy Commissioner's desk lay a thick manila folder. Marshall pulled up a chair and they got down to business.

An orange card, bare details. Name, age. D.O.A. . . . time found 8:40.

Galka was right. It had taken a half hour for Patrolman John J. Schager of the Grand Central Parkway precinct to arrive on the scene.

Found lying on stomach . . . gun in right hand . . . bullet in right temple. Body found by Benjamin Cohen.

Marshall noted the wrong first name but said nothing.

"Tan topcoat, blue suit, white shirt, black and red polka-dot tie, blue socks, red muffler . . . The scene was immediately ordered roped off by Chief of Detectives Leggett."

The recital of details went on, Arm reading swiftly. "Four dollars and forty-five cents found in pocket, clothing was damp, trousers wet. The body was identified by the Reverend Stuart Haskins . . . Doctor Furey of the Queens Medical Office could not fix exact time of death, but estimated it was twenty-four hours prior to discovery of the body."

Peter Marshall did not tell Arm that he had evidence proving considerable error in the estimate.

"His wife, Helen, reported him missing at twelve thirty-seven P.M. Tuesday, November twenty-fourth, to the Great Neck police. He left for work Monday, the twenty-third, about seven forty A.M. . . . In his wallet there was a note dated November, 1959. Arm held up a photostat of the note. Marshall could see that the handwriting was scraggly and jagged.

"It's signed. It's suicidal in nature . . . 'I underestimated the forces I was up against,'" Arm read with difficulty. "'I only wish I could have shown my love for you in action . . . no funeral . . . cremation . . . dispose of the ashes.' Here, can you make this out?"

He could not make it out. The penmanship was small and tight with little jabs up and down. He had already seen several specimens of Bang-Jensen's handwriting and he'd been able to read them. His eye caught what appeared to be a small scribbled notation at the bottom of the page. It said "6A." He wondered what it could mean.

The note was a touching and rather noble farewell, and it seemed to squash his budding theories of foul play.

Walter Arm squashed them even flatter. "Handwriting was checked from sample by Lieutenant Joseph McNally. . . . Ballistics, checked gun twenty-five-caliber colt automatic . . . five shells in clip . . . one ejected, shell found eighteen inches from head . . . He had no permit. Metropolitan Police of Washington said the weapon was purchased June seventeen, 1941, by Paul Barry Jensen. . . . Investigation to date discloses nothing suspicious. It was continued to try and discover where he was prior to his death and motivation of his actions. . . .

"Detectives canvassed bus stop at two hundred fifty-seventh and Northern Boulevard. . . . All persons using buses saw his picture . . . none remembered seeing him that Monday. . . . Neighbor stated he saw Bang-Jensen and gave him a lift to the bus stop at Northern Boulevard and Morgan Street. He was last seen by this man walking toward a waiting bus. . . . Two buses leaving at this time— seven thirty-four and the seven forty-four. Driver said face was familiar, but positively did not see him on Monday. . . . Other buses were checked, passengers shown his picture, no one remembers seeing him. . . .

"Bang-Jensen had been under treatment by three psychiatrists, according to the Police Sergeant's report. The areas of discussion centered on Bang-Jensen's fears for the future. The subject of suicide was brought up constantly. He stopped treatment two weeks before his death. Arthur and Stanley Kernstein, Upland Druggists, at eighty-four Horace Harding Boulevard, had known Bang-Jensen for seven years . . . said he frequently purchased sedatives and tranquilizers on prescription. . . .

"Got a few tips . . . not a great deal, nothing that helped. . . . The red, crusty material on the gun was almost positively identified as blood . . . rust spots but of such variety that it was impossible to say which ones were old, which new.

"Would you like to know what he had in his pockets? . . . Blue Cross card, note with wife's sizes, eyeglass case of black leather, brown horn-rimmed glasses, key case, two keys, wrist watch, blue and white money clip, wallet, Parker ball-point pen, quarter, dime, nickel, four one-dollar bills, two handkerchiefs, black plastic comb . . ."

How normal, how commonplace.

"Police conducted forty interviews. Do you want to see these pictures? I don't want to look at them." Arm held out a manila envelope with photographs in it.

Peter Marshall did not like looking at the photographs either. As he studied them, he tried to shut out their awful reality. He failed, but he also managed to observe . . . the face was clean shaven. Bang-Jensen lay with his head turned slightly to the left. His hands were tucked in under his chest, which apparently meant that the body had been rolled over by the police and then returned to its original position. No man walking down the path could have missed seeing him . . . the pants legs looked soiled and unpressed, wet . . . as did the front of the body.

The foul indignity of a human being brought to this pitiful end! The angry, gaping wound. . . . May God damn those who made these cruel photographs necessary! He handed them back.

"What about the autopsy?" he said.

"Well, you can call Grimes on that if you want. He's the Chief Medical Examiner, but Doctor Soletsky, who is the Assistant M.E., says it was death by gunshot wound, suicidal . . . no solid food found in the stomach."

"How long do they estimate he'd been dead?"

"You'll have to talk to Grimes about that. I think he figures around twenty-four hours from the time he began his autopsy."

"That would make it noon or one o'clock Wednesday."

"Something like that. It could have been earlier."

"And does anyone have any idea where he was during the missing time?"

"Well, we haven't been able to trace him. Cab driver who said he picked him up didn't prove out. Bang-Jensen probably just wandered around . . . making up his mind."

"Is the case closed, Walter?"

"Yes, it's closed. The police aren't boobs, you know, Pete."

Dr. Richard E. Grimes, Chief Medical Examiner for the City of New York, gave Marshall the brush-off, and in so doing, made him realize that his squashed theories might not be dead after all.

It took several telephone calls to reach the busy doctor, who gruffly told him to write a letter and explain what he was up to. Peter Marshall complied and followed it with another telephone call.

"I'm sorry I can't see you," snapped the M.E.

"Can you tell me why?"

"I have orders. All the facts you want are in the newspapers."

"I'm afraid there are a lot of incorrect statements in the papers."

"I don't care. The facts are there, all there."

And that was that for the moment, but not a very long one, for Peter Marshall was miffed by the doctor's brusqueness. He went to a well-placed friend and asked a favor. A week later it was granted in the form of a photostatic copy of the entire autopsy report.

In it he found some incredible discrepancies and omissions.

Two different dates and two different times were given as to when Dr. Grimes started his autopsy—1:00 P.M. on November 26 and 11 A.M. on November 27.

No estimated time of death was given.

The hand-written notations on the first page, the joint findings of Doctors L. M. Soletsky and J. Furey, read in part:

"—turned by police, then turned back to original approximate position.

"Supine—both fists beneath chest, pistol *near* rt fist— rust on gun & palm rt hand—contact wound rt temple . . . body cold (very cold last night)—No obvious P.M. decomposition."

The report of Lt. Paul E. Girardin described the deceased as being found with the gun *in* his right hand.

Dr. Grimes's autopsy revealed: "Face smooth-shaven . . . body diffusely cold and rigid . . . In addition there are brownish colored stains over the thumb, index, and middle fingers of the right hand, and over the thumb, index finger, and proximal portion of the left palm close to the index finger. There is a deep indentation in the skin, linear in type, at the tip of the right thumb, measuring 1 and ½ inches in length . . ."

Two sentences leaped out at him: "The edges of the wound are reddish black. There are no distinct evidences of powder granules in the skin about this wound even after all the blood has been removed."

Did the "black" refer to powder burns, and if there were no powder burns, how did one shoot oneself in the head? The wound was "jagged, irregular, longitudinal . . . measuring 1¼ inches in length, but its entrance was only a quarter of an inch wide."

Was it really a contact wound? Had the gun been in Bang-Jensen's hand? Right now there was only one thing of which he was sure. Contradiction seemed to be the order of the day.

He got more contradiction in short order, giving further inflation to reviving theories. There were *not* three psychiatrists who had attended Paul Bang-Jensen in the last months of his life.

There was Dr. Lawrence Strauss, a general practitioner of Great Neck, Long Island, who had recommended a mild sedative when Bang-Jensen came to him in the summer of 1959.

The prescription was never refilled, and Helen Bang-Jensen took more of the pills than her husband.

The Upland Druggists may have known the Dane for seven years, but tranquilizers and sleeping pills had never been on his shopping list.

There was Doctor John H. Cornehlsen, an industrial psychologist who specializes in vocational guidance. It was true Bang-Jensen was gravely concerned about his future, but Cornehlsen did not find him a suicidal type. They discussed the subject on two levels: the high rate of suicide in Scandinavian countries and the unlikelihood of Bang-Jensen's ever taking that way out.

On the recommendation of a friend, Bang-Jensen did consult a psychiatrist. He was Doctor F. S. Friedenberg of Brooklyn.

"I think it is quite impossible to state whether a person is inclined enough toward suicide to commit it. It was impossible in his case, at any rate," Doctor Friedenberg said.

"Were you surprised when you heard the news?"

"Yes, frankly, I was."

"He came to you about mid-July, didn't he? Was he suffering from a nervous breakdown?"

"He came about that time, yes. But he was not suffering from a nervous breakdown. When one has a breakdown, there is an impairment in the intellect. Bang-Jensen never suffered that. He was always sharp as a whip. I found him a most admirable and unusual person."

"Well, what was his problem then, Doctor?"

"He was worried, depressed about one thing, his inability to find a job with a good future. Yet, he understood the problem perfectly. He told me he took a test to determine his capacities. In intelligence he scored in the upper two percent and, in a special category, in the upper one half percent. But he recognized that in a sense his own qualities contributed to the difficulty of making a new career.

" 'I can't find work as a waiter,' he said. 'I can't find work as a hotel manager. I could find work as the manager of an A-one hotel, but an A-one hotel won't dare hire me.' . . . So he knew it was going to take time."

"He discussed suicide frequently, didn't he?"

"Yes, but not as a way to solve anything."

"Well, do you think there's any significance in it, his bringing it up so much?"

"It would be difficult to say, Mister Marshall. Tell me, have you ever been out of work for a long period? . . . If you have, you know it can be very depressing."

"Yes, it can."

"In fact, if you weren't depressed about a situation like that, it would be abnormal . . . family and all."

"But Bang-Jensen had a job."

"Exactly! Not the job he would take as a new career, but a job. He was not badly off financially, and so his only concern was for the future. Being the kind of person he was, it worried him."

"He had no regrets about the U.N.? He didn't dwell on what had happened to him?"

"I'm glad you raised that point. About the U.N., he was a complete realist. Often we discussed the idea of what he might have done had he to do it over, and he knew he could have done no differently. He was, of course, sorry that he had been dismissed, but he knew that his moral convictions were such that he could not compromise them. He knew also that he had information of sinister forces at the U.N. . . . and that he could do nothing to stop their machinations. He recognized that the political situation there was such that there was no way out. But he accepted it all as a fact of life. He was realistic about the whole thing."

"What about these sinister forces you mention? Did he ever describe them, or express any fear that he might be in danger from them?"

"We only discussed them generally, Mister Marshall. And he never expressed fear. You should understand that after they fired him he was perfectly all right for a number of months, a long time. It was only when he couldn't get a job that he became depressed."

"He stopped coming to see you in September, as I understand it. Did you consider him cured?"

"He called me one day to say that he was not coming back, that he was going to see a Christian Scientist. I was quite surprised, because our relationship had passed the doctor-patient stage and we had become good friends."

"Did he give any reason?"

"No, but I think he was hoping for some kind of miracle . . . a quick cure. . . . He did not give me the man's name."

"And his family, how did he feel about them?"

"He was a very devoted family man, and he recognized his responsibility to his children. I repeat, Mister Marshall, I was very surprised when I heard that he was reported to have killed himself."

Peter Marshall went back to Great Neck and paid a call on William Wetzlar, the last man to admit having seen Paul Bang-Jensen alive.

From where they stood on the macadamed drive, he could see the Bang-Jensens' spacious, handsome, ranch-style house. He knew the shrubs and trees that artfully decked the neatly landscaped property had been planted by Bang-Jensen. The house, though exhibiting an air of privacy, was closely hedged by its neighbors. This was true of the entire community: spacious, tastefully built homes, close together but still giving that feeling of individuality.

William Wetzlar further proved the contention. Short, on the hefty side, he was obviously of a different type from his late neighbor up the street. It was only by economics that they had resided in the same community, and Wetzlar admitted as much.

"I only knew him as someone who lived here, and I used to give him a ride every now and then . . . I'd see him walking and I'd say hello."

"What about that Monday morning?"

"It wasn't a nice morning . . . nasty. I was out here waiting for my daughter, and I called to him. We stood here a couple of minutes in the driveway."

"Did he say anything about Thanksgiving?"

"No, we just passed the time of day. I noticed he didn't have a hat. He didn't seem upset, but it would have been hard for me to tell. He was not that kind of person . . . well mannered, very quiet."

"He didn't say anything significant?"

"Nothing that I recall . . . I got the impression though that he was sort of forcing himself down to where he had to go. You know, some men like to walk down to the bus. I don't think he actually enjoyed that walk. I think he was the kind that if he had to do something—he did it."

"Your daughter came out, and off you went."

"That's right. It's only a couple of minutes down to Northern Boulevard. I stopped for the light on Greenwood behind two other cars. He thanked me and got out, and I saw him cross the street and go toward the bus stop."

"Was the bus there?"

"I didn't notice whether there was a bus there or not that morning . . . but it was usually there, and there were people waiting."

"You saw him cross the street, and that was the last you saw him."

"That was it. I went across Northern Boulevard where my daughter gets the Schenk express bus to Flushing."

"Do you remember what time it was?"

"I think around seven thirty-five."

Peter Marshall thanked William Wetzlar and drove down to Greenwood Street and Northern Boulevard. He found the thoroughfare bordered by a great variety of shops, cemented together in a conglomeration of nondescript fronts. Across from the bus stop, the slightly faded marquee of the Little Neck Theater announced the showing of a foreign film. Next to it, there was a narrow stationery store with a coffee counter at the rear. It had a counterpart halfway up the block on the other side of the street. These two shops opened for business at 6:30 A.M. He found that the big two-tone-green New York City Transit Authority buses left their stop at five-to-ten-minute intervals during the morning rush.

The questions he asked brought no answers of any merit, and by the time he drove away, he knew how utterly cold and dead the trail had become.

CHAPTER 7

EVEN THOUGH he could find no clues to the missing
hours, Alice Widener's article in her comprehensive little
digest *U.S.A.* lit a fire under him. It gave back full strength
to original theories.

It was a special issue, an exclusive, and it contained a
memorandum,[1] written by Paul Bang-Jensen to his wife at
her request and dated November 30, 1957.

The two-page document related how, five days earlier,
Bang-Jensen had been asked to report to Dr. Sze, head of
the U.N. Health Clinic. The doctor somewhat reluctantly
informed the diplomat he had been told that the Dane was
under a great nervous strain, and although there was no obligation to accept the offer, the Health Service did have
psychiatric advisers.

It took no more than ten minutes for Bang-Jensen to
convince Dr. Sze that he was perfectly healthy both mentally and physically and required no medical aid of any sort.

Dr. Sze thanked Bang-Jensen for coming. He repeated it
sounded quite unlikely that Bang-Jensen would succumb to

nervous strain, and then shook hands with him, saying good-bye and wishing him good luck.

In retrospect and in discussing the episode with his wife, Bang-Jensen made it clear that because of his knowledge of certain facts, the enemy was starting to move against him. Because of what he knew, they might possibly want him out of the way. For this reason, he concluded his memorandum with two paragraphs that leaped off the page at Peter Marshall.

"My wife has nevertheless insisted that I should inform a few of my friends that under no circumstance would I commit suicide. I have done so, though reluctantly, since I fear my friends might think I'm getting a little dramatic.

"My wife has asked me to write this memorandum to her, and to make it clear also in this that under no circumstances whatsoever would I ever commit suicide. This would be completely contrary to my whole nature and to my religious convictions. If any note was found to the opposite effect in my handwriting, it would be a fake."

There was the signature, and the date, and Peter Marshall read it over again. It had been written two years before the end—and certainly a great deal could and did happen to Paul Bang-Jensen in that twenty-four month period. But was it enough to drive him over the brink—enough so that, in the note found on his body, he would make no reference to the early denial of such an act?

He didn't know. He'd go ask Alice Widener.

They had met some years before at a rally in which she had been the principal speaker. He recalled that it was she, assigned to do a series of articles for the *Freeman* on Americans in the Secretariat, who had uncovered the mess which later resulted in the dismissal of thirty-three employees. They had been dismissed on disloyalty charges after hearings before the Senate Sub-Committee on Internal Security.

He remembered her as a small, brilliant woman with large unafraid eyes, a French nose, and a tone of voice that, no matter whether it rose or fell, was delivered with incisive authority. There was drama and drive in Alice Widener, and an absolute dedication to the facts. The latter was reflected bi-monthly in *U.S.A.* and a widely syndicated newspaper column.

"A little banty-rooster," an acquaintance had described her warmly. "Once she takes a stand, she'd fight the feathers off an ostrich."

As she ushered him into the nicely decorated living room of her third-floor Park Avenue home and office, he realized his memory of her had been accurate, but he knew she didn't remember him at all.

She sat down and he held the light for her cigarette. "And now," she said, blowing out a puff of smoke, "why do you want to write a book about Paul Bang-Jensen?"

It wasn't female curiosity, pleasant or unpleasant, it was all business, and her eyes appraised him steadily as he answered in generalities.

"A book should be written about him, you're right," she said, "but not any book. It's got to be terribly accurate, you see. If it isn't, they'll tear your head off. Whom have you talked to?"

He told her some of the people he had seen.

She blew out an impatient cloud of smoke. "Are you writing about his death or his life?" she asked with a touch of asperity.

"Both. They go together."

She studied him coolly as she puffed her cigarette. "I suppose you want to know how I got his memorandum?"

"That's not really important. I'd rather know what you think of it."

Alice Widener stood up with a sigh. "Think of it? Do you mean, do I think he was murdered?" She shook her head sadly. "My opinion won't prove anything. You have to deal in facts! Facts, you see! It's what they did to him that's important, not what he did to himself either voluntarily or under duress. Do you see?"

"You knew him well?"

She ignored his question and countered with one of her own. "How much do you know of what happened to him while he was Deputy Secretary for the Hungarian Committee, and after he refused to turn over the names?"

"I'm getting hold of all the documentation I can. I'm going to talk to everyone concerned, Hungarians, U.N. officials, everyone who will talk who had anything to do with him, right from the beginning of his life."

"And you're not going to go off on some flight of sensationalism, just to sell copy?"

"If the facts are sensational."

"They are. They are." She bobbed her head. "But not in the way a lot of people think. Peter Marshall, you'll have to do a tremendous amount of studying if you want to do this right, do you understand?"

"I expect to."

"Have you got the Gross Report?"

"Not yet."

"You'll need it . . . also the minutes of the Assembly Tribunal. There's no point in discussing the case, you see, until you're thoroughly familiar with it." And now she favored him with a smile as she stubbed out her cigarette.

"Would you tell me about how you got to know him?"

She lit another cigarette and sat down again before she replied, starting out obliquely. "Some years ago I was very active around the U.N. I got to know a great many people. . . . I got to know some anti-Communists. I'm going to say something that's horrible, but unfortunately, it's true. Never, never have any of my informants in the U.N., with regard to exposing Communism, been Americans. I suppose over the years I gained a reputation for being an anti-Communist who would not make a statement without proof to back it. . . .

"All right, about two o'clock in the morning the day after they had literally thrown Paul off the U.N. premises—the day they suspended him—my phone rang. . . . I picked up the receiver and a voice with an accent said, 'Mrs. Widener, save Bang-Jensen!' and hung up." Alice Widener paused and stared at him silently.

" 'Save Bang-Jensen,' it went on all the rest of the night. Call after call, and I got little sleep. You see, I didn't know who Bang-Jensen was from Adam. Then a friend called me and told me about his suspension—his eviction. You know about that, how the two guards were ordered to show him out?"

"Yes."

"Well, I said if he wants help, have him telephone me. . . . He did, and we had a long talk. He convinced me of his character and of his purpose. We decided it would be better if we didn't meet, and we never did meet until Christmas of nineteen fifty-eight, when the whole family came here for dinner. It was a lovely meeting." Alice Widener looked down at her lap and concluded quietly, "That's how I got to know him . . . from a phone call in the night . . . 'Save Bang-Jensen.' "

He waited a moment before he asked the next question. "Did he ever mention a Soviet defector, or defectors, to you?"

"Where did you hear that?"

"I read it, and Mrs. Bang-Jensen admitted there was some truth in it."

"He never spoke to me on the subject. There may be a kernel of truth in it somewhere, but don't be carried away by what you read in the magazines."

"Well, if it's true, it would have a direct bearing on the case."

"It could have," she corrected him; "you don't know that for sure. You have to get the facts, you see."

He had the feeling something was troubling her on this line of approach. She lit her third cigarette and stared off at nothing as though trying to make up her mind to add something more.

"You thought he was quite a person, didn't you?" He said it more to gain her sympathy than to get an answer which he already knew.

Alice Widener gave him her penetrating stare before she replied. "I'm going to tell you something," she said softly. "It may sound corny to you, but it's true. To him, honor was not just a word, it was a fact of being. When they impugned his honor, called him mad and sick and all those other things, there was nothing on earth that could stand in the way of his trying to prove them wrong. Do you understand that!" The last came out harshly, and her look was almost one of anger.

"Yes," he said, and thought he should have said more but didn't know what to say.

She puffed on her cigarette and looked away, and when she continued, her voice, though in an even lower pitch, did not conceal the intensity of her feeling.

"He was born out of time. Today we consider a hero a fool . . . a man who uses poor judgment. And my, his judgment was poor because he tried to fight them . . . alone! Alone! How could he expect to win!" It was an angry cry. "He was doomed! . . . He doomed himself! They broke him bit by bit! And when they had him down and finished, they still stuck their swords into him. And look, look, even after he is dead and gone, they throw mud on him to clean themselves!"

He saw the tears welling up in her eyes and looked away as she broke off.

"Il y a un gentil et parfait chevalier, sans peur et sans reproche?" He quoted it as a question.

"Exactly," she said, "exactly. He never knew how brave he was. He thought himself weak. I don't know whether he went out and pulled the trigger of that gun, Peter, because he couldn't fight any more. I think he probably did, regardless of that note. But if his was the physical act, theirs was the moral. They forced him down that wretched path to it!"

"Who are *they*, specifically?"

Alice Widener stubbed out her cigarette. "When you have read all the documentation on the case—when you've talked to everyone concerned—you'll see who 'they' are . . . specifically."

Peter Marshall walked down Park Avenue, oblivious for the moment to the winter chill. Already it was dark, and the myriad patterns of lights scaled the building fronts in early evening display. His thoughts turned inward and neither sight nor sound of the city penetrated past eyes and ears.

Although there still were areas to be explored and vital questions to be answered, concerning the death of the man—particularly the missing hours—he must now turn his full attention to Paul Bang-Jensen's life.

CHAPTER 8

THE CAREY BUS swung into a stop in front of the stylish new BOAC terminal. Peter Marshall alighted with several other passengers; they about to begin a journey, he ending one.

It was a foul night, the rain mixed with snow, and it was pleasant to hurry the few steps from the bus into the spacious, warmly lit waiting room.

He saw a long counter behind which there were three very pretty girls in blue uniforms, checking in those soon to depart. He was ten minutes early for the hastily made appointment, but he began sorting out those present in the hope that the man he was going to meet had also arrived.

A fourth girl, a statuesque blonde, moved in on him with a well-practiced smile.

"Can I help you, sir?"

He said, "Yes . . . I'm looking for a passenger going out on your eight-thirty flight to London. I don't know whether he's arrived or not."

"That's flight three fourteen. If you'll give me his name, I'll check."

She checked. The man in question had not yet arrived, and then she suggested helpfully that Peter Marshall might want to go up to the mezzanine that overlooked the waiting room. There was a bar there.

He thanked her and she stalked off to greet two diplomatic types with the same marvelous control and use of muscle and smile. He decided he would do his waiting where he could keep an eye on the entrance.

The man had not been friendly on the telephone. He'd been brusque and suspicious.

"I certainly don't want to answer any questions on the phone. I don't know you. I don't know anything about you."

"I understand that. If we could meet, I could explain very quickly."

Pause and then, "Have you seen Mrs. Bang-Jensen?"

"I've talked to her on the telephone. To get back to our meeting, you name the place and time and I'll be there."

Another pause. "How do you know about me?"

The explanation brought a grunt, and Peter Marshall decided he was getting nowhere. "Look, you were his friend. What you have to say about him is important."

"And this is a book?"

"Yes . . . on his life."

"You are sympathetic to him?"

"Yes, but I'm not out to tell any fairy tales."

The grunt was less antagonistic. "It's not going to do any good to stir it all up again. In my position, I can't take a stand. I may feel one way, but I can't take a stand. I have my job to think about, my family."

"I appreciate that, but I'm looking for facts more than for opinion. If you don't want your name used, it won't be."

"Well, I'm going away to Europe. Why don't you call me in about a month?"

"I can't wait that long. I have a deadline. It's important I see you now."

"Well, that's impossible. I'm leaving tomorrow evening."

"I'll see you any time you say before that."

"No, I'll be much too busy, getting ready."

It looked like a stone wall, and he was debating whether to give up or to go on arguing when the offer came: "Look, I'm getting an eight-thirty flight, BOAC. If you want to talk to me, I'll see you at seven-thirty in the waiting room."

"Wonderful! I'll be there. . . . How will I know you?"

"Ask for me."

At 8:00 o'clock, Marshall's impatience had become well laced with annoyance. With an 8:30 departure, his contact would have to board the plane a good ten minutes before take-off. It left damn little time to talk after the checking in had been accomplished.

At 8:10, the waiting room's populace filling the air with anticipatory chatter, he decided he'd been stood up. For the fourth time he strode to the counter and checked the passenger list with the attendant.

No show. As he turned from the sympathetic clerk, a squarely built man in trench coat and alpine fedora came toward him, well-traveled valise in one hand, brief case in the other. The man was smiling.

"Mr. Marshall?"

"Yes!"

"I'm sorry I'm late. I'm always late for these things, but usually the flight's late too. I'll be just a minute."

"That's all right," and then, with a smile, "how did you recognize me?"

The traveler returned the smile. "By the worried look on your face."

They sat on a bench, Marshall facing the wall clock, doubly aware of how terribly few minutes they had.

"I must apologize for my rudeness on the phone last night, but it was quite a surprise to get your call." The traveler offered a cigarette. "All right, now I understand about the book, and perhaps it's a good thing someone is doing one just to straighten everything out. What is it you want to know?"

"When did you first know him?"

"Well, I knew about him long before I knew him. During the war—before I was captured—I was in the Danish underground, and Paul was very active in that."

"He was here in America. How could he be in the underground?"

"I assure you he was, Mr. Marshall, and he was well thought of for his part in it. Have you talked to Henrik Kauffmann yet?"

"I'm hoping to see him this week."

"Well, Kauffmann can tell you all about it. You know, of course, that Henrik Kauffmann was the Danish Minister to the U.S., and when the Nazis overran Denmark, he set up a 'government in exile.' Paul became his right hand. But you talk to Kauffmann. Get him to tell you about Greenland."

"How about your association with Bang-Jensen?"

"I met Paul when he came to the U.N. . . . . That was in—ahh—July, 1949. He was the top-ranking Danish political officer in the Secretariat."

"That sounds impressive."

"Well, maybe it sounds a little more impressive than it was, but it was a good job, and at times a very responsible job."

"You liked him."

"Yes, I liked him." The slightly slanted eyes looked into Marshall's steadily. "He had many winning qualities. He was not jealous of his position as many people are. He was not always looking out for himself, if you know what I mean? . . . In fact, he was always going out of his way to help his countrymen, and with no thought of thanks. I don't think there are many of us who can be called absolutely truthful men. We are cynical. Often we use the truth as it suits us. There were times when Paul might have been wrong in what he said, but he never said it without thinking it was the truth. Do you see what I mean?"

"He sounds like Prince Hamlet." Marshall threw it out to get a reaction.

"No." The other shook his head and stuck the butt of his cigarette in the sand tray. "No, that's a bad analogy. The only similarity is the tragedy. In many respects Paul was naïve . . . foolish. He was too sensitive a man, too serious a man."

"He didn't have very good judgment," Marshall said, thinking of Alice Widener's remarks.

"How much judgment does a man have who attacks the U.N. Secretariat . . . and expects to beat it?"

"Was he right?"

"I am not the one to say. I'm really in no position to comment on it." The traveler took off his glasses and pulled out a handkerchief to wipe the lenses. "I know that, once he took a dislike to someone, he did nothing to hide it."

"What about the list of Hungarian witnesses he wouldn't hand over?"

The traveler shrugged. "Do you mean was he justified in carrying it around in his pocket?" There was a hint of sarcasm in the sound of his voice. "Everyone knew those names couldn't be kept secret. The list became a kind of symbol for him."

"He kept them secret."

A beautifully modulated English voice, female in sex, announced Flight 314, asking passengers to board through Gate 4. Marshall could have shot her.

"That's all right, we still have a minute." The experienced traveler smiled.

"When did you see him last?"

"We had lunch, I think it was the Thursday before

Thanksgiving. We ate at Ferdi's. He wanted to discuss a tax problem with me. Actually it was nonexistent, but he was worried about it."

"That doesn't sound like a man who's about to kill himself."

"Ordinarily perhaps not, but if you'd known Paul—"

"Then you have no doubt that it was suicide?"

"None . . . I don't think the Communists could have cared less about him."

"Is that based on something you know for sure?"

"It's an opinion . . . my opinion."

"You saw him frequently?"

"Infrequently after his dismissal. We'd have lunch once in a while."

"And that last time, what did he have to say, aside from the tax problem?"

"Oh, we talked about his job situation. I think he wanted to make his job at CARE permanent."

"Did you make a date to see him again?"

"No."

The final call for 314 was announced, and the two men stood up. "I'm sorry I haven't been more helpful," the traveler said. "You won't find your job an easy one. There are too many people who won't talk," he said with a smile, "even while on the run."

"It's been very kind of you to do this much. May I call you when you return?"

"You may, but I don't think I can add much. Go see Kauffmann. Go see the Danish correspondent, Gunnar Leistikow."

They shook hands. "Have a good trip."

"Thanks, I will." The traveler stepped onto the escalator and began his short journey upward. He gave a half salute of farewell and called down with a smile, "Good luck to you . . . and you be kind to my friend Paul."

CHAPTER 9

FROM MANY PEOPLE, Marshall gathered facts on his protagonist's youth, his rise, his first setback:

From Henrik Kauffmann, former Danish Ambassador to the United States—

From Alfred Maack-Petersen, boyhood friend of Paul Bang-Jensen—

From Adolf A. Berle, Jr., former Assistant Secretary of State and co-worker with Bang-Jensen on Danish matters during the war—

From Gunnar Leistikow, Danish news correspondent and supporter of Bang-Jensen—

From friends of the Bang-Jensen family—

And from others who did not wish their names to be used.

In learning about his man, he began to see him more clearly. From a figure on which adjectives had been draped to cover the bones, he was emerging as a flesh-and-blood human being.

"He had a funny way of walking . . . sort of loose

*jointed. We nicknamed him 'rubber knees.' Paul didn't go
in for sports; it was always books, books, books. He really got
fantastic grades. His older brother Niels was quite different
. . . . outgoing, a little autocratic as older brothers will
be, but Paul knew how to handle him. He was a diplomat
even then. Of course, I was younger. My brother and Paul
and Niels were all about the same age group, so I got left
out a lot, but I remember . . . so well . . . there would be
times when I would be hurt about something—as boys will
be—some childhood slight, some trouble blown up out of
proportion, and Paul would speak to me. Somehow he'd
know. And whatever he had to say would always help. I can
see him now. Tall, thin, quite handsome . . . quiet.*

"I did not see him for many years, but when I came to
this country after the war, he took me out to his home and
I met his wife and family. He showed me around the U.N.,
and I knew he was very proud of being a part of it. He went
out of his way to help me in finding a job."

After Peter Marshall had talked to those who could fill
him in on Paul Bang-Jensen's past, he sat down and capsul-
ized what he had learned. He wrote:

Came to U.S. 1939 to further studies in international law,
economics, politics. Very interested in teachings of Harvard
Law Professor Roscoe Pound, with particular regard to writings
on due process.

Paul, the bright young man of twenty-nine, exuding charm,
warmth, brilliance. Niels Bohr, the noted atomic physicist,
twenty years Bang-Jensen's senior, impressed . . . life long
friends.[1]

Joins Danish Embassy in Washington at start of W. W. II as
First Secretary.

Meets Helen Nolan of Port Jervis, New York. She, graduate
of Elmira College, gifted, idealistic, liberal . . . Executive Secretary to Clark Eichelberger's Committee to Defend America by
Aiding the Allies.

"Paul and Helen met at an Embassy party in nineteen thirty-nine, and after that, they began going out when he could find the time—you know how busy things were in those days. And the money—poor Paul, he had very little of that either.

"But they had so much in common . . . the same ideals, the same hopes. She understood, and they became very close.

"You know, it was quite a joke with them but actually Helen proposed to Paul in nineteen forty. It was leap year, and there's an old Danish custom that says when the woman proposes to the man, if he does not accept, he has to pay a forfeit of a dozen pair of gloves. Well, Paul was so broke that he not only couldn't accept, he couldn't afford the forfeit. But, to make up for it they became engaged."

Peter Marshall resumed writing:

Denmark invaded and conquered by Germany, April 9, 1940. Kauffmann sets up Government in Exile with help of U. S. Administration. Disobeys orders from homeland. Is ordered to return. Refuses. Bang-Jensen becomes attaché. Kauffmann's right-hand man. In Washington circles known as "the key man."

Vital importance of Greenland recognized by Kauffmann and U.S. Bang-Jensen and Adolf A. Berle, Jr., work together in drawing up a treaty by which U.S. will take over protection of Greenland until Denmark again free.

(If Nazis took Greenland, weather stations for submarines of serious consequences to Allies. Aircraft installations a direct threat to Canada and U.S. mainland.)

Treaty signed April 9, 1941. Result—all hell breaks loose in homeland, via Berlin. Letters exchanged between President Roosevelt and King Christian. U.S. not yet in war, uses theory of Monroe Doctrine as basis for treaty, and that Danish Government is acting under duress.

Bang-Jensen also responsible for keeping Danish shipping under its own flag and for use by Allies. No easy job, for English wanted ships sold in prize courts, and Danish captains wanted to lease out to the highest bidders.

Bang-Jensen very active in setting up underground operations inside homeland. Given sums of money by U.S. to gather needed information. Money well spent, information gathered.

On delicate missions to England for Kauffman.

Tireless worker, seven days a week, inspired.

1943 Niels Bohr arrives in U.S. Member of British scientific mission.[2]

Paul Bang-Jensen and Helen Nolan are married.

"It wasn't until nineteen forty-three that Paul felt he was financially able to ask Helen to be his wife. In March, he took five days off and they drove to Staunton, Virginia. They got married there at the birthplace of Woodrow Wilson. It's sort of a shrine, and for Paul and Helen it was just the sort of place for them to marry."

To Peter Marshall, Henrik Kauffmann lived up to the title "diplomat" in the best sense of the word. A tall, lean man with a handsome mane of white hair capping finely cut features, he was perceptive and understanding.

As he spoke of Paul Bang-Jensen, Marshall saw reflected in his striking blue eyes a touch of sadness. "When Paul came to this country in nineteen thirty-nine, he was already known in Denmark as a brilliant lawyer. I, myself, had heard about him. . . . He'd written a book on price fixing, a rather dull sounding subject, but it actually won a prize. . . . And so we met, and in all my career I can't ever recall having been so impressed with a young man . . . so taken. . . ."

Henrik Kauffmann spelled out the details of the war years and how important and vital a role Paul Bang-Jensen had played in Danish efforts to help the Allied cause and rid the homeland of the Nazi yoke.

"When the war ended," Kauffmann related in his soft voice, "Paul hoped for an immediate position as an ambassador. He didn't want to go back to Denmark and start in the Foreign Service with a couple of years of ground work at home. Many of his age group are ambassadors right now and I have no doubt he would have risen to a high post, but he thought he deserved it right away . . . and he missed his opportunity, you might say.

"He stayed on at the Embassy in Washington until 1949 . . . in a sort of special capacity. I kept him on as my second in command because, quite frankly, none of the other people sent out had his capabilities. Of course, there was some grumbling at home. A wartime hanger on. People soon forget."

"With his law background," Marshall asked, ending the pause which followed, "I should think he could have gotten a good position somewhere?"

"Oh, he could have. He could have. He had several fine offers, but he turned them all down."

"The world of diplomacy had gotten in his blood, is that it?"

"The state of the world was, of course, very much in his mind always. He was a member of the Liberal Party in Denmark, which would be analogous to your Democratic Party here. Both he and his wife were closely associated with the liberal philosophy."

"And that was what took him finally to the U.N.?"

From where they sat, there was a good view of the East River. A high-flying gull swept in close to the window, leveling on the gusty wind. The mewing sound of his hungry complaint reached them faintly. The elderly man, whose quality of vigor gave his bearing added attractiveness, watched the gull out of sight before he replied.

"Have you ever heard of the 'Easter Crisis' in Denmark?"

"No, I don't believe I have."

"Well . . . Paul is blamed for that. It happened in 1948. Your Government had called in the Norwegian Ambassador and myself and advised us of their appraisal of the cold-war situation. Czechoslovakia had fallen in February. The

U.S. felt if an anti-Soviet defense alliance wasn't forth-coming, the Scandinavian countries might soon fall as others had.

"It was properly my job to go back and advise the Government, but Paul was anxious to take on the assignment. He hadn't been home in some time, and I thought it might be an opportunity for him to look around, renew contacts.

"Before he left, we sat down and I told him not to paint too vivid a picture. Everything comes out brighter than told anyway. . . . Well, he talked to a foreign minister who was more a politician than a foreign-service man. He didn't know our rules and Paul, I'm afraid, did not paint the picture in pastel colors. It came out very bright. It led to fear sweeping some circles in Denmark that a Soviet invasion was in the offing. It was Easter time, and while there was no mobilization, the troops were kept on duty instead of getting leaves. It raised a lot of tempers.

"The whole incident was unfortunate and Paul came in for a great deal of criticism. It hurt him . . . and of course, later the Communists used it to show how bad his judgment was."

"Denmark joined NATO in 1949, didn't it, sir? Do you think his warning had anything to do with that?"

A faint smile creased the diplomat's firm mouth. "Some will tell you so, I'm sure. It's a pity you can't end your book in 1948."

"That would only be a part of the story. He went to the U.N. in forty-nine."

"Yes, so he did," Kauffmann nodded and again the note of sadness was in his voice. "He believed very deeply in the purposes of the U.N., but he was never happy in his work there. How could he be? It's all red tape, bureaucracy. He always said it was overstaffed. Much of the work he found meaningless, with endless drafts to write. He wanted something more rewarding."

"But still he stayed on."

"Yes." The former ambassador gave him a level stare. "He stayed on."

Peter Marshall continued asking, listening, probing, gathering the kindly man's impressions of all that followed. He learned much, and then, at the end, asked the key question:

"Do you think he killed himself?"

Henrik Kauffmann sighed and gave a short nod. "I saw him about two weeks before his death. He was in a very depressed state. He thought his job with CARE as a consultant was no job at all, and he no longer felt capable of handling a responsible post. He was tormented by the memories of the abilities that he had lost. I'm afraid he dwelt on them . . . and turned inward . . . everything was out of proportion. . . ."

"You have no doubts?"

"After his suspension he told me it was something he would never do . . . but I believe he did it in a fit of depression. Mr. Marshall, you are a young man, but as we grow older, we should mellow, grow more liberal in our outlook toward people, more tolerant, for we are all human. It's a pity that Paul couldn't see that."

Although Peter Marshall realized he'd gained much insight and background on Henrik Kauffmann's understanding of Paul Bang-Jensen's character, the interview left him momentarily disturbed. The contradictions of character plagued him. How did one reconcile the description of a man going out of his way to help his fellowman, without thought of reward, with an individual whose vanity and ambition allowed him no tolerance for human frailty?

Only after long study of the notes he had made from the handful of people to whom he had talked, could he clarify the inconsistencies in his own mind.

It was a matter of time, and a matter of place, and a matter of juxtaposition. Each sees the man from where he sits and the relative relationships between the two. Some see his weaknesses, some his strength, some both. But all emphasize what they see as a constant trait of character because that is what they remember best. Any man of character, when described by those who think they know him, must emerge as a compilation of contradictions with only a few observations consistent throughout.

Taking only the latter, Peter Marshall could say of Paul Bang-Jensen: "He was a man of high purpose who was driven equally by his feelings for his fellowman and his own personal ambition. He wanted a better life for his fellowman, and like so many brilliant men, he saw himself as one capable of knowing how best to attain it. He had a swift, agile mind that saw to the core of the matter, but in reaching it, he was often tactless, rude, and inflexible. He had a true generosity; a selfless spirit that was an inspiration to some and a bore to others. He had a slightly sardonic sense of humor, but no tolerance for those whom he disliked. He was monumentally stubborn, and in this, his courage was unique. His love for his wife and children was deep and abiding."

Peter Marshall stopped there. He knew he could go on, but it was better to let the analysis stand as it was. He'd see if it could stand up against the events to follow and become further amplified.

It was time to look into those events, for they had made Paul Bang-Jensen famous, and they had helped to kill him.

Part Two: Betrayal

70 BETRAYAL AT THE

CHAPTER 10

THEY WENT to the Old Hungary Restaurant at 2nd Avenue and 70th Street, and there Laszlo Varga showed him how to order Hungarian-style. Marshall noted that the former Parliament member had the same clear, flinty blue eyes that he had found so compelling in the looks of Monsignor Bela Varga. He did not think the two men were related, but he knew they had something in common and that the characteristic was shared by all the Hungarians he had met so far, whether blue-eyed or brown. There was no defeat in their gaze. There was firmness. There was humor. There was intelligence, and what pain they knew, they kept well concealed.

Laszlo Varga had come to the United States as a refugee in 1947, shortly after the Communist take-over. He was to be one of those who, in 1956, clamored and pleaded in vain for the U.N. to take action after the Revolution had been won and before the Russian tanks returned to crush the victory.

"It is, of course, not my belief alone," he said in his pleasantly accented way, "that nineteen fifty-six was a turning point in history . . . that the West had its chance . . . its last chance . . . to take action that would have reversed the tide . . . swung it in the other direction."

"But wouldn't that have meant war?"

"No! . . . My friend, what you must do is to learn all about what happened in Hungary, and you must learn what happened at the U.N. Then you will see . . . then you will know. No," Varga shook his head, "there would have been no war. If the U.N. had sent only one observer the Soviet troops would never have come in."

"Doctor Szentadorjany mentioned there was a fact book on Hungary[1] I should get hold of."

"Yes, we'll see that you get a copy of that. It's very good, and there are a number of people to whom you should talk. You see, what happened in the U.N. has a direct bearing on Bang-Jensen. The committee to investigate the uprising in Hungary would not have been necessary had the U.N. acted."

"And in that case, I'd have no book to write." He said it lightly.

Laszlo Varga shook his head. "It is tragic that you have this book to write, but it is good that you are doing it."

"You knew Bang-Jensen quite well, didn't you?"

"I knew him, of course. I don't know how well. I thought very highly of him. . . . I found him different from most U.N. people I have met, in that he was polite . . . and friendly . . . and he was genuinely interested in what you had to offer. He would listen to you, and when he spoke, you trusted him instinctively."

"And his death?"

"You know what Monsignor Varga says about his death? That no matter who pulled the trigger, the terrible tragedy is in the fact that any man in this great country of yours could be forced to such an act . . . either by his own hand or another."

"I read somewhere a description of the U.N. as the tombstone of mankind."

"Well, I don't know about that." Varga smiled. "But you find out what happened there in November, 1956, and you make up your own mind. And now let us have some palacsintas. They're very good, a Hungarian favorite, and I think you'll like them." Varga laughed. "We'll make a Hungarian out of you yet. You look like one."

In the next few weeks Peter Marshall talked to many Hungarians—to Imre Kovacs . . . to Anna Kethly . . . to Janos Horvath . . . to Sandor Kiss . . . to General Bela Kiraly . . . to Thomas Szabo . . . and others.

At night he read everything he could get his hands on concerning the revolt as it had taken place in Hungary, and as it was handled in the conference rooms of the U.N. From his endeavors, he came to know why Laszlo Varga and his countrymen looked upon the United Nations' actions as too few and too late. Whatever the reasons behind such actions, Peter Marshall saw them as the climactic turning point in Paul Bang-Jensen's life. For this reason he set them down as they had occurred.

The autumn of 1956 was a time of confusion and crowded headlines and momentous consequences for the world. In a space of a few weeks, Poland moved to assert its own independent spirit; Israeli and Anglo-French forces invaded Egypt; the United States elected a president; in Hungary, a nation rose up.

The first whispers of the Hungarian revolt came October 23, as students in Budapest demonstrated in support of Poland's newly proclaimed "independent road to Socialism."

A breath of freedom was in the air. The people were looking forward to substantial improvements in the standard of living and perhaps, too, relief from the dreaded practices of the State Security Police—the AVH.

"For me, it was just like a first love," said Jan Greg, a young former Freedom Fighter. "It was beautiful. Everyone just going out, joining in, taking part, doing anything he could."

News of Hungary was flashed around the world. Newspaper readers saw photographs of the huge Stalin statue being torn from its base. Leaders came to the fore, reforms were demanded, manifestoes written. Street fighting swept Budapest. Soviet tanks rolled into action against unarmed citizens.

And in New York, never had the world organization sat so uncomfortably astride its hallowed ground on the East River. For this wasn't a Palestine, with a problem born of the ages; nor a Korea, with fast, incisive United States action to lead the way. This was a satellite Soviet-bloc nation rising against the Kremlin.

Some detected confusion. For one thing, a U.N. staff member recalls, very few understood exactly what the situation was. "There was complete ignorance at this point as to what was going on in Hungary. Hardly anyone knew who Imre Nagy was."

Paul Bang-Jensen was an exception. He had a tremendous interest in what was unfolding, and was often in the U.N. news room checking developments. "He sensed the importance of Hungary almost at once," Helen Bang-Jensen recalled.

Fatefully enough, the case of Imre Nagy, later to be betrayed and lured from safety to eventual execution, was to preoccupy Bang-Jensen until the end of his life. Nagy, with determination masked by a pince-nez and a warm, shy smile, was a veteran Communist with long years of Moscow residence. He also had human insight into the leadership of people.

As Premier for almost two years in 1953-55, Nagy had defied the previous order of communization in Hungary and set about to improve the nation's lot. Most endearing to the people was the stand he had taken against the repressive police and judicial practices. As a result, he had fallen in bad with the Communist hierarchy and had been ousted from his post in the party. He had only been re-admitted to Communist membership October 13, 1956.

It was little wonder that the crowd shouted for Nagy when it marched on Parliament in the later stages of the October 23 demonstration. Nagy's brief and restrained appearance on a balcony disappointed the throng, which did not know he was under the control of the AVH and unable to speak his mind.

But overnight the clamor for Nagy had its effect. He was taken to see Premier Andras Hegedus and First Secretary Erno Gero. They said he was to blame for the popular ferment outside and Gero sarcastically added that Nagy "could now stew in his own juice." Sometime thereafter, early on the morning of the twenty-fourth, Nagy was told he was being named Premier.

With the man of their choice apparently in charge, students and workers of the revolutionary ranks were shocked to hear Nagy broadcasts refer to the Freedom Fighters as "hostile elements." Further, it was implied that Nagy had asked for Soviet military assistance to put down the uprising—although in actuality the Russian armored cars and tanks had been in action since the night of the twenty-third.

What was not known was that Nagy, after being made Premier, was taken to Communist party headquarters and held incommunicado.

The U.N. "Report of the Special Committee on Hungary" says: "During Wednesday, Thursday and most of Friday, 24, 25 and 26 October, Mr. Nagy was, according to the evidence received by the Special Committee, in the Party Headquarters. During the first part of this period, he was not allowed to see anyone from the outside, nor to receive or make any telephone calls. He was, during part of the time, kept locked in a room with his son-in-law."

Early during this period, Nagy was handed a party-line speech and ordered: "Go read this into the tape recorder." He balked when he saw that he was to call the revolutionists "Fascist bandits." Because the situation was worsening for the Communist bosses, Nagy was allowed to make some changes. However, when student worker representatives were admitted to see him on the twenty-fifth, they found him seated at a table behind which stood about fifteen men armed with machine guns.

In succeeding meetings, delegations found civilian-garbed AVH guards standing at Nagy's side. But the tidal wave of the revolution was not to be stopped, and by the twenty-sixth, success appeared to be running with the Freedom Fighters. Gero quit as party secretary and Janos Kadar took over that office. Nagy was free to leave Communist headquarters and go to the Parliament building. The next day he stated that the AVH would be dissolved.

When the chairman of a revolutionary council visited the new Premier on the twenty-ninth, his opening comment was to note that for the first time the AVH were no longer present.

On the thirtieth, Nagy announced negotiations for the immediate withdrawal of Soviet troops and the abolition of the one-party system in favor of a new coalition government. He also said that the permanent Hungarian delegate to the U.N.—Doctor Peter Kos—was being recalled. The fact that Kos was actually a Soviet citizen by the name of Leo Konductorov had never bothered East or West at the U.N. until that day.

On November 1, with Nagy the popular and legal leader

of Hungary—and indisputably, it would seem—a message came rattling into the U.N. communications center. It was direct from Budapest. Addressee: Secretary General Dag Hammarskjold. Sent by Imre Nagy in words that were hard to misunderstand:

RELIABLE REPORTS HAVE REACHED THE GOVERNMENT OF THE HUNGARIAN PEOPLE'S REPUBLIC THAT FURTHER SOVIET UNITS ARE ENTERING INTO HUNGARY. THE PRESIDENT OF THE COUNCIL OF MINISTERS [NAGY] IN HIS CAPACITY AS MINISTER FOR FOREIGN AFFAIRS SUMMONED [YURI V.] ANDROPOV, AMBASSADOR EXTRAORDINARY AND PLENIPOTENTIARY OF THE SOVIET UNION TO HUNGARY, AND EXPRESSED HIS STRONGEST PROTEST AGAINST THE ENTRY OF FURTHER SOVIET TROOPS INTO HUNGARY. HE DEMANDED THE INSTANT AND IMMEDIATE WITHDRAWAL OF THESE SOVIET FORCES.

HE INFORMED THE SOVIET AMBASSADOR THAT THE HUNGARIAN GOVERNMENT IMMEDIATELY REPUDIATES THE WARSAW TREATY AND AT THE SAME TIME, DECLARES HUNGARY'S NEUTRALITY AND TURNS TO THE UNITED NATIONS AND REQUESTS THE HELP OF THE GREAT POWERS IN DEFENDING THE COUNTRY'S NEUTRALITY. THE GOVERNMENT OF THE HUNGARIAN PEOPLE'S REPUBLIC MADE THE DECLARATION OF NEUTRALITY ON NOV. 1, 1956. THEREFORE I REQUEST YOUR EXCELLENCY TO PUT ON THE AGENDA OF THE FORTHCOMING GENERAL ASSEMBLY OF THE UNITED NATIONS THE QUESTION OF HUNGARY'S NEUTRALITY AND THE DEFENSE OF THIS NEUTRALITY BY THE FOUR GREAT POWERS.

There it was: a plea for help unprecedented in the history of the Cold War. It was clocked into the U.N. wire room at 12:27 P.M. and was sent to the Secretary General's office. But Hammarskjold was out to lunch and the message got no special attention. Instead of excitement, it earned a tremendous yawn.

"My God!" a staff member said when discussing it. "Couldn't someone see that here was an out-of-the-ordinary communication—signed by Nagy and sent to the SG? Someone should have known!"

It was only because of the news reports from Europe telling of the Premier's announcement that the cable was brought to light by early afternoon. Correspondents checked the wire room—yes, a Nagy message had been received, and also a second one from him at 12:45.

The Secretary General's office on the thirty-eighth floor at first professed ignorance. A message from Nagy? No one knew anything about that. A U.N. press officer hurried to the office, found the message buried in an "In" basket and made its contents known at 2:00 P.M. But, even then, no special effort was made to alert delegates to the fact that an urgent appeal from Nagy was in the shop. Its text was run off on mimeograph machines and routinely distributed to mailboxes.

The second message, directly from Budapest, was in turn shuffled aside. It was also addressed to Hammarskjold and signed by Nagy. It said:

I HAVE THE HONOR TO INFORM YOU THAT MR. JANOS SZABO, FIRST SECRETARY OF THE PERMANENT MISSION, WILL REPRESENT THE HUNGARIAN PEOPLE'S REPUBLIC AT THE SPECIAL SESSION OF THE GENERAL ASSEMBLY TO BE CONVENED NOV. 1, 1956, AT NEW YORK.

Nagy, in the first message, specified that the question of Hungary be placed before the forthcoming General Assembly, and this was not due to convene until November 12. Yet the rest of his cable underlined the critical situation at hand and spoke for quick action.

His second message seemed to make it clear that he was aware of the emergency session being called on the Suez crisis that day, and his naming of a Hungarian delegate suggested he thought that some move on Hungary should be made also.

If the two cables raised any questions—and they certainly did—Hammarskjold for a few more precious hours would have been able literally to ring up the Hungarian Foreign Ministry in Budapest on the direct cable connection. This he failed to do and the circuit was later broken.

Whatever the U.N.'s analysis of the messages, there was no gainsaying Nagy's urgent words that the situation was becoming critical in Hungary and the government was begging the attention of the United Nations.

"I know Hammarskjold was busy with Suez," Imre Kovacs, former Hungarian Parliament member recalled, "but it certainly was negligent of him not to follow up the Nagy cables at once."

While the Secretariat pondered, some U.N. delegates, united in their desire to oppose Communism, worked feverishly to push the world organization into meeting the Hungarian appeal head on.

Dr. Emilio Nuñez-Portuondo of Cuba and others—joined together in the so-called Cassandra Club—button-holed fellow diplomats to urge fast, decisive steps on the Nagy cables.

Even as the U.N. dawdled, there were the first hints in Hungary of the new Red terror to come: Russian troop movements were reported around Budapest; Kadar was going secretly to the Soviet Embassy for talks.

A bitter discussion had raged at the Kremlin as to how to deal with the Hungarian comrades. The Stalinists called for reimposition of Moscow's total rule by brute force; moderates appeared willing to settle for a pro-Soviet "neutralist" Hungary. The uprising was "a rat to choke over," Khrushchev was to admit later.

At the U.N. the Security Council met three times on October 30 to attempt to thrash out the critical Middle East developments. There were charges and recriminations. The United States called on Israel to withdraw from Egypt; the

Soviet Union conveniently overlooked its own position in Hungary and called for a cease fire as well as withdrawal by the Israeli forces. There was a vote condemning Britain and France's ultimatum to invade the Suez Canal Zone. But by and large the sessions got no place, and Hammarskjold adjourned the final meeting at 10:00 P.M. with no conclusive U.N. action that might have given the British legislators something to think about.

Whatever suspicions Bang-Jensen had previously harbored about the high command of the Secretariat, they were hardening to awful certainty at this time. He felt that Hammarskjold let the Security Council wind up that night despite the fact that speediest action was essential—that the British Cabinet would have been influenced, for British and French military forces were not at that time committed.

The next day (the thirty-first), Bang-Jensen watched the Security Council struggle on. The Russians raised technical points and time was lost. Finally, Yugoslavia proposed an emergency session of the General Assembly.

If the U.N. had hoped to bring its weight to bear, it was too late. That same day the British and French landed their military forces in Egypt.

In those days of double crisis, Bang-Jensen saw the pattern of delay used as a weapon. "Delay, delay, delay, and the purpose is served!" he said. He was equally angered by the casual reception given Nagy's cables.

On November 1, major attention at the U.N. was on the Middle East, and the emergency session opened at 5:00 P.M. (This was the session Nagy had referred to in his second cable.) It was about this hour that many delegates, picking up their house mail, were learning of Nagy's plea to Hammarskjold.

In the following three hours of debate on Suez, the word "Hungary" was mentioned only once, when a British delegate said: "I cannot help contrasting [Britain's action in the

Middle East] with the armed actions of the Soviet Union aimed at perpetuating its domination of Hungary."

After a recess, the session reconvened at 10:00 P.M. and continued to sit until 4:00 A.M. on November 2, finally approving a resolution that condemned Britain, France, and Israel and called for a cease fire.

Almost as if in irony, Hungary was briefly touched on in the final sleepy half hour of that early-morning meeting. Italian delegate Leonardo Vitetti asked to speak "on a point of order." He noted to the weary assemblage that the Nagy appeal "has just been circulated to us"—this was four-teen hours after the first cable from Imre Nagy had arrived at the U.N. He added: "I hope that the U.N.—and if necessary this special emergency session—will take immediately whatever action is possible with regard to the request of the Hungarian people."

Delegates shuffled papers—yes, the Nagy appeal! The Cassandras leaned forward expectantly; the Russians watched with cold eyes; the Indian delegation looked on with disdain—from the outset Krishna Menon, the India Foreign Minister, had labeled the Hungarian revolt a Fascist uprising;[2] the Assembly roused itself as Victor Belaunde of Peru got up and vouched his agreement with Vitetti's statement—and then the world's representatives looked to John Foster Dulles.

"I want to express my endorsement," said the American Secretary of State, "of the intervention made by the representative of Italy with reference to the Hungarian situation."

Dulles, looking tired and strained, had no forewarning that he was to undergo an operation for cancer the next day. But no one knew of his physical deterioration, and perhaps his lack of fervor was taken as listless interest.

He went on: "I hope that this matter, which is on the agenda of the Security Council, will be kept urgently before it, and we shall not be preoccupied with the Middle East to the exclusion of assisting the State of Hungary to regain its independence." [3]

But time was already running out in Hungary, and once again the issue was sidestepped and nothing was done. "It was fantastic," Thomas Szabo, a Hungarian newsman, said. "A complete outsider could notice how, for a week before the intervention, the Russians were waiting for a reaction, of the West, of the United States. I know positively the Russians tried to find out the attitude of the United States on Hungary—and there wasn't any. The tragic thing was that this had been a period of uncertainty; there were no military or diplomatic moves. It was postponed, postponed, until the Russians clearly realized that the United States was not going to do anything."

He added: "There was a great deal of confusion at the U.N. None of the major Western delegations wanted to make a decision. It's to [American Ambassador Henry Cabot] Lodge's credit that, when he was talking on the phone with President Eisenhower, he said: 'We cannot delay this any longer if we want to save our face.' Dulles took another line. He thought the U.N. could keep back, tone it down.

"The general opinion among many at the U.N. was that, if there had been any diplomatic or political gestures, the whole thing could have been changed. Why, even a Pole told me: 'If they [the Hungarians] succeed, we are going the same way—the whole picture of Europe will be different.' "

But so it was that on the morning of November 2, when the exhausted U.N. delegates awoke only a few hours after the wearying Suez debate, they were assaulted by headlines they had not expected to see.

Said *The New York Times:*

SOVIET TANKS RING BUDAPEST; NAGY DEFIANT,
APPEALS TO U.N.

And later that day came Nagy's final appeal to Hammarskjold, for this was his last chance, and he stood with his back to the wall in Budapest:

YOUR EXCELLENCY:

AS THE PRESIDENT OF THE COUNCIL OF MINISTERS AND DESIGNATE FOREIGN MINISTER OF THE HUNGARIAN PEOPLE'S REPUBLIC I HAVE THE HONOR TO BRING TO THE ATTENTION OF YOUR EXCELLENCY THE FOLLOWING ADDITIONAL INFORMATION:

I HAVE ALREADY MENTIONED IN MY LETTER OF NOV. 1 THAT NEW SOVIET MILITARY UNITS ENTERED HUNGARY AND THAT THE HUNGARIAN GOVERNMENT INFORMED THE SOVIET AMBASSADOR IN BUDAPEST OF THIS FACT, AT THE SAME TIME TERMINATED THE WARSAW PACT, DECLARED THE NEUTRALITY OF HUNGARY, AND REQUESTED THE UNITED NATIONS TO GUARANTEE THE NEUTRALITY OF THIS COUNTRY.

ON THE 2ND OF NOVEMBER FURTHER AND EXACT INFORMATION, MAINLY MILITARY REPORTS, REACHED THE GOVERNMENT OF THE HUNGARIAN PEOPLE'S REPUBLIC, ACCORDING TO WHICH LARGE SOVIET MILITARY UNITS CROSSED THE BORDER OF THE COUNTRY, MARCHING TOWARD BUDAPEST. THEY OCCUPY RAILWAY LINES, RAILWAY STATIONS, AND RAILWAY SAFETY EQUIPMENT. REPORTS ALSO HAVE COME THAT THE SOVIET MILITARY MOVEMENTS IN AN EAST-WEST DIRECTION ARE BEING OBSERVED ON THE TERRITORY OF WESTERN HUNGARY.

ON THE BASIS OF THE ABOVE MENTIONED FACTS THE HUNGARIAN GOVERNMENT DEEMED IT NECESSARY TO INFORM THE EMBASSY OF THE U.S.S.R. AND ALL THE OTHER DIPLOMATIC MISSIONS IN BUDAPEST ABOUT THESE STEPS DIRECTED AGAINST OUR PEOPLE'S REPUBLIC.

AT THE SAME TIME, THE GOVERNMENT OF THE HUNGARIAN PEOPLE'S REPUBLIC FORWARDED CONCRETE PROPOSALS ON THE WITHDRAWAL OF SOVIET TROOPS STATIONED IN HUNGARY AS WELL AS THE PLACE OF NEGOTIATIONS CONCERNING THE EXECUTION OF THE TERMINATION OF THE WARSAW PACT AND PRESENTED A LIST CONTAINING THE NAMES OF MEMBERS OF THE GOVERNMENT'S DELEGATION. FURTHERMORE, THE HUNGARIAN GOVERNMENT MADE A PROPOSAL TO THE

SOVIET EMBASSY IN BUDAPEST TO FORM A MIXED COMMITTEE TO PREPARE THE WITHDRAWAL OF SOVIET TROOPS.

I REQUEST YOUR EXCELLENCY TO CALL UPON THE GREAT POWERS TO RECOGNIZE THE NEUTRALITY OF HUNGARY AND ASK THE SECURITY COUNCIL TO INSTRUCT THE SOVIET AND HUNGARIAN GOVERNMENTS TO START NEGOTIATIONS IMMEDIATELY.

I ALSO REQUEST YOUR EXCELLENCY TO MAKE KNOWN THE ABOVE TO THE MEMBERS OF THE SECURITY COUNCIL.

PLEASE ACCEPT, YOUR EXCELLENCY, THE EXPRESSION OF MY HIGHEST CONSIDERATION.

IMRE NAGY

The Security Council was hastily summoned at 5:00 that afternoon and the question then arose—was Janos Szabo the legal Hungarian delegate?

The Security Council posed the question to the Secretariat, and the lack of efficiency and direction was obvious. Under Secretary Protitch apparently knew nothing about Premier Nagy's second cable, for he answered:

"We have not yet officially received in the Secretariat any particular information on any credentials from the Hungarian government itself—"

As he spoke, an aide bent and whispered in Protitch's ear, and the Yugoslav corrected himself: "I have just been informed by the Legal Office that a cable had been received from the Hungarian government appointing Dr. Janos Szabo at the emergency session yesterday."

Was it stupidity or was it something intentional? Whatever it was, nothing was done. The debate went on:[4]

Lodge: "It is sad to state this, but we have heard reports— and they come persistently—that new Soviet troops have entered Hungary, and this makes the situation unclear, if not full of dark forebodings. . . ."

Sobolev: "There is a report today which is being distributed by the press agencies which says: 'Early today a gov-

ernment spokesman said that no new Soviet troops crossed
the Russian-Hungarian frontier during the night.'

"Mr. Lodge, in his statement, repeated time and again
that the situation in Hungary was obscure, but he presented
no facts and no evidence to substantiate his allegations
against the Soviet Union."

The session ended after two ineffectual hours. The next
day the Council reconvened again:

Sir Pierson Dixon (Britain): "It would be quite wrong,
misleading and unfair to the Hungarian people to take the
comfortable view . . . that we can now safely leave the
Hungarian question to settle itself."

Louis de Guiringaud (France): "We have not only the
right but the duty to find out whether [Russian troop
movements] are not a regrouping of Soviet forces so that
they will be able to intervene with such suddenness to
make possible the establishment of a regime to the liking of
the Soviet Union."

Janos Szabo: "I should like to inform the Council with
satisfaction . . . the leaders of the Hungarian and Soviet
Armies met at noon today and both parties expressed their
view on the technical questions of withdrawing Soviet
troops."

Sobolev: "I can confirm that such negotiations are in
progress."

Thomas Szabo laughed bitterly when he discussed this
meeting: "Poor [Janos] Szabo, he couldn't do anything. At
that Security Council meeting he wanted to get up and say
—'It's all true what is in Nagy's telegram,' but he was
scared stiff. He just got up and said—'Now I must read my
instructions,' all the while looking nervously at the Soviet
delegate. Later he told me: 'I have everybody at home. I
wish I wasn't here.' "

And then it was November 4, 1956. In Budapest, at

5:19 A.M., thousands heard the beginning of the end:

"This is Imre Nagy speaking, the President of the Council of Ministers of the Hungarian People's Republic. Today at daybreak Soviet forces started an attack against our capital, obviously with the intention of overthrowing the legal Hungarian democratic government.

"Our troops are fighting.

"The government is in its place.

"I notify the people of our country and the entire world of this fact."

As Nagy spoke, Soviet troops were on the move, crowding across the frontier from Russia, entering Budapest, taking over airfields, road junctions, railways, choking off the spark of revolution.

At 6:00 A.M. Hungarians heard Janos Kadar on the air announcing formation of a new government. Hungarian refugee sources believe he made this address from Uzgorod, in the Soviet Ukraine. Horrible realization swept Budapest as Kadar said he had "requested the Soviet Army Command to help our nation smash the sinister forces of reaction and restore order and calm."

News of Nagy's radio announcement (made at 11:19 P.M., November 3, New York time) reached the United Nations within thirty minutes.

There, interminable debate on Suez was dragging into the early morning hours at the General Assembly's special session. The report of Nagy's last stand shocked the delegates. Australian delegate Ronald Walker read a news dispatch of the Hungarian situation to the Assembly.

Henry Cabot Lodge followed: "And I sat here," he said, "and heard the representative of the Soviet Union talking about stopping bloodshed in Egypt. . . . When I first saw the press dispatches [of Nagy's address] I immediately asked for a meeting of the Security Council. . . ."

The special session adjourned at 3:00 A.M. and a special

Security Council meeting started at once. There were speeches—

Lodge: "Shortly after midnight I requested a Sunday meeting of the Security Council to deal with this agony of the Hungarian people. Five minutes later this request was broadcast by Radio Budapest. That shows how quickly what we say and do here affects the people of Hungary in their struggle. . . ."

Sobolev: ". . . the United Nations and particularly the Security Council have nothing to do in this matter. Interference by the United Nations and by the Western countries in the Hungarian events might only lead to complications, and it goes without saying that such interference would be unlawful and contrary to the principles of the Charter."

—And finally a vote at 5:15 A.M. (it was then 11:15 A.M. in Hungary), with the Soviet Union casting a veto on an American resolution proposing the Council censure the Russian military attack in Hungary. Then Lodge pressed that the General Assembly take up Hungary, and this was adopted. The Council adjourned at 5:24 A.M.

In Vienna, during these intervening hours, the Associated Press newsprinter was tapping out an amazing eyewitness account of the agony of a nation's fight to the death for liberty. By teletype, from the Hungarian news agency building in Budapest, came the running story:

"The Russian troops suddenly attacked Budapest and the whole country. They opened fire on everybody . . . it's a general attack. . . .

"Any news about help? Quickly, quickly, quickly! . . .

"Russian MiG fighters are over Budapest. . . .

"Associated Press in Vienna, if you have something, please pass it on to me. The government waits for your answer! . . .

"*Everywhere Russian tanks are in the street. A Russian infantry division is going toward the Parliament. . . .*

"*If you have an answer, pass it on. Any answer, pass it on. Imre Nagy personally asks help. And diplomatic steps, diplomatic steps . . .*

"*The people have just turned over a tram to use as a barricade near the building . . . young people are making Molotov cocktails and hand grenades to fight the tanks. . . .*

"*The fighting is very close now. . . .*

"*Heavy shells are exploding nearby. . . .*

"*People are jumping up at the tanks, throwing hand grenades inside. . . .*

"*What is the United Nations doing? Give us a little encouragement. . . .*

"*I am running over to a window to shoot. . . .*

"*Our building has already been fired on, but so far there are no casualties. . . .*

"*The tanks are now firing toward the Danube. Our boys are on the barricades and calling for more arms and ammunition. . . .*

"*Now things are silent here, except for a few rifle shots. The tanks rolled away from our building. . . .*

"*In our building we have youngsters of fifteen and men of forty. Don't worry about us. We are strong even if we are only a small nation. When the fighting is over, we will rebuild our unhappy country. . . .*

"*We hope the U.N. meeting won't be too late. . . .*" 5

In New York, the United Nations General Assembly met in special session that very afternoon of November 4 and passed an American resolution. It called upon the Soviet Union "to desist forthwith from all armed attack on the people of Hungary" and "requested the Secretary General to investigate the situation . . . [and] to suggest methods to bring to an end the foreign intervention in Hungary. . . ."

Of course, by this hour it was too late, and if anything, the U.N.'s own action was a pathetic indictment of inability to act when action was needed. Hungarian leaders regarded it as an outright failure of the world organization.

General Bela Kiraly, military commander in Budapest during the revolt, said later: "The U.N. could have announced: 'Hungary, an independent country negotiating with the U.S.S.R., announces its neutrality and places itself under the guarantee of the United Nations.'

"We hoped for such a solemn announcement that the U.N. had taken notice of Nagy's statement that Hungary was asserting itself as independent and neutral.

"If they wished to go further, the U.N. could have sent 300 neutral soldiers to symbolize this international interest. They could have served as a symbolic picket line of Hungary's neutrality."

Thomas Szabo stated: "It was the easy way out, not to do anything or bring up the excuse that 'if you do something there will be an atomic war.' If the U.N. could have named a big nation, Turkey, or similar, to be the U.N. representative in Budapest things might have been different.

"Anyway, it is quite obvious, it was the United States' fault. The Secretary General did not want to take action, only under American pressure would he do anything.

"After the intervention I talked to Endre Sik [formerly a Hungarian U.N. delegate who became the Kadar regime's Foreign Minister] and he told me: 'I feel very ashamed. But you know, my daughter is in Russia, and anyhow, the other side doesn't want to do anything.' "

Laszlo Varga said: "We organized the transmission of over six thousand telegrams to the U.N., asking, begging that it take action. . . . There was no response. It was a turning point for the future of the Western world."

Magyars regret that Nagy's second cable to Hammarskjold designated Janos Szabo as the Hungarian representative, since a stronger individual might have stood up to the Soviets and by force of personality hung on for Nagy.

As it turned out, the U.N. a few days later refused to recognize Miss Anna Kethly, Minister of State in the Nagy government—but has, ever since, permitted the Kadar regime to be seated in the General Assembly. In effect, the U.N. filed Nagy's desperation appeal to Hammarskjold away under old business and smiled benignly on Kadar's bloody-handed men.

In the face of world opinion, the U.N. administered a light slap on the wrist to the Kadar delegates by holding their credentials in escrow—in other words, by taking no action one way or the other. This, of course, does not prevent the Kadar representatives from sitting and voting as Moscow sees fit.

"They're just the same as any other delegation," said a U.N. correspondent. "Perhaps a few remember that they have a slightly special category."

Laszlo Varga lashed out: "After it was over, the one concrete thing the U.N. could have done was to refuse the Kadar delegates their seats in the Assembly. The Russians lost some prestige, but they crushed the uprising and got away with it scot-free. It's fantastic that the issue of the Hungarian representation was handled the way it was—out of sight, out of mind. Dag Hammerskjold bears the brunt of the responsibility."

"Janos Szabo means traitor," growled Imre Kovacs. "It was bad judgment to name this man, since he was under terrific pressure from the Soviet. He was instructed or persuaded one way or another not to push his case. It would have been better if Nagy had named a neutral nation as delegate."

The probable reason that Nagy did not was that the situation appeared to be developing favorably in the last days of October, and he himself had planned to go to the U.N. on Monday, November 5.

But, on this date, Nagy was in refuge at the Yugoslav Embassy, where he had fled the day before. (He left the Embassy November 22, after being promised that he might return freely to his home. Instead, he and a number of others were taken into custody by Soviet forces as soon as they left the Yugoslav building.)

It was on the fifth that Miss Anna Kethly arrived in New York, and her presence raised another dilemma for the United Nations. Nagy was in asylum; a Kadar government had been announced and it had Soviet military support— but fighting was still reported. So where did Miss Kethly stand?

The U.N. should have had no trouble determining this, according to Miss Kethly. She said:

"Previously to November second (date of my appointment as a Minister of State), the Hungarian government still had not settled the question of a U.N. delegation.

"On November third, Imre Nagy proposed to the Council of Ministers that the Vice Foreign Minister and myself should go to the U.N., since I was already—temporarily —abroad in Vienna as the only member of the Hungarian government in the West. He asked the approval of the Council of Ministers to his proposal authorizing me to officially represent the government at the U.N.

"The Secretary General had opportunity to convince himself that our appointment was made in accordance with the Hungarian laws and regulations in existence. Imre Nagy's legal government had the right to decide the question of its own representation at the U.N.

"Although the Secretary General received me after I arrived in New York, he did not find it possible to act on my request to be seated as an official delegate. According to him, if official formalities were not scrupulously observed, my seating would create a precedent causing unforeseeable complications for the U.N., for example, by the unruly and often-changing Latin American regimes. . . .

"In view of conditions in Hungary, to have scrupulously observed all the formalities was something like asking a drowning man to present a petition, duly stamped, in order that he be rescued.

"So, the Secretary General did not recommend approval of the credentials of the Hungarian delegates. And since the Secretary General of the United Nations is a more influential person than the Minister of State of a small East European country embattled for its freedom and independence, I was not permitted to address the U.N. General Assembly either.

"On the basis of the above, one can conclude that the U.N. Secretariat did not attach the importance to the Hungarian revolution that it deserved."

When *Life* magazine, in March, 1957, called "the whole record [of the Hungarian revolution] a sorry one for the United States and the United Nations alike," Henry Cabot Lodge promptly rebutted.

Commenting on *Life*'s assertion, he said: "The record is not a sorry one. The record is a good one. Although it did not succeed in bringing about the withdrawal of Soviet troops, the U.N. has done things for the people of Hungary which no single country or organization could have done.

"The steps which the United Nations has taken have played a useful part in preventing deportations; in bringing food to the people of Budapest; in helping 170,000 Hungarian refugees to find new homes; in persuading many Asian and African countries for the first time to vote to condemn the Soviet Union; in dealing a body blow to Communism all over the world."

Paul Bang-Jensen did not agree. He thought the U.N.'s action had been deplorable and sickening, a mélange of vacillation, unconcern, and disbelief that anything such as an anti-Soviet revolution could ever take place. Bang-Jensen saw its importance, sensed that, on it, might hinge the fate of the West in years to come.

From his exile years, when Denmark was overridden by the Nazis, he knew the agony of Hungary.

He knew of the thousands of letters—of the deputations of shocked citizenry—that had flooded into the United Nations exhorting justice for Hungary.

He was powerless.

The U.N. Charter begins, in Chapter I, Article I:

"The purposes of the United Nations are: to maintain international peace and security, and to that end: to take effective collective measures for the prevention and removal of threats to the peace, and for the suppression of acts of aggression . . . and to bring about . . . in conformity with the principles of justice . . . adjustment or settlement of international disputes or situations . . ."

Paul Bang-Jensen felt the U.N. had failed miserably to live up to its Charter.

That was the point of view from which the forty-seven-year-old Danish diplomat both saw and judged the Hungarian Revolution. Later, he would learn in great detail how it had been fought and lost.[6]

CHAPTER 11

SITTING in Sandor Kiss's tiny cubicle in the offices of the Free Europe Committee, Peter Marshall reflected that here was still another Hungarian whose looks concealed the amazing experiences of his life.

Of slight build, blue-eyed, fair-haired, deceptively mild in manner, Kiss did not give the appearance of a man who had fought in the underground against the Nazis . . . been captured . . . sentenced to death . . . escaped . . . served as a member of Parliament from 1945 to 1947, when there was a free Hungarian government . . . imprisoned in 1952 on charges of plotting to form a coalition government minus the Communists . . . tortured . . . spent over three years in jail . . . and, finally, a leader in the revolution from beginning to bitter end.

"I know you were the fourth witness to testify before the U.N.'s Special Committee on Hungary," Marshall said. "I want to know what you told them . . . what you told Bang-Jensen. I want to know what you did during the revolution . . . how it went."

"Yes . . . I see . . . I shall try." Sandor Kiss spoke

slowly, and then paused, getting the English words sorted out in his mind.

"Well . . . at the time nobody thought it was an uprising, but they did think it was a new movement.

"On—ahh—Sunday evening, that would be the twenty-first of October . . . I was at the University Club and I went out and found a great crowd, waiting in the street to get the morning paper to find out—ahh—what was going on in Poland.

"I went to the Margaret Bridge. It was about eleven o'clock, and the crowd grew and grew. It—it was something —you might say, electric, and it ran through everyone. An excitement—a-a wonderful feeling.

"When the newspaper vendor appeared, everyone surged forward to get a copy. There weren't enough papers, and the news vendor got frightened and ran down into the men's room under the bridge to hide from the crowd." Sandor Kiss smiled at the memory and continued slowly, carefully, searching for the right words.

"Papers that were selling for one forint at eleven were selling for ten or more by midnight . . . The—ahh—desire to know what was going on was like—a-a great hunger.

"The following day—Monday—all evening there was a meeting at the Technical University. And it was there the students wrote the sixteen points which was—ahh—manifesto by which they hoped to bring about the reforms all Hungarians were seeking.

"That next day, on every main street and boulevard, there were trucks with students carrying Hungarian flags with the Soviet emblem cut out of them. . . . The students chanted, 'We want freedom! We want freedom!'

"They sang the national anthem.

"The crowd grew around the Parliament building. It pressed right up to the front door. We chanted 'Nagy! Nagy! Let us hear Nagy!' The sound was like—like the roar of water plunging down a falls. It rose and fell, but it did not cease.

"When it grew dark, the police put out the street lights to make us go home, but the crowd rolled up newspapers and made torches of them . . . thousands of little lights.

"Around eight o'clock Gero gave a statement over the radio that said the crowds were made up of Fascist counter-revolutionaries. A roar went up. Everyone was infuriated! . . . It was oil on the fire . . . Some shouted that Gero was a Fascist-Communist . . . I could see the little torches —ahh—bobbing up and down in the darkness, furiously.

"The idea was born to go to the radio station and read the sixteen points over the air, so that the whole country could hear that it was not a Fascist movement, but a movement from the people for freedom. . . .

"While most of the crowd went to the radio station, I went with some to the printer. We were going to make— ahh—copies of the sixteen points. When we got there, there were soldiers guarding the door with—ahh—what do you call?—ahh—submachine guns. Our group grew larger, and there were some who wanted to rush the soldiers. It became quite tense, but by talking, we finally convinced the soldiers that we weren't out to damage anything, and they let a few students into the building.

"Suddenly we heard the sound of shooting in the distance. A truck came. The people in it cried out, 'The AVH is shooting! They're killing students at the radio station!'

"We went there in a hurry, angry, excited. It was two and a half kilometers. . . . When we arrived, I saw a great many burned-out trucks and cars. They were AVH vehicles, about twenty to thirty of them. The students had set fire to them in retaliation. The AVH had rushed in its special—ahh—riot police and they were throwing smoke bombs down from the roof. The air was thick with smoke. At that time, we had no weapons.

"An ambulance drove up to the building. Some saw that it was a trick and blocked it from entering. It was full of ammunition for the police, but there were no guns.

"It was near eleven o'clock when the Csepel youth arrived in trucks. They said, 'Oh, we can get guns. Some of you come along with us.' One group went off to the Csepel Arms Factory and the other went to the Arsenal at Pestzsenterzsebet.

"While we waited, the cry went up that the Army was sending troops to help the AVH. It was an armored column with—ahh—infantry in trucks, about a thousand men in all. . . . It came rumbling down the Danube Road from the north and turned into Kossuth Lajos Street. . . . It halted at the head of the street, blocked by a single truck the students had parked there. . . . As the word spread, the shouting and talking broke off . . . it became very still. . . . There were a few street lights, and we could see the long massed column with its armored cars, stretching back into the darkness. . . . No one spoke. The officers came and stood at the end of the street. . . . They stared at us and we stared back. . . . I could smell the smoke very strongly. It was thick, like the tension you felt inside . . . and all around. I wondered how so many people could be so still. . . . Out of nowhere a man appeared, and we watched him climb up on the truck. . . . He was an old man with gray hair, and he wore blue working clothes.

"He stood on the top of the cab, facing the soldiers . . . outlined against the night . . . all the faces looking up watching him, wondering. . . . And then, his voice rang out and you could hear it everywhere it was so clear, so strong:

> Don't shoot, my son, because
> I, too, will be there. . . .
> Flesh from my flesh, blood from my blood,
> how could you lift your hand against me,

> when I am calling out to you,
> crying out to you!
> Don't shoot, my son, because
> I, too, will be there.

"It is a well-known Hungarian poem by the poetess Zseni Varnai, and he recited it all . . . his voice like a song, rising and falling . . . a little old man, a worker . . . and all around people were suddenly crying . . . soldiers, too . . . men, women, my wife. . . . When he ended, someone began to sing the National Anthem, and the whole square rang with it. The soldiers crossed over to join us . . . even some of their officers. The old man had vanished. . . . Soldiers began passing out their guns, but they too had no ammunition. You see, the AVH kept it strictly controlled.

"At midnight the trucks returned with both guns and ammunition.

"The attack began.

"The street lights were shot out.

"Our people went into apartments across from the radio station and started shooting from the windows.

"Everybody wanted to fight, but there were not enough guns.

"I could not get one. I stood in a doorway with my wife, watching.

"We left about one A.M. . . . We had two children at home to take care of.

"Our fighters captured the radio station about three A.M.

"I walked back toward the center of the city at about five. There was heavy fighting going on . . . Freedom Fighters on the roof tops and behind windows. Russian tanks shooting into buildings.

"I got hold of a rifle. I went up to the third floor of an apartment with nine others . . . no one was in charge. We were all strangers. It was spontaneous.

"We were shooting at tanks and armored cars, trying to hit the drivers. The tanks returned our fire with cannon and machine guns. Three in our party were wounded. About six-thirty, we heard a great boom!! and two Russian tanks went up at the end of the street. Grenades and mines were very effective.

"At eight, the Russians broke off fighting. We went out along the walls and heard shooting on the other side of the city. . . .

"There were three high school girls walking down a street, waving Hungarian flags and singing. An AVH car came roaring by and shot them down. A bus driver saw it happen . . . he blocked the street with his bus. The crowd got the three AVH men. . . . It tore them to pieces."

And so it was that Sandor Kiss, in his slow but careful way, described to Peter Marshall the revolution as he had observed and taken part in it, from beginning to end.

"We ended the fighting because the Russians went after the population, shooting at everyone and everything in range of their guns. . . .

"We went to the forest outside of Buda. We went a few at a time, running, hiding. There were five or six hundred people in the forest, but we did not have guns or ammunition . . . it was hopeless.

"We got food from nearby towns. . . . We went into the mountains for six or seven days after the—ahh—fourth. . . . The Russians, they bombed our positions for three days.

"I came out a week later. . . . It was finished. . . . My friends told me I had to leave. I had made a—ahh—radio broadcast. . . . I went with some others to the western border. There were Hungarian soldiers there, but they let us go through.

"My wife with my two children got out with the help of a friend who was a train conductor."

Sandor Kiss stopped talking and Peter Marshall came back from the sadness of a man having to flee his homeland, yet safe with his wife and children. He looked at his scribbled notes and knew that, even if he couldn't read them, he could remember this Hungarian's story.

Could you call a man a "patriot" today? Or was that word reserved for the history books and Lexington Common? He was a "patriot" if he won, but many would call him a poor damn fool if he lost.

"Have you talked to Janos Horvath?" the calm, undefeated man asked.

"No, not yet."

"You must see him, yes. He—he's very—ahh—important to what you are doing. He knew Mister Bang-Jensen very well."

"You knew him too, didn't you?"

"Ahh, yes . . . He was a very sincere man. . . . He wanted to get the facts. He was very helpful to us . . . to me in particular when I testified before the Committee."

"All of your countrymen to whom I've talked think that the Report on Hungary that the Committee put out afterward is very good."

"Yes . . . I think it is very good, and in many ways because of Bang-Jensen."

"But he wasn't satisfied with it. He thought there were a lot of things left out, a lot of errors."

"Some facts were left out, but for us . . . we had expected nothing"—the blond man smiled with gentle ruefulness, almost apologetically—"so we were pleased to have something . . . even if it was words on a page."

Whereas Sandor Kiss was slight and blond, Janos Horvath was stocky and dark. Like Kiss, Peter Marshall found Horvath to be a quiet man with a stillness and impassivity in his black eyes that, at first, was misleading. He gave the impression of listening carefully but not quite understanding. His face was expressionless until he spoke or smiled, and then it came alive and quickly revealed the brightness that lay within.

When Marshall first met the Executive Vice-President of the Kossuth Foundation, he did not know of the close bond, the Damon and Pythias parallel, that lay between the careers and lives of Sandor Kiss and Janos Horvath.

The two had fought the Nazis together, been captured almost at the same time, sentenced to death together, and escaped together with the aid of Zoltan Tildy, whose democratic government they later served as Parliament members.

After World War II, Horvath had represented the Thirteenth District of Budapest in the Parliament and in the City Council as the chairman of the Smallholders Party. This was the proletarian stronghold of the Communists. Horvath, like Kiss, was imprisoned by the AVH and spent four years behind bars. The uprising found him employed in Budapest's largest electronics factory.

Horvath turned the factory, called "Red Sparkle," into a strategic position of defense which raised havoc with the attacking Russian forces.

Known and respected through the Thirteenth District, he was appointed Revolutionary Chairman for the entire area.

Had Imre Nagy's government remained in power, he would have become Minister of Agriculture. As it was, he fought with his command against the second onslaught of Russian armor until all ammunition was gone. Then, like Kiss, he escaped to Austria with his wife and daughter.

Now he sat in his office and quietly talked to Peter Marshall, as he had to the U.N.'s Committee on Hungary.

"The curiosity of the people was a kind of strength. People everywhere talking, asking questions. 'What did you see? What did you hear?' . . . The Russians promised freedom, and look what we've got. The Russians say they are our friends, but is this the way they show it?

"People moving in crowds . . . a great sea of people . . . Russian tanks in the middle of the streets and the people moving around them, stopping to stare at the soldiers.

" 'Devaih! Devaih Te!', the Tankers shout.

" 'Why should we move!' the people shout back. 'This is our city! Why are you here?'

"Sometimes the tanks open fire. They shoot to kill, and amidst the screams and frightened shouts, the crowds run away . . . but in a little while, they flow back . . . a heavier tide. They come to help the wounded, to strew flowers and flags on the dead, to cry shame at the white-faced Russian soldiers:

" 'Do you know who this is you have murdered! He's nineteen years old . . . a factory worker! See, here, look! Here is his card. He's a member of the Communist party, and you killed him! Why did you kill him!'

" 'We have come to help you!' The strident cry is drowned in jeers. 'Your country has been occupied by reactionary Fascists! The landlords and the bankers are trying to seize control!'

" 'Tee durak! Durak! Durak! You fools! Fools! Where are they! We are all workers here! This is our city! Leave us alone!' "

That, too, was the nature of the revolution as expressed by Janos Horvath, who concluded with the somewhat ironic fact that the only allies who fought on the side of the Hungarians were those Russian soldiers who saw the wrongness of what they were doing and could not stomach it.

To get further insight into those few so crucial days—to try to see and feel them in some small part as Paul Bang-

Jensen must have come to see and feel them—Peter Marshall met with another Hungarian who had played a major role in their passing.

Except for his gray-white hair, he found that General Bela Kiraly did not look his forty-eight years. Very conservatively and neatly dressed, the General made an imposing figure as he sat comfortably ensconced in a corner of the Biltmore men's bar, a scotch and soda before him.

Marshall wondered if the scar under his left cheek was a memento of the more than five years he had spent in Communist jails. That Kiraly had been under the death sentence, that he had been tortured, Marshall knew, but here, as with Kiss and Horvath, there was no outward sign. The man's face was vigorous, fresh, full of strength. The blue eyes that looked out at him from the handsome, squarely set, Slavic features were alert and amiable.

From Horvath and others, Marshall had learned something of the General's background. Released from prison on September 5, he had not taken part in the early fighting, for he had been confined to a hospital bed. Then, at a meeting of the Revolutionary Council, directly after the badly mauled Russians had withdrawn from the city, it was suggested that, should the Soviets return, the Hungarian fighters had better be organized. Who was a good man for the job? A young lieutenant from Kiraly's home town brought up the name of the former Commanding General of the Hungarian War College.

A deputation of students was sent to the hospital to ask Bela Kiraly if he would serve. Kiraly accepted the offer, and Nagy, on hearing the General's name proposed for the position of Military Commander, had remarked, "As long as Kiraly is with us, we are all right."

Although Imre Nagy had little in common with the General, he knew that, as a young career officer, Kiraly had been one of a few selected by the Russians for special training. His rise had been swift, but in the dangerous arena of Communist power politics, so had his descent.

Now he sat at a table across from Peter Marshall and in excellent English told him of those last few days.

"After the first fighting was ended, I set up my headquarters in the office of the Budapest Chief of Police. It had an excellent communications system. I could pick up the phone and get the Prime Minister's office.

"At eleven A.M., on November second, I received a call at my headquarters from the Prime Minister. He said, 'Dear friend, if you have ever had an important task, now you have one. Andropov [Russian Ambassador] has handed us a note saying that mobs are threatening the Soviet Embassy and that if we are unable to control them, they shall call in their troops.'

"I assured the Prime Minister I would have order established within a half hour. I then dispatched a tank and a mechanized battalion to the Square of Heroes, which is close by the Embassy, and drove directly there myself. There was absolutely no one anywhere near their building. I went up to the door, and when it was opened, I said, 'I am the Military Commander of this District. I've come here to defend you, but whom am I to defend you against?'

"Andropov appeared all smiles, calling me 'Comrade!', trying to make a joke out of the whole thing. He said we mustn't be taken in by nervous civilians.

"I realize now," Kiraly told Marshall, taking a sip of his drink, "that the move was simply a device to find out how ready we were to act—how well organized, and the Soviet Ambassador, in finding us prepared, immediately changed his approach.

"He then led me upstairs, insisting that the real purpose in having me come was to make arrangements to start negotiating the withdrawal of Soviet troops from the country. He was very friendly. We were all good comrades.

There was nothing to worry about. Everything was going to be all right.

"He took me to the room where they had their 'K' code system for telephoning. I picked up the number one phone and had a direct line to Imre Nagy. I reported what had happened, and it was arranged that the Russians would come to the Parliament Building to start negotiations. Of course, they were simply stalling for time. I believe, just as in Korea when the Chinese Reds attacked, the Soviets knew they could get away with it. . . . Now all they had to do was delay.

"I am fully convinced," the former Hungarian soldier said without any sign of bitterness, "had the U.N. acted on Prime Minister Nagy's telegram of November first, the Russians would have accepted the revolution as a fait accompli. By the second, however, it became a matter of lulling us into the belief that we had won our point, while they prepared to crush us."

Kiraly then went on to explain to Peter Marshall how the conference between Hungarians and Russians got under way about noontime on November 3, and how well the first session progressed.

"At one point, General Pal Maleter came out and told me, 'Everything is all right. We're going to get what we want.'

"And so it appeared to us as the proceedings were recessed. The only important detail left to settle was the exact date of the Russian troop withdrawal. If the Russians insisted it be January fifteenth instead of December fifteenth, we weren't going to argue too strenuously about it.

"Well, the first negotiations had taken place at the Hungarian Parliament Building and the Soviets asked that the second meeting be conducted at their headquarters at Tokol . . . that's located on Csepel Island about ten miles south of Budapest. The purpose of the meeting was to agree on a deadline, sign the papers, and then we could all live happily ever after.

"Our delegation arrived in four cars about ten P.M. and was greeted by an honor guard. A short time later, Pal Maleter called me to say everything was going well.

"Then nothing.

"When I called back and got no answer, I feared the worst had happened. I had two amphibious craft held ready on Haros Island. When we lost contact with Maleter, I had these sent to Csepel to proceed to the Soviet base camp at Tokol. Radio communications were maintained all the way.

" 'We are arriving on Csepel.

" 'We are proceeding through the streets outside Tokol.

" 'We are arriving at Tokol.

" 'We are in sight of Soviet headquarters.

" 'We are entering the—!'

"Then, finished, no more. That was it. They were inside, prisoners." Bela Kiraly moved his glass on the table as one might move a chess piece in a final checkmate.

"The main Russian thrusts came from the east and the south. We fought in the city as long as we could, and then we retreated to a position in a village overlooking Budapest. After that, we fell back to the Vertes Mountains . . . and then northwestward toward the border. . . . I came out on the nineteenth of November."

There was no defeat in the General's voice. He was simply relating a tragic fact. Its reality he could face. He would not dwell in the past. He could look ahead. God had given him not only a heart and a mind. He had also given him a spirit that would not be broken. He shared it with men like Sandor Kiss and Janos Horvath. . . . And Paul Bang-Jensen?

"You knew him, of course?" Peter Marshall asked.

"Yes, right from the time I arrived here. After I testified before the Committee, I wrote to Hungarians in Europe. I told them this was a new stage of the struggle. First, fighting was our duty; now, bearing witness to help the U.N. Report was our duty.

"I know that Paul Bang-Jensen took the personal responsibility of safeguarding the identity of the witnesses. He talked with a tremendous number of people, and he gave them that assurance."

"When did you see him last?"

"It was on the twenty-third of October at Hunter College on the anniversary of the revolution." A month before he disappeared, Peter Marshall noted to himself.

"I saw him sitting alone in the last row. I brought him to the front row and introduced him as a guest of honor. I know that he was pleased . . . but I saw deep sorrow in his face."

"You think he killed himself?"

Bela Kiraly shook his head thoughtfully, "I don't know. I know when they had me in prison, they gave me something in my food to make me do anything, say anything, they wished. . . . And I did it, knowing it was wrong . . . as though I were sitting there watching myself, powerless . . . and not unhappy that I was powerless. It was a terrible experience to get over."

"But what motivation could there have been for anyone to kill him?" Peter Marshall asked the question to see if the General knew of the defector story.

He did. "As I understand it, Bang-Jensen was approached by a Soviet staff member of the U.N. who wished to defect to the West. He wanted assurances of asylum. He had valuable information to trade. You must know about it."

"Yes, I've heard."

"Well, if that story is true, and Paul had knowledge of that kind . . . well, they'll kill you for less than that."

"Where did you hear the story, General?"

"From one of your government officials. Are you trying to get facts on it?"

"Yes . . . before I'm through I hope to track it down."

"Good. Anything you can do for the memory of that fine man will be good, and we shall help you all we can."

Peter Marshall saw that the Hungarian revolt and the failure of the United Nations to aid in its success were acts of world history, which overshadowed and dwarfed the individuals concerned in their passage. But he knew that, to Paul Bang-Jensen, Hungary had a deeply personal meaning: the wheel of his life had come full turn. It had all happened before. It had happened first on his third birthday, and the memory was branded into his soul.

In brother Niels's hand, there was a poker. "Come, grab the other end."

"No . . . I don't want to."

"But it's a present . . . for your birthday."

"I don't want to."

"It won't hurt. It's not hurting me. Something wonderful will happen. A surprise!"

"You promise?"

"Of course. Take it."

The little boy reached out gingerly and grasped the end of the white-hot metal. His shrill, agonized scream rang through the house.[1]

When the Special Committee on Hungary was formed and Paul Bang-Jensen was offered the position of Deputy Secretary—with assurances given as to his role—this, he later came to believe was a repetition of his childhood betrayal. It had happened several times in the past. Now it repeated itself again.

"The coincidences in real life are often, as we know, more striking in the dramatic effect than any unlikely coincidences in a novel." So wrote Paul Bang-Jensen.

CHAPTER 12

"MRS. BANG-JENSEN, this is Peter Marshall."

A second's pause, and then, "Oh . . . yes . . . how are you?" In her voice was the same soft graciousness of their earlier conversations.

"I guess you haven't found the time to answer my letter."

"No . . . I'm afraid not, Mr. Marshall . . . It—it's just something I can't face right now."

"Well, you said once I might call if I had any questions."

"Yes." It was a reply that said neither "yes" nor "no."

He resolved to make another plea before he got down to his main purpose. "Mrs. Bang-Jensen, I don't want to bother you, but you know what I'm doing, and the last time we spoke, I tried to explain why I'm doing it. This book is going to be written. It deserves to be written, but much of its impact will depend on its accuracy. You, more than anyone, know the facts. Will you let me come and talk to you?"

"I can't!" The pain in her reply hit him harder than the disappointment of it. How could he argue with someone

like this; whose every word seemed to be asking for understanding.

"I'm sorry, truly, I'm sorry," she said. "I know what
you're attempting. I know how hard it must be, but—I—I
simply can't."

"Would you answer a question, Mrs. Bang-Jensen?"

"I'll try."

"Your husband was made Deputy Secretary of the Committee on Hungary. Did this appointment come about for
any particular reason, or in any particular way?"

"We talked about that many times," Helen Bang-Jensen
admitted quietly, and then went on without pause.

"We did a lot of conjecturing on it, but it was simply
logical that he be selected. He didn't think it was good procedure at the time because Alsing Andersen of Denmark
was the Chairman. However, my husband was the most
informed in his department. When the Secretariat wanted
to know what was happening—when Doctor Protitch
wanted to be briefed—Paul was the one he turned to.

"That was his job, of course, but he would have known
what was going on anyway out of interest. If there had
been a committee on Suez, he would have been just as well
informed on that situation.

"It was fantastic how busy people were in the U.N. at
that time. Paul wouldn't even come home to bed. So when
you ask why was he selected, it was primarily because of
his knowledge and his experience.

"Then, too, Hungary was an East-West problem, and
you'll recollect that the Committee members all came from
countries not directly affected. You wouldn't have expected
to see an American on the Committee.

"We never knew if there was any more reason than that
. . . sometimes things just happen. It's been a question to
many people in view of what followed. Everybody looks for

an underlying meaning to everything when, more often than not, the meaning is obvious. . . . Perhaps it was just fate."

A.'s eyes were blue. Cold blue, Peter Marshall thought as they stared at him. The voice was noticeably thin and raspy in such a big man.

"I don't know why the devil I'm doing this!" The hostility was directed as much toward himself as it was toward Marshall. "If it ever got out—"

"It won't."

"That's the chance *I'm* taking, not you!" A. snapped rudely. "My job is a good job. The pay's the kind that few foreign-service officers ever see any place else. My wife, she likes the way we're paid, the way we live."

"They'll throw you out of the U.N. for talking to me?"

"Maybe not the way they gave Paul the bum's rush. My contract just wouldn't get renewed next year, that's all. So, by God, if you use my name or tell anyone I talked to you, I'll deny it!"

Marshall felt his own temper starting to rise. "You have my promise . . . and I don't see any reason to get so tough about it."

"I said it's not your job that's at stake."

"Well, why did you come, then!" He said it knowing he was probably putting an end to the interview before it began.

A. grunted and then said sourly, "I suppose I came because my curiosity outweighed my better judgment."

"Well, then, since we're both curious," Marshall said with a smile, "what do you say we get down to cases?"

A. gave him his long, cold stare again. "All right," he said, not quite so truculently; "you tell me what you know about Paul, and we'll see."

After he had told him, A. said nothing for a long moment. Then, his eyes on his drink, he asked quietly, "What do you want to know from me?"

"I want to know how the Special Committee on Hungary came into being. I want to know about the people who were on it, and all the things that happened during the months it was taking testimony. I want to know Bang-Jensen's part in it."

"You don't want much, do you?"

"I want everything I can get."

"I could use another drink."

"Right. And I'm going to take notes." He planked the notebook on the table.

A. glared at it, "Don't you ever use my name. He was my friend. He got a rotten deal. I'd like to see some good come out of it, but not at the expense of my job."

He chewed the piece of ice in his glass and set the glass down emphatically. "Okay, the Special Committee was formed by a General Assembly vote on January tenth, nineteen fifty-seven. Your country, other countries pressured the U.N. into the Committee's formation. After all, by then it was both the least and the best the U.N. could do." A. spoke swiftly, fluidly, without pause.

"The purpose of the Committee was to find out what had happened in Hungary now that it was too late to do anything about it. Hammarskjold sent Philippe de Seynes, as his representative, to Geneva and asked Kadar to allow de Seynes to enter the country as an observer. Kadar told Dag to go to hell, and the Committee knew that it was going to have to get its facts from documents and refugees. Out of what it learned, it would write a report. The report would be read by Hungarians and a few others. Then it could be filed away and forgotten. Now the point to remember is this: it was a *special* committee. The U.N. had never had a committee like it. I don't care what anyone might say about Korea, or Palestine, or anything else. It was a special committee with special problems, and therefore it required special handling. Do you understand that?" A. glowered at him.

"Yes, I think so. When you say handling, you're referring to the problem of witnesses who wanted to keep their identities secret."

"That was only one of the problems. There were others. You understand the Secretariat's job was to give aid and assistance to the Committee in gathering the information for its Report. More than seventy of us were assigned, and Paul was appointed as the number two man, Deputy Secretary. His boss was William Jordan, and you're certainly going to want to talk to him."

"They didn't like each other, did they?"

"No, they did not like each other, but forget the personalities for a minute. The reason they fought, and the reason things got so thoroughly fouled up later on, was the simple fact that special instructions to the Secretariat group were pretty well nonexistent. Even after insistence by Jordan and Bang-Jensen, these instructions were not entirely clarified."

"Who issued them . . . or didn't issue them?"

"They came through Dragoslav Protitch, who was Under Secretary for Political and Security Council Affairs. He, in turn, took his cue from Hammarskjold and Cordier. I'll fill you in on Protitch later, but it was through him that Jordan, as Secretary, and Paul, as his Deputy, tried to get things straight. . . . Now you mentioned the witnesses, and I said there were other problems. Security would be the first problem, wouldn't it? If you were the Russians, don't you think you'd be interested not only in knowing what was going on but in doing all you could to make the job a tough one?"

"Sure, and I know, from Bang-Jensen's own statements,

he didn't think the security was very good, but doesn't the Secretariat have set rules to follow along those lines?"

"I said this was a *special* Committee, didn't I?" A. grated sarcastically. "Special, like in special! It required special instructions on security and it didn't have any. It didn't even have a security officer when it went to Europe. And Paul was absolutely right in his statements about it.

"Now . . . security was one thing. The screening of witnesses was another. Originally, one of Paul's assignments was to schedule the appearance of witnesses, without giving any preliminary interviews.[1] Well, the Committee began to hear a lot of information repeated. Paul saw that it was a big waste of time. He began to do his own screening, actually against instructions. Jordan stuck to the rules such as they were, even though he didn't agree with them.

"Of course, the most important of all the instructions had to do with the anonymity of those who testified. It wasn't until the Committee had started taking testimony that it realized a lot of Hungarians weren't going to talk if they couldn't be sure their names would be kept secret from the Russians. It was strictly a life-and-death matter in their eyes. After what had happened at the U.N., a good many of them had no trust in it at all. And isn't it just a little bit naïve to think that a Soviet is a U.N. official before he's a loyal Communist?

"Well, Paul sought assurances from Protitch on this score, and he thought he got them. But the only thing he got in writing was a memo by Cordier to the Controller. It said that P. Bang-Jensen was authorized to keep a secret list of names for travel expense purposes, and that this secret list was his own responsibility.

"Now get this, my friend—you can say Paul used bad judgment in not getting something in writing from Protitch or Cordier or Hammarskjold. I assure you that's not good form for a civil servant. You obey instructions, you don't make them, and if you don't have instructions in writing, you don't act. Well, he acted. If the best that Hungary could expect from the U.N. was a report—all right, Paul was determined it would be an excellent report. If it was necessary to promise witnesses that only he or the members of the Committee might know their names, okay, he'd promise them that. And that's just what he did, and all the legal semantics that got thrown in his face later simply obscure the fact. He got the best instructions he could, and he acted on them in the best way that he knew how.

"Why, hell, to show you how bad it was, one time when Prolitch tried to give Jordan verbal instructions instead of putting them in writing, the Englishman turned off his hearing aid and just sat and whistled in his face."

A. extracted a page from the envelope beside him. "Now you've probably read this statement, but I think you should read it again in view of what I've just said. This was to Hammarskjold from Bang-Jensen."

Marshall picked it up. "Yes, I recognize it." He read it over.

Early in February, 1957, Dr. Protitch informed me after several discussions with him, you had finally agreed that I could promise the witnesses that, while their names would be available on request to the members of the Committee on Hungary, I would be the only person in the Secretariat who would know their names, unless, of course, the name in the individual case had already been known to others before the witness decided that he preferred to be anonymous. I had no cause to doubt that you had told Dr. Protitch to give me this instruction; there was in fact no reason why it was necessary for anybody else in the Secretariat to know the names of the witnesses; Dr. Protitch's statement to me was supported by the memorandum of February 8th from your Executive Assistant, Mr. Andrew Cordier, which stated that you had approved that I would "be responsible" for maintaining a secret register showing the names of the witnesses.[2]

"Protitch denied all this, didn't he?" Marshall said, handing back the paper.

"Yes, he did."

"So you take your pick, is that it?"

"That's it." A. nodded.

"One thing Bang-Jensen says, and you said, is that the Committee members might ask for the names. That's six people, even though five of them are not in the Secretariat. That's not much anonymity."

"Don't get it wrong. The Committee members could ask for a name, although they seldom did, but it was Paul who kept the list and knew who the people were. You've got to make that clear. You have a term, 'snafu.' Well, my friend, that's what it was, a big snafu."

"Was it just another case of bureaucratic bumbling?"

"Look, I'm a bureaucrat, too. . . . As you must know, Paul thought it was much more than that. It's up to you to figure that out. Now, as to who was on the Special Committee on Hungary and who were the important Secretariat people who assisted it, I'm not going to tell you until you place that order." And for the first time since they'd met, A. smiled.

That night Peter Marshall made his own list. He referred to it in his mind as "The Cast."

MEMBERS OF THE U.N. SPECIAL COMMITTEE ON HUNGARY

CHAIRMAN: Alsing Andersen, Defense Minister for Denmark during World War II. Had known Bang-Jensen for many years.

RAPPORTEUR: Keith C. O. Shann, U.N. Australian Delegate. Responsible for preparing the Report, liaison between Committee and Secretariat Group.

MEMBER: Ambassador R.S.S. Gunwardene of Ceylon. Conscientious, hard-working U.N. diplomat.

MEMBER: Ambassador Mongi Slim of Tunisia. Very anxious to bring the true facts of Hungary's plight before the world.

MEMBER: Delegate Enrique Rodriguez Fabregat of Uruguay. He would have a dramatic announcement in Rome.

SECRETARIAT GROUP

SECRETARY: William J. Jordan, Englishman, former teacher, former Foreign Service researcher. Been with the U.N. since its founding days, devout Secretariat official. Primary job, to direct efforts of his subordinates and to act in liaison between the staff and the Committee.

DEPUTY SECRETARY: Paul Bang-Jensen. The U.N.'s position was that he was a "glorified clerk" in this job, that he was to schedule meetings and arrange for appearances of witnesses, plus other allied and not very responsible duties. This characterization not borne out by facts.

INFORMATION OFFICER: V. Duckworth-Barker, Englishman, had spent his early years as Foreign Service Officer in Hungary. Had fallen in love with the country. Hard-working, considerate, liked Bang-Jensen.

LEGAL OFFICER: Marc Schreiber, Legal Adviser to the Committee, native of Antwerp.

STAFF MEMBER: Philip Messinesi, Greek national. Aided in the drafting of the Report.

Although, as A. had pointed out, the Secretariat Staff to assist the Committee numbered over seventy in all, Peter Marshall felt his cast was sufficient for the time being.

CHAPTER 13

"I MET PAUL for the first time in Alsing Andersen's office at the U.N.," Janos Horvath said. "It was shortly after the Committee on Hungary had been formed and I went there with Anna Kethly and some others to learn what we must do to help."

"Was the Secretary, Jordan, there too?"

"No, just Alsing Andersen and Paul. Paul was introduced to us as the man we must talk to if we had any questions, any difficulties. You understand, it was all very new to us, and we weren't exactly sure of ourselves."

Marshall nodded and smiled at the understatement. "And your first impression of him was good."

"Yes, it was. I liked him. I sensed his sincerity. Sometimes you can tell that about a man very quickly."

"Okay, you got your instructions on what you were to do from Alsing Andersen, and then what happened?"

"A few days later Anna Kethly testified in open hearing. She was followed by General Kiraly. He was followed by Jozsef Kavago, who had been the Mayor of Budapest.

Well," Horvath smiled faintly, "we knew, after those three, we weren't making a very good impression on the Committee. It seemed to some that the Committee was not sympathetic and wanted to believe the Russian story."

"I've read a part of what Madame Kethly had to say—she wrote me a long letter too. And General Kiraly told me about his testimony; what do you think was wrong?"

"Nothing wrong. But all three witnesses talked at length about the failure of the U.N. and the history of the Revolution. None of them were what you would really call the man in the street, and they all talked too long. Of course, at the time, we did not realize this. What we did realize was that the Committee seemed unfriendly to us in their questioning. We knew we weren't doing well, but we were strangers. Not many of us spoke English, or spoke it very fluently. It was a new experience, and there was distrust on our part."

"I shouldn't wonder."

"Well, it was here that Paul Bang-Jensen first came to our aid. We had a meeting at somebody's place up on Riverside Drive, I remember, trying to figure out what we must do. Sandor Kiss was going to testify next, and I was going to follow him. I brought up Bang-Jensen's name. I said I thought we could trust him, and that we should ask his advice on how we must proceed to get the Committee on our side. The others agreed, and Sandor and I had a meeting with him the next day before the Committee met." Janos Horvath laughed softly. "Sandor had a two-hour statement. Bang-Jensen said he must cut it in half! 'You must not repeat all that's been said,' Bang-Jensen told him. 'The repetition is bad. You must tell them what happened to you. Give them facts, no opinions.'

"He stressed the repetition over and over. He said it was better if the Committee asked Sandor to come back a second time. Well . . . they did just that; they asked him to come back three times. And when he had finished his statement, the Chairman and the Rapporteur and Mr. Gunwardene all congratulated him. Mr. Gunwardene said, 'Now, my young friend, I understand what the Revolution was all about.'

"Unless you understood the situation, you might think this was a little thing on Paul's part. But to us it was a big thing. He gave us good advice. He told us what to do, and we, whom you might call the leading Representatives of the Hungarians in Exile, we trusted him."

"And this trust worked down to the witnesses themselves who wanted to remain anonymous?"

"Not as you might think, Mr. Marshall. Not as most people seem to think, especially inside the U.N. It was through people like myself and General Kiraly and a few others that the word was passed from camp to camp. 'You can trust the Dane.' The word went across the ocean . . . not only written, I took it myself."

"And did they trust him?"

"More did not than did, because they were frightened people, and they would not trust anyone. Also, at that time, there were some who did not think the Revolution was over, and they did not want to give out information. But, as you know, eighty-one people trusted him. However, it was because the word was passed."

"The witnesses must have liked him."

"Quite the contrary. Many came to me afterward and said, 'Why is he so cold? Why is he so formal? He does not care about us.' Well, I told Paul that, and he said to me, 'I must act this way. I can't let them see how I feel . . . how their stories tear my heart out! . . .'" Janos Horvath sighed.

"And, of course, in your mind, and in the minds of all Hungarians who have had to leave their country, you think he was absolutely right in keeping the list secret?"

"Yes . . . knowing the situation in the Secretariat, we certainly do. He was a loyal man who would not betray a trust. That was his crime. And there is something else I might say. I have heard he was ridiculed for keeping the list in his pocket. Any man who has been in the underground will tell you that is just the place to carry a document. As long as you have it you know just where it is. If it is taken from you, you are the first to know, and if you are killed for it, your friends know, and they can take steps."

"Do you think he killed himself?"

"Never, even the last time I saw him, did I think that about him. But I can see how a man in his position might have come to that."

"When did you see him last?"

"I remember exactly, it was the night of September twenty-fifth. We had a meeting of our Foundation, and we had a speaker who had traveled in Russia. Paul came to that meeting, and when it was over, we sat down and talked. He wanted to talk, I could tell that, and though I was somewhat tired myself, I did not want to stop him."

"What did you talk about?"

"Mostly it was Imre Nagy. He went over and over it, as though he were seeking for something or trying to prove something. After a while, we left here and walked down to Grand Central together, where he was to get his subway. Well, instead we went into a coffee place there, and it was not until one o'clock in the morning that we said goodbye."

"You didn't know what he was trying to get at exactly?"

"No, I did not, and perhaps it is from experience, but I do not ask questions like that. If he wanted to tell me what he was getting at, he would have."

"And that was the last time you spoke with him?"

"The last . . . and when I heard the news, I was surprised . . . and I felt very badly."

Again Peter Marshall could see that Janos Horvath was a man of understatement; a man whose face did not betray his feelings.

Peter Marshall sat at the bar at Ferdi's Sidewalk Café. From behind it, co-proprietor Yale Ferdinand passed the time of day chatting about his U.N. clientele.

"We get a lot of people from over there—" He nodded toward the United Nations building directly across First Avenue.

"Andrew Cordier, he comes in. Even Dag Hammarskjold once in a while. He likes a window seat, but he'll take any place that's free if necessary—just like anybody else."

Ferdi's, with its attractive décor—except for a garish temporary exhibition of amateur art done with chewing gum —is a convenient and popular eatery for U.N. folk of all ranks. Its menu is modestly priced.

A little after 1:00 P.M. a short, brown-haired man approached the bar. Marshall, watching for an unknown face, turned to him.

"Mr. K.?"

"Right. Mr. Marshall?"

They shook hands. K. was not of the handsome, manicured variety of diplomats, nor was he an imposing man. But Peter Marshall sensed his friendliness.

"Do you mind being seen with me?" Marshall asked him as they took a table in Ferdi's inside room—"not that anyone knows me but—"

He didn't add the word "yourself" because K. had already understood. "Who's to know? People are always seeing old friends here. It's a lot better to meet in a place like this where no one looks twice. . . ."

Marshall said: "You know what I'm doing?"

"Yes. Remember, I am a dedicated U.N. career man. The organization has a function, it has a part to play in our world. I don't know what you think about it. But I know Bang-Jensen believed in it—and that's what he fought for. That's the irony of his case. . . ."

K. was facing Peter Marshall. He looked across the latter's shoulder, out through the window toward the tall building across the street. He went on: ". . . it was just something I couldn't stomach."

Marshall realized how sincerely the man had spoken. He waited for a moment. Dishes were placed before them on the table.

"Well, maybe you would like to ask me some questions," K. said abruptly. "What have you done so far?"

"I've talked to Hungarian leaders who testified. I've learned about the formation of the Committee on Hungary," Marshall said. "I hoped you might be able to fill in some details about the hearings in New York."

"The Committee heard thirty-five witnesses here. Sixteen of them testified secretly. Perhaps you know that it was over one of these witnesses that Bang-Jensen and Jordan had their first disagreement."

"I've read Bang-Jensen's side of it. But this is one reason I want to talk to you. Tell me how it happened."

"You see, during the first part of the Committee's hearings, the members felt uncertain whether any Hungarians had been deported to the Soviet Union.

"Both Andersen, the Chairman, and Shann, the Rapporteur, had told Jordan they were very eager, naturally, to hear any witness that might corroborate the fact that deportations had taken place.

"Accidentally, Bang-Jensen learned that Jordan had received a letter about a young Hungarian who had actually been deported. Paul was bowled over—the fact that such wanted testimony was to be had and that Jordan had not made it known . . ."

Peter Marshall interrupted—"but why did Jordan do that?"

K. put his knife and fork across his plate in European fashion. He shook his head. "Right there you get to the heart of it: Bang-Jensen taking the initiative and Jordan proceeding cautiously, worrying about the rules. You know what Jordan said—that it 'was quite undesirable for the Secretariat to give the impression of stacking the evidence . . .' Jordan admitted that he was doubtful as to whether the Secretariat should even furnish names of potential witnesses. He didn't think it was within the instructions.

"But you can bet that Bang-Jensen did. He saw to the scheduling of the witnesses on his own responsibility. Naturally that didn't please Jordan at all. It was a bad situation. At first, Jordan denied that he had received the information about the deportee. Later he admitted that Miss de Hedervary, a political affairs officer who was acting as an interpreter, had given him the name.

"And don't think Bang-Jensen let Jordan off easily. He said it had been agreed on that he should handle witnesses and that the testimony of this particular witness had been concealed not only from him but from the Committee.

"In a nutshell, he believed that some would have been just as pleased if the deportee witness had never testified. I guess you know he included this incident in a listing he called 'suppression of witnesses.' In a memo he later wrote to the Secretary General, he bluntly called it 'sabotage.' "

K. paused. Coffee was on the table. "I take it black. . . . I wish you could have heard that witness. He was regarded as one of the most important to appear in New York. Here it was—on the line—first evidence that Hungarians had been deported. And the lad instantly won the Committee's sympathy. The boy was about sixteen, tousled hair. He was smiling with infectious, undefeated cockiness.

"Believe me, the delegates listened with something close to wonder as he told his story. It went something like this:
When were you captured?

On November tenth. It was about over—there wasn't any more to do.

Where?

Near the Morice Zsigmond Circle in Buda.

How?

I jumped out of the fat into the fire. There were hundreds of people who were living in the cellars of a movie theater and a department store. No place else to go. I had been sleeping there, moving around in the daytime. One morning the Russians came and ordered all the men to come out—they were needed to fight fires, according to the word passed around. I knew it was a trick. I got away from this . . . but was picked up by the AVH.

And then?

We were loaded on a freight train. Myself and others who had taken part in the revolt. Men and women, boys and girls. There were Russian guards. No food, no heat, no sanitation. We traveled three days and three nights. We were taken fifty kilometers into the Soviet Union. They had a camp there.

Could you tell the Committee about the camp?

Not very much—

What!—Excuse me, what do you mean?

I didn't stay long enough to get to know that place.

You escaped. Tell us about that then.

I couldn't stand it. There was a window in a shower room that could be forced. Five of us decided to try it. We got out all right. It was in the dark.

Were you fully dressed?

Oh, yes. It was cold. We had on our overcoats.

How did you manage to get out of the camp? Weren't there guards?

Lots of guards. But we saw this Russian jeep parked nearby. We all got into it and drove out the gate.

Drove out the gate!

Yes, you see our overcoats looked very much like the coats of Russian soldiers.

And no one did anything to stop you?

No, there was quite a bit of traffic going in and out. We just waved to the guards—and called out to them as we sailed by.

And they just waved back?

They're not very bright, sir.

Well, what did you do then?

We drove off and caught up with the rear of a big Russian truck convoy. It was heading toward home. . . .

Yes?

So we went along.

You attached yourself to the convoy?

Yes, sir. It seemed like a good idea. We went right back to Hungary with it.

No one stopped you, no one questioned you?

Not once. It wasn't so far to the border. In the dark the Russians thought we were Russians.

What did you do when you reached Hungary?

I made my way back home. My mother was there.

Hadn't she worried?

A little, I guess.

Just a little?

Well, not so much. You know, she didn't know what had happened. She knew I was hungry, though. She gave me something to eat.[1]

A few days later, Peter Marshall met K. again for a leisurely evening in New York.

"So now you want to know about the Committee's trip to Europe?"

"That's right. I've met several people who were there with the U.N. group. I've read the Report and every paper I could find. What I need is—"

". . . is, as you people say—the inside. Correct?"

"Exactly. I know the Committee heard testimony for more than a month in Europe during March and April."

"There were hearings in London, Geneva, and Vienna. But we started in Rome. Oh, we had a good laugh there," K. said. "You see, the Committee had set up a snack bar for refugees—they were living in camps near the city, and I must say they were underfed. But when they came in to testify and visited the snack bar—and found that cognac was being served, why they did more drinking than eating. That's the way Hungarians are—it was the spirit of the thing. Bang-Jensen had to settle up the bill and he couldn't get over it. . . ."

K. laughed silently, shaking his head at the remembrance. "And then we had the bomb incident."

"What!"

"Oh, I should say, 'bomb scare.' The Committee was preparing to take off from Rome's Ciampino Airport for the flight to Vienna when it happened. The Uruguayan delegate, Rodriguez Fabregat, advised us, just before we were to leave, that he had a report a bomb was on the plane.

"Some of the U.N. people—there were about twenty-five aboard—were incredulous. Others took it as a serious matter. Two Secretariat members, Duckworth-Barker and Schreiber, were assigned to search the plane.

"There was grumbling—and laughter. Someone said, 'Let's go get a cup of coffee.' Everyone stretched his legs and whiled away the time."

"And what did they find?"

"Nothing. No bomb, at least. Although the presence aboard the plane of two Polish Communist officials, en route for Warsaw, was noted with some suspicion.

"By the time the plane took off, about an hour and a half late, there was a good deal of uneasiness, nevertheless. This was heightened during a stopover at Milan when Italian police, now fully alerted, rushed out to cordon off the area.

"By the time we got to Vienna, late on a Friday afternoon, we were all cracking a few nervous jokes. It was beautiful weather there, but everybody sensed a new tension. You know, the airport at Vienna isn't more than a few miles from the Hungarian frontier—and we could feel the difference, the atmosphere. Here there were thousands of refugees located in a small area—and the Committee was only minutes from the very scene it was trying to explore.

"The Austrian government provided a nice old building for the Committee's use. It was located at 6A Wallnerstrasse, a short, cobblestoned street. It was near the Graben, with its famous pastry shops. 'Whipped cream,' I remember a refugee saying. 'We haven't seen that for years!'

"It was these contrasts that the witnesses saw—and that we knew they felt. Outside our headquarters, there was a strong guard . . . Police in their long, leather coats and plainclothesmen, too. Hungarians came to us with trepidation—they were afraid, yet they wanted to help.

"You probably know about the arrangements that were made to hear them?"

Peter Marshall nodded. "I know the Committee sent out telegrams and letters.[2] I also talked with General Kiraly, Monsignor Bela Varga, and Anna Kethly—they told me how they sent letters to refugees, urging all assistance be given the Committee. Janos Horvath visited Vienna personally and advised Hungarians that they could rely on Bang-Jensen—that if Bang-Jensen promised anonymity, he would never betray his word."

K. gave his light smile. "Well, then you probably also know about the Sunday morning argument between Bang-Jensen and Jordan?"

Peter Marshall nodded his head.

"I wasn't there—in the room. But it affected everybody. I understand they were fairly yelling at one another. Everybody heard about it, of course, in no time.

"You see, the Committee held its first meeting on Saturday morning, and there was a general expression by all the delegates to get down to business as soon as possible. It was felt that a great deal could be accomplished in Vienna.

"Well, on Saturday night, there was some discussion between Bang-Jensen and Jordan as to how many people from the staff would be needed for Sunday.

"Let's say there was a misunderstanding; Bang-Jensen thought there would be a full crew—and there wasn't. Bang-Jensen raised his voice; Jordan replied in kind.

"It was slightly incredible, two men snapping at one another like that. It happened in a big, high-ceilinged room. I think that was the breaking point between the two. They had further words Sunday night—"

"I've seen Jordan's personal notes of that Sunday night," Peter Marshall said. "Jordan said that Bang-Jensen was 'shouting loudly in a ridiculous tone.'"

"They were probably both shouting . . . and both ridiculous. You see, what happened was that Jordan had decided to prepare short summaries of what potential witnesses might offer the Committee—instead of lengthy translations. Bang-Jensen argued that this was unacceptable, that the Committee should have the complete record of what each witness had to say.

"This all came to a head just at a time when the Committee was attempting to make rapid progress—and was having a difficult time making any progress at all. Although through Horvath, Thomas Pasztor and others had prepared a tentative list of witnesses, the Hungarians were wary. They were scared. They had good reason, too. The city was full of spies. You know, they found one Hungarian Communist on a rooftop opposite the building, taking photographs of witnesses.[3] Hungarian refugees had plenty to worry about—a wife or a parent in the homeland, or close friends. . . .

"On Monday, Jordan told the Committee that there was some difficulty about scheduling the witnesses. He said the

Secretariat staff members would continue giving preliminary interviews, and to try to speed up things he assigned Duckworth-Barker and Schreiber to take part in the screening also. He claimed that Bang-Jensen's arrangements for pre-interviews had broken down. He also admitted that he was 'baffled'—he used that very word—by the fact that witnesses wished to remain anonymous."

"I know that only one out of forty-three allowed his name to be used," Peter Marshall said.

K. let his eyes drift away. "It was something I shall never forget. Those few days, those men and women and young people that came to the building on Wallnerstrasse; the brave, the fearful, the anguished.

"The prospective witnesses would arrive and show their invitation to guards in the entrance foyer. Then they went up a winding staircase to the rooms used by the Secretariat team. As I said, it was a fascinating building, Marie Thérèse style; I remember the doorknobs placed rather high up on the doors.

"For the pre-interviews, the witnesses were taken into small offices. Some of them broke down even at that point and fled from the building! Others wept.

"That's when we became aware of how poor our security was."

"There were no rules?"

"We had to make our own rules. Notes taken during the day were burned in ash trays before going home. Bang-Jensen was continually worried about the security problem. A thread he placed across a filing cabinet was broken . . . he kept the list of witnesses on his person. . . ."

"Was it generally known he kept the list?"

"The key people knew it—Jordan, Shann, and other top Secretariat staffers. They've made many references to this —the fact that Bang-Jensen had a list."

"It was a special situation. . . ."

"Right . . . in more ways than one." K. mused, "You'd be surprised, I remember one day when one of our people came rushing in, breathless, frightened—said an attempt had been made to run him down. Sounds foolish? Maybe."

"Well, what about keeping the witnesses' names secret?" Peter Marshall asked.

"At the Committee hearings, Andersen always started off by assuring the witness that his or her desire for anonymity would be completely respected. . . ."

"There wasn't any question about this?"

"None whatsoever. Of course, the promise of secrecy had already been given in the screening interview. That was the critical time. The individual would come in, the men would often click their heels . . . perhaps an interviewer would say: 'Please do not give me your name. You are to be designated by the letters AA.' "

K. interrupted his flow of thought. "Again the incongruity. They were honest, sincere, proud to be there . . . but so afraid. They would explain their position in detail . . . 'I'll tell you all I can, but never, never must my name be known. . . . I've just arrived, all my family are back there.'

"A few were more candid: 'It's not a question of relatives with me, it's a question of Communists.' "

"Specifically, what words were used to promise secrecy?" Peter Marshall asked.

"Bang-Jensen would answer them: 'Nobody will know your name but myself. However, I have to keep your name at the disposition of the Committee. And if the members ask for it, I have to give it to them. But up to now, nobody has ever asked.' "

"Just like that?"

"Exactly like that." K. pursed his lips in his soft smile. "I know."

Marshall waited silently for K. to go on.

"Yes." K. said. "Some spoke for three minutes, some for

almost thirty. Some of the witnesses told such hair-raising or tragic accounts it was feared we would be accused of weighting the scales, so to speak. But what to do. We came to know the horrible facts; we couldn't escape either . . .

"There was the time one man pulled out his false palate to show the agony of the torture he had undergone. Bang-Jensen got up and left the room. . . .

"Every kind of case, fantastic situations. Of course, if you've read Bang-Jensen's reply to Hammarskjold's letter of dismissal, you know he said there were two high-ranking Hungarian Communists who would testify only on the condition the Secretary General would never know their names. Well, that's absolutely true. They were both political figures. One of them gave his testimony in German.

"You realize, Bang-Jensen later offered to tell Hammarskjold why they wouldn't give their names—but the Secretary General never wanted to find out." [4]

Paul Bang-Jensen's career as Deputy Secretary encompassed two distinct phases. The first had to do with his part in the screening and protection of witnesses and the gathering of information. The second had to do with the writing of the report on the problem of Hungary.

To Peter Marshall, it was this second phase that held the most significance in Paul Bang-Jensen's career. Contrary to accepted belief, the major portion of the U.N.'s case against the Deputy Secretary revolved around his actions during the writing of the report and the immediate months following. His refusal to turn over the list of anonymous witnesses to the Secretary General was not the main issue.

The big question in Marshall's mind concerned the validity of the Secretary General's basis for firing the Danish diplomat. Was it simply a smoke screen for the obvious, or was it founded in fact?

Just as he had found it necessary to make clear in detail

what had taken place in the U.N. during the final stages of
the Hungarian uprising, now he felt it necessary to recount
Bang-Jensen's activities during the spring and summer of
1957.

Part Three: Accusation

CHAPTER 14

THE COMMITTEE and its attendant staff returned from its travels in the early days of April. In its three months of investigation, it had acquired over two thousand pages of testimony and allied data. From this great mass of documentation, the report on Hungary must be honed down into a readable, factual account of events.

Plans for the writing of the report, however, had been formulated early in the proceedings.

"A preliminary outline of the report was drawn up between 26th February and 1 March before the Committee left for Europe," Jordan points out. "Responsibility for the individual chapters was assigned to members of the Secretariat at this stage.

"Mr. Bang-Jensen was given no assignment with regard to the report."

Later Jordan continues, "The Committee approved the outline of a draft report at its meeting in Geneva. It gave approval first to a summary outline, and, at a further meeting, to a fuller outline.

"Mr. Bang-Jensen was not involved in the preparation of this outline."

The next statement by the Secretary is not only touching in its magnaminity, but when considered in the light of Paul Bang-Jensen's knowledge of the Hungarian Revolution, which was second to no one's, it is positively brilliant.

"The question of Mr. Bang-Jensen's participation in the preparation of the report was discussed with Dr. Protitch in London. It was agreed that some part of the work should be assigned to him in order that he should not feel left out."

Actually it was Shann, the Rapporteur, who was responsible for what went into the report. It was he who must approve the work of the Secretariat in drafting the seventeen chapters.

Here, too, the instructions from the 38th floor on the duties of the Secretariat Group with regard to their functions and responsibilities in writing the report caused conflict and dissension.

In a defense of his actions that were to follow, Bang-Jensen wrote to Dag Hammarskjold:

As to Mr. Jordan, I have in fairness to him pointed out to you from the beginning that, correctly or incorrectly, he maintained that he was acting under instructions. At times he appeared to be extremely unhappy and told me, for instance, in detail how he had had several heated discussions with Dr. Protitch, and twice had threatened to resign, as Secretary of the Committee on Hungary, unless his instructions regarding the preparation of the draft to the Committee's report were changed. . . . As he reported it, you first had directed that the Secretariat should leave the drafting completely to the Rapporteur; when Dr. Protitch had pointed out to you that the members of the Committee no doubt would protest against this, you had agreed that the Secretariat could prepare a first draft to the various chapters, but you had insisted that the Secretariat then should leave it to

the Rapporteur and the members of the Committee to correct
that draft.

I expressed several times to Mr. Jordan my disbelief that you
could have issued such instructions, but he maintained that this
was the case and that he was, in fact, going beyond your instructions when he had some of the drafts redrafted after consultation
with the Rapporteur.[1]

"The point behind it all," explains a staff member, "was
that the real authority came from the Secretary General,
and he wanted the Secretariat to have nothing to do with
the writing of the report. He wanted it to be left up to the
Committee, and naturally the Committee couldn't have
done it without a great deal of assistance." [2]

William Jordan must have gone way beyond what was
expected of him, for, from Political Affairs Officer Philip
Messinesi, there is the statement "Most chapters underwent more than ten drafts."

If Jordan went far beyond what was expected of him, relating to the preparation of the report, he went just as far
in changing his original plans for Bang-Jensen's participation in that preparation. The reasons he gives for this
change are valid enough, but there is a strong doubt
whether they are the only reasons.

"Assignments were revised on April twenty-fifth. Mr.
Bang-Jensen was assigned responsibility for the first draft of
Chapter one.

"Mr. Bang-Jensen's first draft of Chapter one was completed on May eighth.

"It was hectographed on May ninth.

"It was reviewed by Mr. Shann on May tenth.

"It was redrafted by myself between tenth and fifteenth
May.

"The redraft was extensively discussed with Mr. Bang-
Jensen and revised in the light of his observations.

"It was hectographed on fifteenth May as a third draft.

"On fifth May, in order to expedite completion of the report, assignments were re-distributed. . . . On this date, Mr. Bang-Jensen was asked to re-draft Chapter X, the earlier draft of which had been prepared by Mr. Poullain.

"Mr. Bang-Jensen's draft of Chapter X was hectographed on fourteenth May . . . The fifth draft was completed on twenty-fourth May.

"Since the subject matter of Chapter VI and Chapter X were closely related, Chapter VI was passed to Mr. Bang-Jensen for review in the light of Chapter X.

"Mr. Bang-Jensen objected that Chapter VI contained many errors which he could not correct without rewriting the chapter.

"Though the Rapporteur was substantially satisfied and even gratified by the existing draft, I had no alternative but to agree to Mr. Bang-Jensen's proceeding with a general revision of Chapter VI. This resulted in a draft of Chapter VI by Mr. Bang-Jensen, hectographed on May nineteenth, 1957. This draft was extensively revised by Mr. Shann and myself. The revision was reviewed by Mr. Bang-Jensen and other officers. . . ."

In all William Jordan's comments concerning his Deputy Secretary runs the suggestion of incompetence. First, Bang-Jensen is to have nothing to do with the writing of the report. Then he is to have a small part in it. And then, because of the pressure of time, his contribution grows to major significance. But, even here, the impression is given that what Bang-Jensen wrote had to go through numerous revisions and that a considerable portion of what he wrote was a waste of time.

In the light of Jordan's observations and the explosion to follow, the impressions of some of Bang-Jensen's co-workers are of value.

Philip Messinesi says: "Mr. Bang-Jensen on many occasions proved helpful. Though not formally assigned to help his colleagues in their drafting, he knew their assignments and often sent us little notes reminding us that in such a verbatim record the witness had given particular information that was useful to us. I myself benefited on a number of occasions from the information he gave me. He also sent in his comments on the drafts that were circulated by Mr. Jordan to most of the officers assigned to the Special Committee."

Duckworth-Barker says: "We worked under tremendous pressure at the end of a particularly extensive mission (Chapter XVII was written in one evening) and I sought and received generous help and cooperation from all my colleagues who had been engaged in drafting various parts of the report. I think that all of us had the experience of Mr. Bang-Jensen's repeatedly expressed anxieties regarding what he called numerous errors in our texts. In some cases, I found his comments of help to me. His close association with the witnesses and his reading of their testimony enabled him to suggest various alterations in some of my drafts which seemed to me improvements. . . ." [3]

"He called me many times, checking, checking," Janos Horvath reveals. "I knew he was worried.

" *'What is the trouble, Paul?'*

" *'You have no idea what is going on over here.'*

" *'You are worried the report will not be satisfactory?'*

" *'If we are not careful, it will be full of errors.'*

" *'Well, you can correct errors.'*

" *'I can try, but I believe some of it is being done on purpose. It is very difficult.'*

" *'What sort of errors?'*

" *'Not big errors, lots of small ones. But if they're allowed to remain in, then the Soviets can discredit the report . . . laugh at it. I tell you, my friend, I am having to fight.'* "

To fight? About what? What small errors?

Here is one example Bang-Jensen offers: "It was stated in an early draft that Imre Nagy was Premier for the first time in 1946-47.

"I pointed out to Mr. Jordan that the Premier at that time actually was Ferenc Nagy, who is living in exile in the United States and, according to the Kadar Government, is one of the persons abroad who instigated the revolution.

"After long argumentation, Mr. Jordan agreed to delete the incorrect sentence; a day later I found, however, he had not done so.

"When I again took up the matter, he refused to make the deletion before the Rapporteur had seen the draft. However, after prolonged discussion, he promised that he would call the error to the Rapporteur's attention.

"When the draft came back from the Rapporteur, the error had not been corrected. Mr. Jordan first claimed that he had pointed the error out to the Rapporteur; when I had expressed doubt that he had done this since it had not been corrected, he admitted that he had not but declared as follows:

"'When the Rapporteur has approved a draft, and it states that Imre Nagy was Premier in 1946, then as far as I'm concerned, Imre Nagy was Premier in 1946.'

"It took several arguments the following days before the incorrect line was deleted." [4]

Duckworth-Barker believes that William Jordan's over-all knowledge in the writing of the report was highly authoritative. From the example above, there seems justifiable doubt.

The staff was working an average of eighty hours a week. Nightly that spring the cluster of lights high up on the side of the smooth-faced edifice glittered into the small hours.

Time was the pressure. If the report was going to mean anything, it had to be presented as soon as possible.

Fatigue was an enemy. It frayed nerves; made tempers

short; made it arduous to observe the polite ground rules of protocol.

But along with the shortness of time, and the debilitating effects of an unusual work schedule, there was another enemy; the ever-unadmitted enemy, the obvious enemy.

A two-year-old would recognize that the Russians would be totally remiss if they did not do everything they could to wreck the writing of the report. If Bang-Jensen's colleagues seemed unable to sense the obvious, the Dane made up for their lack of sensitivity. Of course, he had been acutely aware of the problem from the outset, but now he hammered it home at an ever-increasing tempo. Conscientiously, consistently, he raised his voice and made a shambles of correct procedure.

Errors and omissions became, to him, acts of dishonesty and deliberate sabotage. "Sabotage!" became his battle cry.

The two most significant chapters in the Hungarian report—Chapters II and VII—triggered the emotional uproar that, in the last day of May and the first days of June, resulted in open warfare between Bang-Jensen and William Jordan. They had disagreed and fought in the past, but nothing compared to this.

The effects directly embroiled Messinesi and Duckworth-Barker. They erupted on to a higher official level and embarrassed and angered Rapporteur K. C. O. Shann. They thoroughly upset and confused Chairman Alsing Andersen. Andrew Cordier, for all his agility, was rattled by them, and while he pondered a counteracting course, they came to rest squarely in the lap of Secretary General Dag Hammarskjold.

Chapter VII was drafted before Chapter II. It dealt with the second Soviet intervention, and its position of consequence goes without saying.

Philip Messinesi was its principal compiler. Though Greek, Messinesi looks and speaks like an Englishman. He is a serious, rather reticent person who had a fine war record and whose forte is labor and economics.

"Chapter seven," Messinesi recalls, "was already in its first draft early in May. I gave it to Mr. Jordan, who seemed quite pleased with it. I then gave it to Mr. Bang-Jensen for his comments, as I wanted to get his reaction.

"A few days later he told me he had found many errors and omissions. We discussed a number of points that he brought up, but I soon realized that our discussion was leading nowhere due to his uncompromising attitude.

"It appeared to me that much that he was advocating would stand up if (a) we had more testimony to prove the veracity of our contentions and (b) this chapter were to expand from twenty to forty typescript pages. . . . It was obvious that he was striving to achieve the maximum condemnation of the second Soviet intervention in Hungary, and for this purpose he believed that if the report were to demonstrate that Mr. Kadar had come completely under the influence of the Soviets as of ten P.M. of first November, the culpability of the Soviet Union would be greater than if the report allowed it to be interpreted—as it does —that Kadar pondered the question of his future role during the second and third of November.

"I was of the contrary opinion, and I pointed out to Mister Bang-Jensen that his reasoning was at fault . . . I argued the point repeatedly but Mr. Bang-Jensen rejected my view and insisted instead that I should have stressed that the Kadar Government had been formed in Moscow on or about third November. To this I replied the evidence was too flimsy (the surmise of two witnesses) and that it would be dangerous for the report to open itself to any kind of attack on the basis of fact. . . ." [5]

Oddly enough, the report on Hungary, as finally published, seems to bear out Bang-Jensen's conclusions more than Messinesi's. With regard to Kadar's time of betrayal, it reads:

"After the broadcast announcement about 9:50 P.M. on 1 November, in connexion with the establishment of the Hungarian Socialist Workers Party, Mr. Kadar went to his home. Witnesses stated that, at some time before 10 P.M., Mr. Munnich asked that a car be made available to him from the car pool attached to the Parliament building. He picked up Mr. Kadar and together they proceeded to the Soviet Embassy. It was reported that outside the Embassy they entered another car which was parked behind that in which they had arrived. . . ."

The implication is certainly clear that, as of approximately 10:00 P.M. on November 1, Kadar had become the Judas of Hungary.

As to when Kadar formed his government in Moscow, the report states: "From evidence given to the Committee, it would indeed appear, if Kadar had not already proceeded to Moscow, he was in Moscow on the 4th. . . ."

Another issue which Messinesi considered pointless conjecture on Bang-Jensen's part was whether Kadar's broadcast from the town of Szolonk was given live or by tape recording.[6] It is, of course, necessary to know this fact in determining Kadar's whereabouts at the time, as the report now recognizes: "The Committee has no evidence of the presence of Mr. Kadar at Szolonk on the morning of 4 November, and assertions by witnesses that the broadcast was made from a tape recording may well be correct."[7]

"Mr. Bang-Jensen stated that there were many omissions," Messinesi continues. "I then suggested that he bring all these points to Mr. Jordan's attention and we would discuss the matter further."

From Jordan's own account, he went over his Deputy Secretary's comments with three other officers.

"All these comments were reviewed and incorporated, in so far as necessary, in a fifth draft, which was placed before Mr. Shann. All major changes proposed by officers, including Mr. Bang-Jensen, but not accepted by me, were expressly drawn to Mr. Shann's attention. . . ."

This fifth draft of Chapter VII then was handed over to the Committee for its approval, and if Jordan was about to sigh in relief, he checked it, for into his office strode Bang-Jensen with an uncompromising gleam in his eye and a copy of the chapter in his hand.

"I am sorry, Mr. Secretary, but I have detected serious mistakes in this draft."

"It is presently being reviewed by the Committee . . . with Mr. Shann's approval."

"But it is wrong! It can't stand the way it is!"

"To what are you referring specifically? And I would appreciate it if you would be specific." There was the quality of taut wire in Jordan's tone as he stared coldly at the tall, unyielding Dane.

Bang-Jensen's gestures, like his voice, were abrupt, his accent heavier than usual, the words harder to understand.

"There are forty—forty, I repeat—misstatements of fact! There—!"

"Please lower your voice. I may be hard of hearing but not that hard!" One crime Jordan could not forgive or tolerate was what he considered an unseemly show of emotion. Of late, he felt his Deputy Secretary had been committing it with increasing regularity. "I asked you to be specific."

"There are also twenty omissions that, if allowed to remain out of the chapter, will—!"

"Name one, please."

"What good does it do to name them, if you only ignore them?"

"Mr. Bang-Jensen, will you please do as I ask?"

"All right, the text of Istvan Dobi's address to the Presidium on May ninth." (Dobi was Chairman of the Presidium of the Hungarian People's Republic under Kadar.)

"What about it?"

"I consider it the most important omission in the entire report as it now stands."

"Unfortunately, there are other people, including the Rapporteur, who do not share your judgment."

"It is proof that Kadar was with the Soviets on the third!"

"At least as you see it." The sarcasm was razor sharp. "Perhaps you'd like to make another list of your errors and your omissions."

"I'll not make another list. I'll redraft the chapter. It's not that the conclusions will be so different, but it will strengthen them."

"I can't prevent you from redrafting the chapter, but I hardly think it will make any difference to the Rapporteur. He is satisfied with the present draft."

"He doesn't know."

"No, it seems only you know. Above all others, you know."

"I know what is wrong. . . . And I think you do too, sir."

"It seems I've heard you sing that song before. What you need is a rest."

"No, all I need is a little cooperation."

After their fruitless meeting, the Deputy Secretary went back to his office to redraft the chapter as he thought it should be done. But, looking out over the city mantled in its gentling spring haze, he resolved to make one last attempt to get the cooperation he so determinedly sought. To get it, it should be noted, he made his first offer to resign his position. What follows is a portion of a memorandum he wrote that May afternoon to William Jordan.

As you know, I have not put the various warnings I have given during the past four months down in writing, since I felt that the matter was much too delicate. After our conversation today, it seems, however, that the time has come where I am forced to put the facts of our conversation down on paper. I ask you to be assured that, when I take this step, it doesn't mean that I am not still prepared to co-operate with you, and assist you, so that matters can be straightened out without causing a scandal which, since it hardly could be kept inside the building, would have a harmful effect to the United Nations. I repeat again that I am willing to do whatever you desire, the only thing I demand is honesty. I am willing to resign quietly as Deputy Secretary, or if you prefer, you can ask the Secretary-General to relieve me of my duties. I am, however, also willing to continue, and to do my best to correct the many serious errors of fact in the draft Report.

Chapter VII, which is the key chapter of the Report, contains, as I have repeatedly told you, more than forty errors of facts, of which some are very serious; some could easily make the Committee look ridiculous. There are also more than twenty omissions of very essential facts and several contradictions in the text. Among the omissions is one, which is perhaps the most important fact in the whole Report. As I told you, I can prepare a re-draft and have it completely ready for the Rapporteur and for distribution to the Members in about three hours. The draft could easily be prepared in such a way that the Rapporteur could state in good conscience that it was fundamentally the same, but that some new material we have found later has been added, certain errors corrected, and the suggestions of the Members of the Committee incorporated, but that otherwise the material is the same. The present paragraphs would be arranged a little more chronologically so that it would be easier for the reader to follow. If you think this is more desirable, I am also willing discreetly to help Mr. Messinesi to prepare this draft so that it can be considered to be his.

Obviously, I am also prepared to continue to tell you of other errors of fact I have found and I am finding in other Chapters.

With regard to the form of the Report, I shall as hitherto leave it completely to you without long discussions. However, I do maintain that as Deputy Secretary, it is my duty to point out errors of fact, and it is your duty to find out whether my statements in this respect are correct by checking the record. This you hitherto have not done. . . .

Jordan did not reply in writing, but Bang-Jensen points out that the Secretary never refuted any of the statements in his peace offering, which ran, in all, over five pages.

Of Bang-Jensen's redraft, Jordan states it was "reviewed by the competent officer [Messinesi] on May twenty-ninth, who advised me in writing as to the degree to which Mr. Bang-Jensen's changes were desirable."

Messinesi resisted the changes and recalls, "I spoke again to Bang-Jensen and pointed out that most of his suggestions brought about no change in substance, and in view of our extreme fatigue, we should be practical and try to get the draft ready instead of arguing. To this he replied he would have to speak to the Chairman of the Committee and to the Secretary General as the report was being destroyed."

Jordan adds, "The Rapporteur, when attention was drawn to Mr. Bang-Jensen's redraft, asked whether it was necessary for him to study it. My reply was that it was not essential. It was a matter for him to decide."

Paul Bang-Jensen, never one to be stopped by half measures when he felt the issue warranted action, now had the temerity to run around Jordan's right end and tackle the long, gangling length of Rapporteur Shann.

It was not difficult to locate the Rapporteur, for, from all accounts, he spent a considerable amount of time in the Delegates' Lounge, which actually is a glorified bar room.

Shann, in recounting the meeting, refers to the location as the "Delegates' Area of the United Nations," the supposition being that, like the quarter deck of a sailing ship, the special delegates' area should be off limits to underlings.

From the autocratic, rather imperious Australian's report, the encounter was not a pleasant one. Bang-Jensen, he maintained, was in a state of "some excitement."

The Deputy Secretary repeated his strong feelings about Chapter VII and described it, according to Shann, as being full of "grave errors." With forty mistakes of fact in it, he claimed that in its present form it would bring the Committee into ridicule. Then, tossing discretion out the tinted windows, he accused Jordon of deliberately trying to mislead the Rapporteur. Shann got the unfavorable impression that Bang-Jensen was implying that, in the present situation, he Shann, was incapable of proper judgment as to what was a fit document for presentation to the Committee.

Shann was not amused. He thought the Deputy Secretary had one big nerve coming to see him in the first place, and he said so.

"I think your position in coming to me is anomalous and administratively improper. I think you're also guilty of disloyalty to the Secretariat."

Bang-Jensen was adamant. "I'm sorry, but I know my duty. And if you won't listen to me, I'll take the matter up with the Chairman."

"In the first place," the thoroughly insulted Rapporteur snapped, "it is my responsibility to put what I think before the Committee in the report. And secondly, in my opinion, you have no right whatever to approach Chairman Andersen."

And that ended the diplomat-to-diplomat exchange for the moment, but it did nothing to deter the Dane. He had the kind of hard-tempered metal that would have given him the strength to dare the Devil himself. Now he did pay a call on Chairman Alsing Andersen and repeated his allegations.

Andersen was greatly disturbed. He thought it was "incredible" that anyone would deliberately try to undermine the report. Better than anyone else in the U.N., he knew

Bang-Jensen's background and temperament. Though they had belonged to different political parties in Denmark, Andersen certainly recognized his countryman's superior intelligence, and at the time he respected, and perhaps even envied, the younger man's abilities.

Andersen went to see Shann, and it was agreed that the Rapporteur would get Bang-Jensen's redraft from the Secretariat, and they would go over it and discuss it in detail as soon as possible.

Evidently Andersen spent a troubled night, for the next morning he took his worries again to the Rapporteur.

"I think the meeting for this afternoon should be canceled," he told Shann. "It would not be right to approve Chapter seven until we have had a look at Bang-Jensen's draft."

"But that's not necessary," Shann argued. "We're terribly pressed for time as it is. If you want, we'll sit right down now and go over his draft before lunch. Then we won't have to cancel anything."

Andersen was not sure they could get it done but Shann convinced him, and they accomplished it in time for the noon whistle. In Shann's words, he and the Chairman could find nothing in the Deputy Secretary's draft that pointed to grave errors. In fact he states that Bang-Jensen made some himself, and many of the proposed changes were of a trivial nature.

Nevertheless, when the Committee met that afternoon, Shann admits that "Some changes were brought to it [Chapter VII] and in principle it was approved."

After the meeting, the Chairman and the Rapporteur talked again, the former still gravely troubled.

"I wish you would be good enough to do me a favor, Mr. Shann."

"If I can, sir."

"I'd like you to go with me and see Mr. Bang-Jensen.

I'd like us to go over his draft again and hear his point of view."

Shann's reply was flat and unequivocal. "The man is in an excited and hysterical state, sir! Besides, if I may say so, I think the procedure is improper. In fact, your suggestion reflects a great lack of confidence in me. After all, I'm the one who is responsible for presenting the Committee with a draft." The Australian's sense of protocol had been stepped on again. Never mind if there was any merit in the Chairman's suggestion. It was insulting, to say the least. He concluded frigidly, "And furthermore, I have no desire to see Mr. Bang-Jensen."

But, in spite of his fervent wish, see him he did, and of course, the setting for the collision was right smack in the middle of the Delegates' Lounge.

There have been varying versions of the donnybrook that ensued. There are some, including Bang-Jensen, who insist it was no donnybrook at all, that Shann's report of the affair is thickly painted with a brush full of vituperation.

To Shann, Bang-Jensen was again in a hysterical state. He was a man engaging in the wildest of allegation, claiming, among other things, that the officers of the Secretariat engaged in drafting the report felt the way he did. (Some have admitted they did.) From Shann's account, it appears that the Dane pulled out all the stops. He was going to the Secretary General. Jordan was subject to Communist pressure. Jordan was dishonest. If things went on as they were going, he, Bang-Jensen, would have no alternative but to resign. . . . His drafts would become known and maliciously used in attacks on the report.

Shann pictures himself as a man being set on by a lunatic, with the Chairman of the Committee standing by helplessly. "My reaction to all this," he says, "was quite firm, and I maintained my position that he was acting improperly, hysterically, and foolishly. I asked the Chairman on one occasion to be excused from a painful discussion which I had previously asked should not take place but was given no assistance to disengage myself. On occasions this would have been physically difficult, as Mr. Bang-Jensen grasped me firmly by both arms, spilling his papers on the floor of the lounge."

Thus spoke Ambassador K. C. O. "Mick" Shann.

Chairman Andersen, as far as is known, has never made a public statement on the debate.

Bang-Jensen did not consider it of such magnitude as to refer to it later.

The ironic and unusual anticlimax to the duel is that, after it was over, Bang-Jensen suggested to Shann that he write a memo to the Secretary General, describing their opposite points of view. In this way, the entire matter could be looked into from a higher level. Shann took Bang-Jensen's advice, but he wrote an entirely different sort of report, recommending, among other things, that disciplinary action be taken against Bang-Jensen if he didn't cease and desist his agitation forthwith. Instead of sending the memo to Dag Hammarskjold, he sent it to Jordan. And then, a day or two later, in a complete reversal of character, on seeing this wild man who, in his opinion, had "already done considerable harm" he threw his arms around his shoulders and said, "Do you feel better now? I've sent the memo off."

At a much later date, when Shann's document was used against him, Bang-Jensen told friends it was a completely exaggerated account of what had taken place. They had argued, it was true, but there were no shouts and screams. It was also true that by accident he had dropped the papers he was carrying, and since the lounge was crowded at the time, the mishap did attract attention.

A U.N. official says, "Everyone was tired at the time. Tempers were short, and on occasion, voices were raised. I raised my own a few times. But one thing must be remembered about Paul, he was gentleman through and through—which is rare enough these days—and he was never childish. If he called Shann a damn fool, he did it politely. He was not the kind to ever lay hands on anyone. In my opinion, one reason he never answered Shann's description of what took place was because, by nature, he was extremely discreet . . . and kind."

Later that same evening Bang-Jensen visited Alsing Andersen at his hotel.

The next morning, Thursday, May 30, Andersen presented Jordan with a paper containing some ten alleged omissions and twenty alleged errors in Chapter VII.

The following day, May 31, these were discussed at the Chairman's insistence by himself, Shann, Jordan, and Messinesi. Andersen wanted Bang-Jensen present, but the latter was refused admittance by Jordan.

According to Jordan, "The Chairman and the Rapporteur were satisfied that the amendments were unnecessary and the allegations of errors baseless."

Bang-Jensen says of the meeting: "Mr. Messinesi apparently was called into the meeting and stated that the draft was correct. I pointed out . . . that this was most unfair to Mr. Messinesi and also to the Chairman and the Rapporteur, since it is impossible for Mr. Messinesi to know what facts I have found which proves in an indisputable manner that many of the facts in the draft are incorrect. . . . I do not think that he should be blamed, because the material is enormous. . . ."

The question arises, if the material was so enormous, why was the Deputy Secretary any better qualified to judge it than his colleagues? One reason was that—incredible as it may seem—Bang-Jensen actually memorized much of the verbatim testimony. And another was that he was ceaselessly checking and rechecking the great mass of documentation.

He goes on to say about that meeting, which he had hoped to attend, "The Chairman, who afterward expressed concern to me about what had happened at the meeting, stated he had at least been promised that the extraordinarily important admission of Istvan Dobi [who headed the Hungarian People's Presidium under Kadar] would be included.

"Dobi had stated in a speech, reported verbatim in the Hungarian press, that the Presidium had not appointed Kadar as Premier until the Russian troops on 4 November had already arrived in the Parliament building. Consequently, it cannot be correct when Kadar alleges that the second Hungarian intervention took place in response to a request issued by the Kadar Government on 3 November." (This fact is not stated in the published U.N. Special Report on Hungary, although it is made perfectly obvious in the Report that Kadar was the tool of the Russians.)

And here, finally, is Bang-Jensen's reasoning behind his insistent demand for accuracy: "I might add—that these errors in fact were in no way of importance for the conclusions which the members of the Committee have drawn. *On the contrary, the correct facts would in many cases further support the conclusions.*"

Bang-Jensen was forcing his attack on two levels: first, as has been pointed out—many small errors would undermine the reliability of the report; secondly, as just stated—correction of these errors would not change the conclusions reached, only strengthen them.

He was seeking the will-o'-the-wisp "perfection" in a spider web of pettiness, personality differences, and everlasting protocol.

Jordan lectures waspishly: "Mr. Bang-Jensen has quite

improperly pressed his views on the Rapporteur and the Chairman. *Even if his views were sound, his conduct would be reprehensible.* I have made it clear to Mr. Bang-Jensen in the past that he is not at liberty to discuss the report with the Chairman. I do not regard myself as free to do so, nor do I regard myself at liberty to discuss the report with any members of the Committee. Contact between the Committee and the Secretariat should take place exclusively through the agency of the Rapporteur, who alone is responsible for the report."

By this reasoning, it can be concluded that had William Jordan found what he considered "grave errors" in a given chapter of the report and the Rapporteur either did not agree or would not take the time to check the records, Jordan would promptly forget the whole thing.

CHAPTER 15

HALF AN HOUR before the Committee meeting on the afternoon of Friday, May 31, Jordan called his recalcitrant Deputy Secretary to his office.

"In your own interest I would rather you did not attend this afternoon's meeting," Jordan told Bang-Jensen.

"Oh? Why is that?"

"I have received a complaint from Ambassador Shann about you. I'm not quite sure yet how it should be handled, but I think it much better if you stay away this afternoon."

"Is the complaint in writing?"

"Yes."

"May I see it?"

"I can't show it to you at this stage."

"Well . . . all right. But may I see it later? I hope there is no misunderstanding over our talks. Is it Ambassador Shann who doesn't want me at the meeting?"

"I can't tell you anything now. I'm just saying it will be very much to your own interest if you do not attend."

"But this is silly, particularly in view of all that's happened in the past few days. It will look as though I had a bad conscience, that I'm to be criticized for my stand. Besides, I definitely should be present because my draft of Chapter ten will be discussed, and I might have to answer questions."

"I called you here to ask you—for your own good—" Jordan repeated tendentiously.

"But I can't accept that. It's childish. Please tell me the reason."

"The reason is that I'm asking you."

"You're asking me—you're not giving me instructions, is that right?"

A long silence followed in which Jordan looked thoughtfully at nothing. Finally he said, "I'm not issuing you instructions—I'm making a request—in your own interest. After I speak with Mr. Narayanan [Officer in Charge of the Department of Political and Security Council Affairs—in the absence of Protitch], I might change the request to an instruction."[1]

There it stood until ten minutes before the scheduled conference, when Jordan phoned Bang-Jensen.

"I'm now formally instructing you not to come to the meeting. Instead, you are to study the draft of Chapter sixteen."[2]

"Oh, come now! I told you this morning, I stayed till past midnight studying it, and I think it's excellent. . . . I really see no point in studying it any further."

"Nevertheless, those are your instructions."

Jordan's insistence on "stay away" and "I can't tell you why" continued, and Bang-Jensen argued that he would do so only on the repeated proviso that Jordan take the whole matter up with the Secretary General.

Jordan evidently did not give this assurance, for, in spite of the order, Bang-Jensen disobeyed it and attended the meeting as planned. Later, the Deputy Secretary concluded that Jordan's motives in the act had been dishonest.[3]

An examination of Bang-Jensen's final draft of Chapter VII as compared with the published text reveals even to the untutored eye a number of major differences. His version hammers home more definitely the double dealing of the Russians. Most importantly, it contains a number of points which are not found in the authorized version.

One is an omission which Bang-Jensen felt strongly should not be cut. It is the final paragraph of Imre Nagy's last speech to the Hungarian people:

"I say this as Prime Minister and as a Communist. It is the revolution which has revealed to me the true will of the people. The Russian pressure exerted on us during the revolution, and the interventions that took place against my will, have enlightened me in full of the ultimate aim of Russian imperialism."

"The report," says Bang-Jensen, "also omits the last and most important part of Mr. Nagy's last governmental act, in which he declared that Madame Anna Kethly should be given all help since she was the only member of the Hungarian Government outside Hungary. This statement obviously was not without significance in relation to the efforts of Madame Kethly to be recognized by the General Assembly in some manner as the representative of Hungary."[4]

Two other striking omissions, other than the failure to include Dobi's speech, concern Kadar. And here the failure in the report is more misrepresentation than omission.

At a meeting held on November 1, 1956, between Imre Nagy, Soviet Ambassador Andropov, and Janos Kadar, according to the published report, Kadar is reputed to have said that he realized now that his future was obscure, but that as a Hungarian he was prepared personally to fight.

What he actually said, according to Bang-Jensen's draft, was "As a Communist I know I no longer have a future."

To a Jordan and a Shann, this might seem like an inconsequential point, but when it is compared with other events that took place that day, it takes on far greater meaning. In fact, it could be of paramount importance, for it was on the evening of November 1 that Kadar took his mysterious trip to the Russian Embassy. And here again, the published report fails to clarify the episode as Bang-Jensen felt it should be. It simply says that Kadar and Münnich got into a car that was parked behind them . . . it says nothing about a man coming out of the Embassy and speaking to them, and their driving off to places unknown.[5]

It is quite possible that, between the time Kadar confessed his future as a Communist was ruined and the time he went for his ride, he talked with Andropov, and the Soviet Ambassador said something to the effect that Kadar could have a very bright future as a Communist, indeed . . . if he cooperated.

This was a point that Bang-Jensen insisted should appear in the report. Needless to say, it did not.

No, there is more here than a "hysterical" Danish diplomat crying out imprecations in a wilderness of sound-proof conference rooms. And, statements to the contrary, there is good reason to believe that at least some of the changes he first recommended in Chapter VII were indeed incorporated in it, even though he was never satisfied with the final version.

Now, as the fur continued to fly, Bang-Jensen became similarly embroiled in the drafting of Chapter II.

"Chapter II was to be a kind of condensation of the report," he explains. "It would give the main developments during the Hungarian uprising. The Rapporteur had told Mr. Jordan that he considered the chapter very important, since many readers might find it sufficient to read this; his own government, in fact, had planned to reprint Chapter II in a special pamphlet."[6]

V. Duckworth-Barker, the staff's Information Officer, was the chapter's draftsman, and he relates its evolution: "While we were still in Europe, Mr. Jordan asked me to undertake a kind of general editorial responsibility for the presentation and style of the report, and he arranged for the authors of individual chapters to send me copies of their drafts.

"Mr. Bang-Jensen states quite correctly that the writing of Chapter two was delayed until near the end. This was partly because my editorial functions on the other chapters were keeping me very busy, and partly because Mr. Jordan thought it better that the chapters summarizing the whole should not be drafted until the report itself had assumed its final shape."

William Jordan phrases the situation vindictively, with one decided contradiction and with one puzzling conclusion: "At the time when the presentation of Chapter two became due, both the Rapporteur and I were involved in the wastage of three days by reason of Mr. Bang-Jensen's conduct. *I had intended to undertake the drafting of the chapter myself.* Fortunately, Mr. Duckworth-Barker agreed in the difficult circumstances in which we were placed to undertake the assignment. By reason of his close work with me throughout the report, he knew the contents of the report as a whole better than any other member of the staff. Mr. Duckworth-Barker and I were both concerned about Mr. Bang-Jensen's mental state, and to avoid difficulty, we specifically agreed that Mr. Duckworth-Barker should consult with Mr. Bang-Jensen as he went along. . . ."

Two questions arise: If the Dane's mental state was so serious, why consult him at all? Why not accept his offered resignation and get him to a doctor? Moreover, since Jordan repeatedly implied there were other more competent officers on the staff, why did he and Duckworth-Barker "specifically agree" to check things out with the Deputy Secretary?

Bang-Jensen is wrong and stoops to the same vindictiveness as his principal antagonist when he says that Jordan arranged by "various excuses" that not even a preliminary draft of Chapter II was prepared until a few days before the report was to be adopted. But he is right in what happened next.

"Late one night, after Jordan had left, I was able to assist him [Duckworth-Barker] with some parts and call certain misunderstandings to his attention . . . [Later] Mr. Jordan instructed his secretaries not to let me have a copy of Mr. Duckworth-Barker's final draft. I received one anyhow. I noticed that a number of factual errors, some quite serious, were contained in the draft."

Bang-Jensen called these errors to the attention of Duckworth-Barker, who suggested that the Deputy Secretary, to save time, put his notes in writing.

"I did so," continues Bang-Jensen, "and went to lunch. When I returned, I was told that, just as the secretary was finished typing it, Mr. Jordan had come and taken the memorandum and the copies from her. . . . I went to Mr. Jordan. He refused to give it back to me or to give it to Duckworth-Barker. He also refused to give me any reasons. Nor was he willing to discuss the errors of fact. . . ."

Bang-Jensen then states that Jordan himself corrected two of the most glaring errors that he had pointed out in his memo, and ignored the rest. Jordan says that Bang-Jensen's comments were reviewed by a competent officer, and of some eighteen changes, he advised acceptance of two.

"During the meeting of the Committee when the draft was being adopted," Bang-Jensen goes on to say, "I told Jordan it was his duty, since he knew the draft contained factual errors, to make reservations to the Committee, saying that the draft was still being checked for errors."

" 'I would never think of it,' " came the reply.

And at the end of the meeting, when the Deputy Secretary raised the point again, Jordan's answer was final. "The draft is now adopted, and is thereby finished as far as I'm concerned."

The problem was not settled, and Jordan knew it as well as Bang-Jensen. He knew the Dane would indeed carry the fight to the Secretary General.

CHAPTER 16

PETER MARSHALL got off the U.N. elevator at the thirty-fifth floor. William Jordan's office was to his right. He entered the outer office just as a tall, tweedy man went through the inner door. A somewhat flustered secretary ushered him along behind.

The slight nervousness he'd felt since entering the building was still there, but in their earlier telephone conversation Jordan had seemed interested and almost eager to talk to him.

"I'll be glad to see you." The words were clipped and staccato, in a high key, and the English accent was pronounced. "I could talk all day and all night on the subject . . . ten hours or ten minutes."

"Wonderful. Would you be able to go out to lunch with me?"

"I think that can be arranged."

The office was a spacious place of business for anyone, and the little man who greeted him seemed lost in it. Carpet on the floor, maps on the walls, a grand view of Queens.

William M. Jordan moved downstage with a frozen grin on his face.

"Mr. Marshall, I would like you to meet Mr. Messinesi, a member of my staff."

Marshall shook hands with the tall man who had preceded him into the office. Messinesi looked more English than Greek to him, and had the sad-eyed expression of a bloodhound.

Jordan was the complete antithesis: diminutive, knobby-featured—his baldish dome framed by a mass of gray-white hair.

It was a very mobile face, the wide smile turning on and off like a faucet. It was a shrewd face, stubborn and sardonic. "Impish" was the word that came to mind.

They sat down and Marshall thought it best to get things straight right away. "Shall we talk here, sir, or do it over lunch?"

"Oh, I'm afraid I can't make lunch. I'm very busy."

So someone had passed the word, or else William had had second thoughts. Messinesi was present to play back-stop.

"Well, I'm sorry."

"What is it you'd like to know, Mr. Marshall?" It was asked with a big grin, but no grin in the heavily pocketed eyes.

"I'd like to know your version of what happened when Mr. Bang-Jensen served you as Deputy Secretary of the Hungarian Committee."

Marshall didn't know whether it was the question or the memory that made William Jordan let go with the first of his cackles. He seemed vastly amused. Mr. Messinesi, with his expression of sadness, stared at the floor.

"Mr. Marshall," the former teacher began in his best and most sympathetic lecture-hall manner, "you must realize that I, as an international civil servant, have to abide by certain rules and regulations. Do you know the difference between the two?"

"With regard to the U.N.? No, I don't."

"Our regulations are set up by the General Assembly, and our rules are a matter of refinements arranged by the Secretariat. Is that clear?" The grin was back. "All right, now I, in my position, must act within the bounds of those rules and regulations, and they simply do not permit me to discuss this case with you."

"There is a regulation that covers talking to the press," Mr. Messinesi added with an unhappy sigh.

Peter Marshall held his rising annoyance in check. "Well, even so"—he returned Jordan's grin—"I should think you might want to say something to clear up some of the confusion."

"Confusion! Confusion!" The grin snapped off. "What confusion?"

"Well, let's say difference of opinion."

"Difference of opinion, nonsense! It's all there. He was going in the face of all the evidence. There's no mystery here, no mystery at all. My dear man, you simply have to read the Secretary General's letter of dismissal. That will tell you everything."

"Not quite, Mr. Jordan. Bang-Jensen wrote a few things himself."

Jordan looked at his subordinate and cackled, and Peter Marshall found himself beginning to take an active dislike to the man. He cautioned himself he was here to get what facts he could, not to form a personal opinion.

"You and he had quite a falling out, Mr. Jordan, and I wonder if there aren't two sides to every argument."

Jordan used his fingers to tick off the reply. "Mr. Bang-Jensen went over my head to the Rapporteur. He went over the Rapporteur's head to the Chairman of the Committee.

He went over the Chairman's head to the Secretary General. It's all there, and it is no mystery."

"And he believed he had his reasons."

"We know all about his reasons. He said there were omissions. Good heavens, we couldn't put everything into the report. Would you want to listen to a three-hour speech instead of one lasting an hour?"

Peter Marshall didn't say it would depend on the speech.

"We were afraid that it was going to be too long as it was," Messinesi said quietly.

"Exactly; we had to get it down to size. It was a matter of judgment, and Mr. Bang-Jensen wanted to impress his judgment over everyone else's. I believe there were five people who had more to do with the writing of the report than Mr. Bang-Jensen. The records are all there."

Having seen a good many of the records, Peter Marshall doubted the statement, and with such a fine emphasis upon there being no mystery, he was beginning to think there must be one.

William Jordan rocked back behind the desk that seemed too large for him. "You know, Mr. Marshall, we look upon ourselves here as a kind of Priesthood. We're dedicated to it, because after all, the only way we're going to have peace in this world is through world diplomacy. This organization is directed toward that end. We've taken our orders, and in any Priesthood or any business, for that matter, where someone breaks the orders, chaos results. We can't have it."

A Priesthood, Marshall thought, looking out the window at the panoramic view of modern cliff dwellings. A Priesthood worshiping what, and at whose expense? Who was God of this Priesthood?

"In the last analysis"—Jordan fiddled with the wire of his hearing aid and again wore his grin of satisfaction—

"the Committee had to approve the report. And it was the Rapporteur's responsibility to see that it was the kind of report it would approve. The Committee approved it. The General Assembly approved it by a large majority. It was a good report. I think that about answers everything."

He saw that it did answer everything for William Jordan. The report was the thing. But for Bang-Jensen, it had been more than that. It was what could be done with the report to make it more than words on a page. Bang-Jensen saw it as a possible weapon, and this member of the Priesthood simply saw it as a job well done because it had been approved.

Jordan picked up the newspaper on his desk and laughed in sardonic glee. "There's an article in here about me by a man named Manley. It says I'm subservient to my superiors and arrogant to my subordinates. I'm a typical bureaucrat." He had another laugh. "Mr. Messinesi is one of my subordinates. Do I treat you arrogantly, Mr. Messinesi?"

The subordinate shook his head without comment.

"Mr. Messinesi is a Greek. I'm an Englishman, but we work for the Secretariat, and we're both dedicated to its aims."

CHAPTER 17

THE EDITOR put down the last page and sat back in his chair, looking thoughtful, but betraying no indication of pleasure or displeasure.

Peter Marshall, who had waited in impatient silence said, "Well?"

"I have several questions." The editor drew noisily on his pipe, getting it re-lit, "But first, how authentic is your description of what went on during the writing of the Hungarian Report? Certainly Jordan didn't give you much."

"No, but other people did. I guess I didn't tell you, but the Gross Report helped a lot too."

"You got hold of it!"

"Yup, I did that. Thirty-five pages of hatchet work, and one hundred sixty pages of annexes to sharpen the blade. And all neatly marked 'Confidential.'"

"Well, how did you get it? Who gave it to you?"

"Frankly, I don't know," Marshall said blandly. "It came in the mail one day. . . . Registered name was unfamiliar and so was the address. I just thanked the mailman."

"You must have made friends."

"Tom, a lot of people want this story told."

"So you keep telling me," the editor said dryly. "I thought the Gross Report was an indictment of Bang-Jensen."

"It is, in spades. It's brutal. When I first read it, I nearly called you up and said let's forget the whole thing. I'm glad I called Alice Widener instead."

"What did she tell you?"

"To calm down, to read Bang-Jensen's statement on page sixteen of his brief before the Administrative Tribunal, and to make a close study of the Annexes."

"What did his statement say?"

Marshall smiled, opening his notebook. "I knew you'd ask me that. Quote: 'The Gross Report is so erosive that readers will be aware that it cannot all be true; however, it will nevertheless have an effect on any reader, even on the most intelligent and alert, because nobody would be able to believe that a document prepared by three seemingly reputable persons could be so thoroughly incorrect and misleading.' Unquote."

"Humm." The editor nodded.

"Humm is right. They sent a copy to the Danish Government long before Bang-Jensen ever saw it."

"And the Annexes, you found them valuable?"

"In the light of other documentation, and the things people in the know have told me, very valuable. As Alice says, it just takes homework."

"All right, fine, but what about Bang-Jensen's cry of sabotage? From reading this, you give the impression that he was a perfectionist, and that's all very well. The points you've listed are well taken, but were the omissions and errors he talked about really acts of sabotage?"

"Well, here's something I haven't mentioned. One of the key Hungarian witnesses to testify before the Committee was with Imre Nagy continually from October twenty-third until the fourth of November, fifty-six. He's called 'the fourth man' because Nagy is dead, and two others who were also in Nagy's presence most of the time are in a Hungarian prison.

"Okay, 'the fourth man' was with Nagy when he telephoned Anna Kethly, who was in Vienna. He heard Nagy appoint Kethly as the Hungarian representative to the U.N. 'The fourth man' told this to the Committee, told it clearly and succinctly. But this fact appears nowhere in the Hungarian Report."

"You're sure of this?"

"Positive. Also, when Bang-Jensen informed Janos Horvath about it, Horvath got in touch with the Committee. Andersen, Shann, Slim, all assured him he shouldn't worry, everything would be all right. You can call the omission anything you want, but Bang-Jensen called it sabotage."

"I suppose the omission proves that the Committee, following the Secretary General's lead, was really taking a soft line toward the Kadar regime."

"To say the least. Now there's something else you have to bear in mind about Bang-Jensen's accusations, you have to take them not only in the time but also under the circumstances in which they were made."

"How do you mean?"

"Well, you know from what you've read so far, security was lousy on something where security should have been the watchword. You've seen the laxity in Europe, the attempts made to learn the identity of the witnesses. Alsing Andersen himself later said in a letter to Hammarskjold that he had no doubt the Russians would pay most anything to get the names. I haven't mentioned it yet, but Bang-Jensen knew of at least two attempts where they tried to do it. Someone offered one of the staff members his own price if he'd turn over the verbatim records for the night. That happened right here in New York."

"Do you know who the staff member was?"

"Bang-Jensen would never say, because he felt if the member backed him up, he'd get in trouble. Stavropoulos, Under Secretary for the U.N. Legal Department and one of the signers of the Gross Report, later asked everyone who served on the Committee if they had been approached. Everyone said, no."

"Do you know that it happened?"

"Bang-Jensen's word would be good enough for me, but it's backed up from other sources, too. But let's not get off the track. He knew what was going on, and when he saw things that he felt were important being left out of the report, he started raising merry you-know-what. And he had something else on his mind at that time too."

"Is that where the Soviet official who wanted to defect to the West comes in?"

"Yes, it does, but I'm not saying anything about that yet —not until it's all nailed down."

"You've got to be accurate about it, you know."

"Now, Tom . . . It's a true story, and I'll be accurate."

"One more question. You say Bang-Jensen and Jordan knew that the problem wasn't settled. What followed?"

"I call it the battle of the memos, and I think we should use most of them as a part of the Appendices.

"Bang-Jensen let fly first, on June fourth, with a two-page blast[1] to T. G. Narayanan, who was in charge in the absence of Protitch. Bang-Jensen said that the Committee had adopted a preliminary draft report, and a final meeting was scheduled for Friday, the seventh. Then he took off. He said the report, as it stood, was full of errors, and that correcting the errors wouldn't change the conclusions, only strengthen them. He thought it was his duty to speak out, and he recommended ways that the corrections could be made quickly. He asked Narayanan to pass on his statement to Cordier or Hammarskjold and Protitch.

"Jordan wasn't going to be outdone, and the next day he countered with a broadside of his own. It included Shann's three-page stinger, relating his side of the meeting with Bang-Jensen in the Delegates' Lounge. I call it 'Shann's Complaint.' It also included Bang-Jensen's personal peace offering over Chapter Seven, a long memo Jordan had written to himself about Bang-Jensen, and a covering memo,[2] stating that he thought Bang-Jensen should be relieved of his duties. And with the nice little tag that Bang-Jensen ought to be given sick leave because, in his estimation, he was a very sick man."

"Bang-Jensen had offered to resign, hadn't he?"

"Twice by that time. Well, Narayanan passed both bundles of joy on to Cordier with 'a plague on both their houses, and don't involve me.'[3]

"This next one you'll have to read. It was written on the sixth and Bang-Jensen sent it direct to Hammarskjold. . . ."

For the eyes of the Secretary-General, only

TO: Mr. Dag Hammarskjold   6 June 1957
             Secretary-General
FROM: Povl Bang-Jensen

This memorandum, in supplement to the one of 4 June which I forwarded through Mr. Narayanan, is addressed to you by me, not as an officer down the ladder, but as a fellow-Scandinavian of the same generation and belonging to about the same circles, with many mutual friends in Sweden. I think you are aware that my position and standing in public life in Denmark is not indicated by the modest position which I, for certain reasons, have been satisfied to hold in the Secretariat for the time being. I am also writing to you as a sober lawyer, who has a great deal of criminal practice, who has had quite some experience with international duplicity through his former anti-nazist activities, and who knows the difference between circumstantial evidence and conclusive proof. With the danger of sounding like a boasting ass, I might add, in order to give more weight to my words:

As a lawyer, who during the years he has been here, have received quite a number of tempting offers of partnership in some of the most prominent law-firms in United States and Denmark.

Since the person in question probably will realize that he hardly can make many believe that I am liar, he will no doubt insist that I am imagining things on account of overwork. I think Lennart Finmark, with whom I had lunch today will be able to reassure you, if necessary, that I, at least, have maintained my sense of humour. In fact, after having lacked sufficient work for years—I wonder if you realize *how* overstaffed the Secretariat is—I have enjoyed tremendously coming back to a brisk working pace. May I assure you half facetiously, but truthfully, that I feel better, eat better and sleep better than I have done for years.

Mr. Cordier will no doubt have reported to you our conversation this morning and explained that the situation is considerably more serious than I found it wise to spell out in my memorandum. It is a methodical attempt to suppress certain essential facts and to insert erroneous facts and contradictions in the report, particularly in the key-Chapter. I offered to give to Mr. Cordier all the evidence, if desired, about these efforts which are both consistent and flagrant. All errors and omissions all point the same way, except one small one, which might be a little unfair to Mr. Kadar. (I was, however, told this evening, that that one is being corrected). The accumulation of errors of fact and contradictions are bound to undermine the authority of the report.

The situation, indeed, is very delicate. Sabotage of the Committee of various kinds has gone on from the very beginning. For instance, a number of efforts were made to prevent the Committee from hearing certain witnesses. At times these efforts were extremely clumsy, and I know that in one case several officers on the staff began to realize what was taking place. Some of the many people working on the report certainly do now. There is, therefore, reason to fear that when errors, contradictions and omissions are pointed out after the report is published, it will soon be known around the building and to the press that these errors of fact were pointed out in advance, but that it, strangely enough, in spite of all efforts, was impossible to make anybody spend the few minutes it would take to look at the record and find out whether it was a tired man's wild assertions or were they actually errors of fact. This will seem the stranger, I am afraid, since the report, factual as it is, is politically explosive. Outsiders would undoubtedly think that the utmost care would be taken to assure that all the facts are correct.

May I now touch upon another aspect, which is the deeper reason for this memorandum. Many diplomats will no doubt feel that this shows an extraordinary lack of sapience on my part, since we are rarely thankful, although we should be, to the person who has the courage enough to bring unpleasant information to our attention. You probably know the story of King Gorm and Queen Thyra from Danish history. Mr. Jordan has told me several times during the last four months, that he was in fact acting in accordance with your instructions and has intimated that it would, therefore, be rather foolish of me to take the matter up with you. I have good reason to believe that he has made the same statement to others. Anyhow, the same assertion has been made by another person.

I wish to assure you that I am at your disposal beyond, but not contrary to, my duties as an officer of the United Nations to straighten out everything. My only condition, as I have several times told Mr. Jordan, is honesty. I have seen enough to know that people can do terrible things, and still have other admirable or attractive sides to their character. I am not excited, I am not angry, not indignant, I have no animus against anybody, I only feel sorry for those—whoever they are—who perhaps by some mistake, have placed themselves in a position from which they find it difficult to retrieve themselves.

"Did Hammarskjold ever answer this?"

"Not until he'd gotten two more memos[4] of the same sort. By then the Committee had adopted the report, and Bang-Jensen was leaving for Denmark on his home leave with his family."

"Not sick leave?"

"Absolutely not! It was his regular vacation, and although a Danish State radio correspondent named Christian Winther tried to sell that idea, it's untrue. More than that, there isn't one person to whom I've talked so far, who knew Bang-Jensen, who says he was anything but normal."

"Except Jordan and Shann. All right, when did Hammarskjold answer him, and what did he say?"

"He answered the day after Bang-Jensen left, and this is what he said":

18 June 1957

Dear Mr. Bang-Jensen,

Upon receipt of your last memorandum dated 17 June, I attempted to contact you but found that you had already gone to the boat. The telephone conversation due to the noise at your end was unsatisfactory. I promised to write to you, which I do now.

You make in your various memoranda several serious charges. Through my inquiries thus far I have not got them corroborated. They will require further attention upon your return.

It is, of course, the Secretariat's responsibility to provide the best possible service for the Committee which covers, *inter alia*, factual accuracy and high quality of drafting, but it is the Committee that must assume, and always does assume, the final responsibility for whatever is contained in the report. This view is certainly shared by the Chairman, as I know it to be the one held by the Rapporteur who has been guided by it also at his consideration of your critical observations of which I believe him to have been fully informed.

I shall be glad to discuss all matters with you which you regard as relevant upon your return from home leave.

Very sincerely yours,

[signed]   Dag Hammarskjold
Secretary-General

Mr. Povl Bang-Jensen
c/o Mrs. Ahnfelt-Ronne
Kirsebaervej 2
Espergaerde
Denmark

"So Bang-Jensen went home."

"Right. For two months. He didn't come back until the middle of August, but that's as far as we go for now."

"Don't you think you'd better talk to Hammarskjold?"

"I've tried, but it's like attempting to get an appointment with God. Anyhow you should be happy to know I'm seeing his left-hand man on Tuesday."

"Cordier!"

"Andrew Wellington Cordier, late of Manchester College in the State of Indiana."

"What have you found out about him?"

"He's a real mystery, Tom. Up until 1944, his whole career was teaching. Between 1938 and 1941 he did a lot of traveling in Europe and South America. He wrote surveys on the Sudetenland, Danzig, and the Chaco, but I don't know whom he wrote them for."

"What did he teach?"

"History and political science. He was Chairman of that Department at Manchester from '29 to '44, and he also lectured at the University of Indiana."

"Well, what's so mysterious about all that?"

"In 1944 he gave up his teaching and went to work for the State Department—in the Department of Political Affairs, run by Alger Hiss. Cordier lists himself in *Who's Who* as an expert on International Security."

"Interesting. Who hired him?"

"I don't know. I checked the Civil Service Registry for the years he was in Washington. According to law, every government employee in an administrative or supervisory position is supposed to be listed, and he's not. That means he wasn't Civil Service, so I suppose he was hired as a consultant."

"Have you got any dope on what he did?"

"I've got this photostat of the Americans who took part in the founding conference of the U.N. at San Francisco in

1945. Cordier is listed here along with Ralph Bunche and seventeen others as a 'Technical Expert.' "

"Alger Hiss was the first Secretary-General."

"And in 1946 Andrew Cordier became number-two man of the U.N., and that's what he's been ever since."

"So he had a rapid rise. He's undoubtedly a brilliant man. Why is he so important to Bang-Jensen?"

"Because it was Cordier who finally organized and directed the attack against him."

CHAPTER 18

"MR. HAMMARSKJOLD wanted to give him every chance. That's why Bang-Jensen wasn't discharged immediately when all this came up." Andrew Cordier, short and stocky with full features and a large beaklike nose, laughed abruptly.

"I don't know how many U.N. officers recommended his dismissal many times to the SG. Of course, if we had fired him, that would have made us villains. And now, it seems, we are accused of torturing him."

Cordier shifted his position in his easy chair and laboriously recrossed his legs. He paused as he leaned forward and eased his leg up over a knee by grasping a trouser cuff.

"Mr. Hammarskjold said, 'No, let's give the man every opportunity.' Isn't that right, he went as far as he could to give Bang-Jensen every chance?"

He looked over at Wilder Foote, the U.N. Press Officer, who had hurried into the office just before Peter Marshall was received.

The Executive Assistant to Dag Hammarskjold didn't

wait for a reply. "I remember one day Bang-Jensen was sitting right where you are." Cordier pointed to where Peter Marshall sat in the corner of a comfortable sofa in the spacious thirty-eighth-floor office. "It was June first, 1957. He was nearly hysterical, charging that sabotage had been committed in the formulation of the Hungarian report. . . .

"I said: 'Listen, Paul, let's talk this over. You've made some serious accusations. You can't go around accusing people.' We talked, but I couldn't change his mind. He refused to be reasonable about this whole thing. The state he was in, it was no use. He claimed willful sabotage. . . ."

"By whom?"

"By his boss."

"Well, who was that?"

"Why—Jordan."

"Mr. Cordier, how about his allegations of errors and omissions in the report?"

Cordier broke into a smile. "Ha! You know, these points were checked and rechecked. In the final evaluation, a lot of these were matters of personal feeling. . . .

"I look at this one way, you another. The particular points did not mean sabotage as far as the report was concerned. Here was a matter of having thousands of pages of material and the necessity of boiling it down to—how long was the report?—say a hundred pages. Not everything could be utilized.

"When Bang-Jensen advocated something and it was not used, he might have cried sabotage. What you call it may depend on what side you're on. . . .

"His motivations? We can only wonder about that. He acquired a fixation that he alone was right. . . ."

"How about the list of witnesses the U.N. Controller's Office authorized Bang-Jensen to keep?"

"They would have followed a set procedure. . . . There was nothing in writing about it."

"Well," Marshall asked, "when Bang-Jensen was relieved as the Committee's Deputy Secretary, how is it that no one asked him for the list? Wasn't this a violation of security procedure?"

Cordier waited an instant before answering. "We were more concerned about the man than anything else. It was a matter of being correct. A matter of not telling him he was all through and to hand over everything he had. . . .

"Everyone had been working under terrific pressure. We thought his two-month home leave would have calmed him down, given him a chance to relax. . . ."

Cordier let his foot slide off his knee to the floor. He leaned forward: ". . . but it didn't. Bang-Jensen came back making the same accusations, and we thought the best thing to do was to get him away from it altogether."

"All right," said Marshall, "but the U.N. didn't seem to show much concern for the man when guards hustled him off the grounds after his suspension."

"Ahh—" Cordier raised a hand—"yes, that was an unfortunate action. Director of Personnel Robertson was responsible for that. As soon as I heard that Bang-Jensen was barred from returning, I personally made it known to him that he could come back into the building. When I found out that someone had started to change the locks on his office, I personally ordered that the original lock be replaced and that everything be left as before.

"He could come back any time and get anything he wanted from his files . . . 'My files,' he said—what were 'my files'? . . . just personal documents, I suppose. Memoranda, records, and so on." Cordier shrugged and smiled. Wilder Foote sat in a chair against a side wall, smoking silently.

"Well, what about the security at the U.N.?" Marshall asked.

"I'm going to say to you what I say to everyone else about

that," Cordier replied—"Nothing!" He grinned. "You can't have security if you talk about your methods. And we have never had any security lapses in the history of the U.N."

Cordier tugged a trouser cuff, crossed a leg.

"Now I've gone on missions, to Korea for instance, and I know there are certain procedures to follow regarding security. It's not a matter of concealing one's papers under a rug or in some odd manner around a hotel room. . . .

"That list. Think of it this way: I'm a Hungarian refugee. We don't know each other—" Cordier motioned toward Marshall—"and here we are meeting for the first time. Why would I trust *you* any more than anyone else? Why would I say, 'I only want *you* to know my name and not anyone else in the U.N.?' "

Cordier paused for emphasis, then went on. "I wouldn't say it, and I don't believe the witnesses did say it."

Peter Marshall looked past the Executive Assistant through the large windows. He knew how completely wrong was Andrew Cordier's contention.

"How about his background," he asked, "his previous work?"

"Well, it wasn't until later, after he got here, that we found the Danes had unloaded him on us. You know the trouble he caused the Danish Government when he went home from Washington in 1948? He came with us in 1949 and never did any particularly outstanding work. I'd describe his work as 'colorless.' He was a poor draftsman and his reports were not well done—oh, passable enough, but not outstanding. He served on some committees. . . ."

"He was on the Palestine Conciliation Commission," Marshall said.

"That's correct," Cordier agreed. "He was Secretary of the P.C.C. and he did a very competent job."

"Well?" said Marshall.

"Well," said Cordier, "the whole thing was unfortunate. It was the first time anything like this has happened in U.N. history." He paused. "It was a tragic case."

CHAPTER 19

IN THE COURSE of his investigation, Peter Marshall had
come upon what he considered some appalling facts. Now
he came upon another whose magnitude was nearly lost on
him in the welter of material at his disposal. It followed the
pattern of U.N. failure; failure to act when Hungary called
for help; failure to issue clear-cut instructions to the Secretariat Group of the Special Committee; and now, in the late
summer of 1957, failure to hear a witness whose testimony,
if publicized properly, might have saved the life of General
Pal Maleter.

Paul Bang-Jensen had cried "sabotage!" in the writing of
the report, and Marshall had told his editor that he thought
the accusations had considerable validity. But if this incident
now before him was not sabotage, it was the most callous
neglect, and its result amounted to the same thing.

Janos Horvath had met the young career soldier, Captain
Pal Maleter, in 1945 when the latter was aide de camp to
President Zoltan Tildy. Horvath, as head of the Economic
Department of the Smallholders Party, and the Captain
had become quite friendly.

Later, when the Communists took over, Maleter remained in the Army. He was a member of the Communist Party, but he was also very much a Hungarian patriot, who became disillusioned with Communism in practice. Horvath says, "It was one reason he did not rise to a high rank in the Military.

"After the fall of Tildy's government, I did not see Maleter again until the twenty-fifth of October, 1956, when I joined him at the Killian Barracks to report on the situation in my own district. He was directing the defense of the barracks, which the Russians had under heavy attack.

"We had not seen each other all those years, and yet, when we met, it was like we had been together only yesterday. It made no difference that he was a Communist and I was not. He said, "This is good, this is right. Now at last I have a real purpose in my life."

To that purpose, Pal Maleter became Minister of Defense to the Imre Nagy government. On the night of November 3, while negotiating the withdrawal of Russian forces from Hungarian soil, he was betrayed and taken prisoner by Serov, NVD Chief under Khrushchev.

Nine months later, on August 6, 1957, the U.N. Secretariat received a cable addressed to the Special Committee on Hungary. It was sent by the former Under Secretary for Foreign Affairs under Nagy, Gyorgy Heltai. It stated that General Maleter's bodyguard, who had been arrested with his Commander during the armistice negotiations and taken to Soviet Russia, had escaped and was available as a witness. The cable suggested he be immediately contacted.

The urgency of such an offer was academic, but it was even further inspired by the knowledge that Maleter, at the time, was undergoing secret trials in Budapest, and it was rumored he would be executed shortly.

On August 16 Bang-Jensen returned to the U.N. from Denmark. On the twenty-fourth he was informed he had been relieved of his duties as Deputy Secretary. No reason was given. But this not-unexpected act did nothing to deter him in his purpose.

Later, he related to the Secretary General his own efforts to have the witness heard.

"After I returned from Denmark on August sixteenth, I learned, despite Mr. Jordan's efforts to conceal it from me, that a communication, apparently a cable, had arrived from Mr. Heltai.

"On the twenty-fourth of August, the Chairman, Alsing Andersen, with whom as a fellow countryman I have been acquainted for some twenty-five years, wrote me from Copenhagen as follows: 'I have not received any telegram from Heltai, nor have I heard about it.'

"After further checking about the contents of the cable, I called this matter to your personal attention on nine September, and furnished you and one of your Under-Secretaries [Dr. Ralph Bunche] with all pertinent data."

This was his memorandum:[1]

URGENT
STRICTLY CONFIDENTIAL

TO: Mr. Dag Hammarskjold   9 September 1957
           Secretary-General

THROUGH: Mr. T.G. Narayanan
           Officer in Charge of the Department
           of Political and Security Council Affairs

FROM: Mr. Povl Bang-Jensen

I have unfortunately received what appears to be conclusive proof of another serious act of sabotage by the Secretariat. In this case it will be possible to ascertain the correctness of the evidence in less than five minutes.

Since I have been threatened with disciplinary action and dismissal if I "continued"—by which I understood: continued to bring acts of sabotage to your attention—I shall in the circumstances take no steps until you indicate that you wish to be informed.

It is my duty to add that it is apparently also being maintained in this instance that the sabotage is carried out on your instructions.

(Hand written note)

Dr. Bunche
Under my previous request that you
investigate the obligations on my
behalf, please ascertain what the
action mentioned in paragraph 1 is supposed
to be.

H.D.   *Dr. Protitch*
[Dag Hammarskjold]   I am passing this on
                         to you for your action
                         and consideration.
                            T. G. N[arayanan].

Bang-Jensen continued in his later account to the Secretary General: "Just about this time [September 1957], Mrs. Maleter and her three children had come from Canada to New York to seek your intercession to save her husband's life.

"The day after you had received the information from me about General Maleter's escaped bodyguard being available as a witness, you received Mrs. Maleter and her children and promised her, according to an interview in *The New York Times,* that you would do whatever you could to save her husband.

"I heard nothing from your Under-Secretary who was to investigate the question until I had a conversation with him about other matters on the seventeenth of September and I asked him: he then told me that I had been 'all wrong.' When I insisted on knowing why, the explanations he gave were not to the point. . . .

"In December 1957, rumors again circulated that General Maleter was to be executed; and the Committee on Hungary was convened to a special meeting on twenty December, 1957, to discuss what it could do. My information is that the officers and members of the Committee were not even then given a copy of the cablegram of August sixth.

"Mr. Jordan's excuse is that the cable was included in the list of Communications received by the Secretariat, allegedly distributed on sixth August: the only reference, however, to the cable in that routine list is as follows:

> Cable dated 6 August from Heltai suggesting
> the hearing of a witness.

"The following might be pointed out: How could the members of the Committee suspect that 'a witness' was General Maleter's bodyguard, whose testimony possibly might be helpful in the efforts to save the General's life?

"Apart from this, Mr. Jordan could not be unaware that it was likely that the members would not study the list carefully before they had filed it away. It is merely a kind of index and the members, and particularly the Chairman and the Rapporteur of a Committee, are entitled to expect that all communications of importance which might interest them will be circulated, and be drawn specifically to their attention by the Secretariat.

"The indications are, in fact, that the list was not, as asserted, sent to the members on sixth August. When I returned from Denmark on the sixteenth, I was assured by both Mr. Jordan's two secretaries and the other members of the staff of the Committee that no 'List of Communications received' had been sent to the members while I had been away. . . ."

Paul Bang-Jensen had said the testimony of the bodyguard

"might" have helped to save the General's life. Peter Marshall, in weighing the course of action the Committee could have taken, had the bodyguard been present to testify at its special session, felt that "might" was indeed a conservative word.

Upon hearing the testimony of this witness, the firsthand account of Russian treachery, the Committee could have released his statement to the press of the world. All means of communication could have been brought into play. Global public opinion could have been focused against Moscow. It is quite possible that the Kremlin, ever sensitive to outside reaction, would have spared the General's life.

Supposition on Marshall's part, to be sure, but at the very least, it would have been worth the effort. No effort was ever made. The witness was never heard.

Next, in studying the exchange of memos that took place between Bang-Jensen and Ralph Bunche, concerning in part the former's attempt to have some action taken on the Maleter matter, Peter Marshall was amazed by the double talk on the part of the Under Secretary.

Hammarskjold had instructed Bunche to investigate Bang-Jensen's charges of sabotage.

Bunche's method of investigation was, first, to ask Bang-Jensen to list his charges specifically, and then refuse to accept them, with the statement, "I have never informed you that I was 'investigating' the Maleter or any other allegations made by you. . . ."

Bunche's explanation of why the General's bodyguard was not heard was borne out, Peter Marshall found, by William Jordan and, he supposed, every other U.N. apologist.

Shann, the Rapporteur, had stated in a letter that he did not want any supplementary report or more hearings. And once the cablegram had been duly listed, the responsibility of the U.N. Secretariat was forever discharged.

Naturally, any U.N. officer who went around making statements to the contrary was insane, or so it seemed that September to Dr. Ralph J. Bunche:

Note on Informal Talks on 19 September with de Hedervary, Duckworth-Barker and Schreiber

I had informal talks this afternoon with three members of the Secretariat of the Hungary Committee—Claire de Hedervary, V. Duckworth-Barker and Marc Schreiber. All three are well-known to me and I talked with them on a personal basis. Each of the three, in his own words, stressed the following:

1. Unqualified denial, in response to my question, that there has been at any time, in any fashion or by any one, sabotage of the work of the Committee.
2. Mr. Bang-Jensen suffers from an obsession about sabotage and Jordan's connexion with it.
3. Mr. Bang-Jensen has been overwhelmed by the work of the Committee and on occasion has given evidence of hysteria.

These talks have strongly confirmed my opinion that Mr. Bang-Jensen is mentally ill. I am not at all sure that he is very far from a state of mind which could lead to physical violence, either to himself or to others.

[signed] R. J. Bunche

Peter Marshall knew that Paul Bang-Jensen had referred to Under Secretary Bunche as "a sacred cow" and one of his chief vilifiers. He knew some other things too.

The "Doctor" in front of Bunche's name had nothing to do with proficiency in psychiatry.

Of twenty-three persons to whom Peter Marshall had talked, as being closely associated with Bang-Jensen at that time, not one had observed any symptoms in the Danish diplomat that would support the devastating verdict reached by Under Secretary Bunche.

On September 13, the U.N. General Assembly adopted the Report on Hungary by unanimous vote.

On September 19, Bunche found the former Deputy Secretary of the Special Committee on Hungary not far from violence.

On December 13,* the Special Committee on Hungary held an emergency session to discuss what steps it might take to aid General Maleter. No mention was made of the availability of the General's bodyguard to testify.

On Monday, June 16, 1958, the execution of Lieutenant General Pal Maleter was blatantly announced by the Soviet press.

* Bang-Jensen gives December 20 as the date.

Part Four: Judgment

CHAPTER 20

OCTOBER 9, 1957, marked the beginning of the end of
Paul Bang-Jensen's career as a U.N. diplomat.

The climactic uproar to follow started quietly enough. At
a meeting of the Security Council, James Pratt of the United
States delegation made a confidential inquiry through Dragoslav Protitch. Pratt informed the Yugoslav that the U. S.
Immigration Department was considering the deportation
of a Hungarian named Karoly Szabo. Szabo had told the authorities that he had testified before the Hungarian Committee. Pratt asked Protitch if he could find out whether
this was so or not.

Before the end of the meeting, Protitch got his first bad
jolt of the day. In asking William Jordan to check through
the records to get the answer for the American delegate,
Jordan calmly replied that he had no way of checking
whether the witness appeared before the Committee unless he had appeared under his own name. Mr. Bang-
Jensen had the secret list together with the relevant correspondence.

The Under Secretary for Political and Security Council

Affairs expressed his surprise. What were files belonging to the U.N. doing in the possession of Mr. Bang-Jensen?

Peter Marshall stopped writing and reflected for a moment. Bang-Jensen had been relieved of his job as Deputy Secretary for the Committee on August 24, continuing as a Secretariat member. In his possession were papers of life-and-death consequence, documents which required security to the last degree. Now suddenly, to the very man who had been one of the principal authors of the instructions given to Secretariat members of the Hungarian Committee, was made known the startling fact that something was badly out of whack. If James Pratt had never made his inquiry, Marshall wondered, would anyone ever have asked about the secret list?

Dragoslav Protitch got an even ruder jolt later in the day. After Jordan reported that Szabo had not testified under his own name, Protitch called Bang-Jensen. He later wrote of that conversation:

"Mr. Bang-Jensen's reply was that he could not check on this name as he did not have the list of anonymous witnesses with him, but that this list and some pertinent material was in a safe place outside the United Nations. . . . Mr. Bang-Jensen claimed that he was a trustee of the list of anonymous witnesses and of the relative correspondence, and that he is not in a position to disclose any names to anyone, to show the list and relative correspondence, nor to hand it over. . . . I asked him to bring these files in this morning and said that I would put them in the safe of the Department of which I am in possession of the code and the keys for opening it.

"This morning I informed Mr. Cordier of what had happened yesterday and of my request that Mr. Bang-Jensen should bring these files in and that they should be secured in the Department safe." [1]

Marshall paused again and noted that Dragoslav Protitch

*handed over his code and keys in July, 1958, to his replace-
ment, Anatoly F. Dobrynin of the Soviet Union, and Dobrynin, in turn, had passed them on May 10, 1960, to his
fellow countryman and Communist Georgy Petrovich Arkadev.*

In reporting the continuing shocks of the following day,
Protitch had quoted Bang-Jensen as calling him "naïve" in
believing that the files would be secure if they were in the
safe of the Department or somewhere in the United Nations
Headquarters.

The Dane flatly refused to turn them over.

On October 10, the Secretary General dispatched a terse
note to Bang-Jensen: "In view of the information contained
in Mr. Protitch's memorandum, I request you to explain
your reasons for your refusal to obey an explicit order from
the head of your Department."

The disobedient diplomat replied with a two-page explanation to Protitch in which he outlined the history of his
activities as Deputy Secretary, stated his belief that he had
been made the sole Secretariat trustee of the witnesses, and
concluded that, because of the laxity of U.N. security, he
would be criminally negligent if he left the list in the
building.

The Secretary General made no reply. Instead he wrote
letters to both Chairman Andersen and Rapporteur Shann,
asking for clarification.[2]

On November 1, Alsing Andersen answered Dag Hammarskjold and made the suggestion which Bang-Jensen had
already offered as a solution. *Burn the list.*

Copenhagen, November 1st 1957

Dear Mr. Hammarskjold,

Your letter of 18 October about Mr. Bang-Jensen and the attached copy of Bang-Jensen's letter to Dr. Protitch meant a regrettable surprise to me.

I knew, it is true, that there had been some disagreement and even some controversy between Mr. Jordan and Mr. Bang-Jensen during the work of the Hungary Committee. I also learned, as you know, that Bang-Jensen as a consequence of these controversies had been relieved of his position as Deputy-Secretary of the Committee.

I did not know, however, that the matter had developed into such a strange situation, as appears from your letter and from Bang-Jensen's letter.

From the outset in New York Bang-Jensen undertook to screen the witnesses and to present the lists to Mr. Shann and myself for our final decision. He also talked with them or corresponded with them in order to establish, whether they knew anything of real interest based upon their personal experience, and in order to fix the time of their hearing before the committee and so on.

I do not remember any discussion with Mr. Jordan or Dr. Protitch about this procedure. So I have always been of the opinion that it was agreed upon between Mr. Jordan and Mr. Bang-Jensen how this question should be handled, and I hope I am not mistaken. At least I found it quite natural for the Deputy-Secretary to undertake this practical task, and I want to add that neither Mr. Shann nor I would have dreamt of approving this arrangement without the consent of Mr. Jordan. I hope that there is no misunderstanding on this point.

When later on both Mr. Shann and I were informed of the fact that certain difficulties had arisen as to the collaboration between Mr. Jordan and Bang-Jensen, we deplored it the more, as both of us held the opinion that Bang-Jensen had done a very difficult work in an admirable way by preparing the appearance of the witnesses.

It is correct and well known by all who attended the meetings of the Committee, that the witnesses who had wished to remain anonymous were concerned on this point.

I do not think that I opened any hearing of such witnesses without assuring them on behalf of the Committee that their desire to remain anonymous would be absolutely respected!

Many of them, in spite of that, stressed their wish by explaining their motives to the Committee.

Thus, not only Bang-Jensen, but also I myself on behalf of the members of the Committee and of the Secretariat and the Staff as a whole have given "firm commitments" that the names of those witnesses should remain secret.

I suppose that everybody will agree, that as a matter of course this promise should be solemnly kept!

So far, I am convinced, there is no possibility of any disagreement.

And I must confess, that until I had read your letter and Bang-Jensen's "memorandum" to Dr. Protitch, it had never occurred to me, that any problem could arise in this context. Quite frankly, I took it for granted that all documents: the verbatim records—which are almost as significant as the lists of names—the correspondence, and the names and addresses of the witnesses already were kept in safe custody at the United Nations.

Now it appears from Bang-Jensen's memorandum that he feels a very personal responsibility after his talks with and his oral and direct promises to the witnesses. This is quite understandable for everybody who during the hearings has heard and seen what a serious matter this question was to the persons in question.

Thus, from a purely human point of view, Bang-Jensen should in my opinion not be blamed for his feeling of responsibility.

But it also appears from Bang-Jensen's letter that his repeated denial to deliver the documents to the United Nations Secretariat springs from a profound doubt or rather suspicion as to the ability of the United Nations to protect the interests of the witnesses. He maintains in this connection that his locked desk has been opened, documents removed and so on.

I am, of course, quite unable to have any opinion of such contentions.

On the other hand it is a fact, that military and political spies are found everywhere. Some have recently been discovered in peaceful Denmark who has sent them home to the Soviet-Union. Therefore it cannot be denied in advance, that spies in certain cases might be at work also in the world's political headquarters in New York. And I do not doubt that the communists would be willing to pay a high price for the documents of the Hungary Committee, particularly for the names of the witnesses!

This should be borne in mind and taken into serious consideration by the Secretariat. The United Nations have a heavy responsibility towards human beings in this matter.

To conclude:

1. In my opinion all documents concerning the Hungary Committee ought to be placed in the custody of the United Nations.

2. This also applies to the names of the witnesses—if they should be kept any longer at all!

   The safest thing is of course to burn these lists.

   Why not do that in this case instead of taking any risk on behalf of other human beings?

   I would not object to this procedure. On the contrary I suggest to do so!

3. If this procedure cannot be accepted, the lists of names, the correspondence and similar documents now in Bang-Jensen's possession should be carefully packed and sealed under the personal supervision of the Secretary-General of the United Nations and be placed in a secret safe in the U.N. building under the personal guarantee of a high, responsible member of the Secretariat.

—Dear Mr. Hammarskjold, I have now honestly tried to understand and to contribute to the solution of this both strange and important question. I sincerely hope that both my comments and my suggestions may prove helpful.

Yours sincerely
[signed] Alsing Andersen

More than five weeks passed before Bang-Jensen got a reply to his explanation. It came in the form of an order from Dragoslav Protitch, "Unless you turn over the list tomorrow morning, your actions will be considered a clear case of insubordination against the Secretary-General."

Instead of complying, Bang-Jensen wrote a three-page memo to the Secretary General, reiterating his stand in detail. He had been given the authority of a trustee. He could not legally, morally, or physically hand over the secret papers. "To repeat: A promise was given to the witnesses on behalf of the United Nations by an officer of the Organization. There was no reason for the witnesses to doubt that he was authorized to do so. Whether he actually was authorized or not is of no legal consequence. In the circumstances, all lawyers, I should think, will agree that the United Nations and I, legally as well as morally, are bound by this promise, and that it cannot be modified without the consent of the witnesses themselves.

"Dr. Protitch has not been able to show me how this legal situation can be circumvented. I trust that you will let me know if you can."

Peter Marshall couldn't help but wonder how this act of stubborn defiance affected the upper reaches of the U.N. Who had ever heard of one man going counter to the power of the largest bureaucracy in the world?

The memo to the Secretary General had been dispatched on Friday, November 22, 1957. On Monday morning, Bang-Jensen was asked to report to Dr. Sze, the head of the U.N. Health Clinic. He supposed it was something to do with a bout of the Asian flu he'd had the month before.

It was after this meeting, in which Dr. Sze found him in good health mentally and physically, that Bang-Jensen wrote his unusual memorandum to his wife. (Peter Marshall realized that anyone reading it at the time might well ponder its necessity. It was only in view of later developments that its validity took on ominous meaning.)

On Friday afternoon, November 29, Paul Bang-Jensen received a last direct order[3] by Protitch, handed down from the Secretary General. He must deliver the list of witnesses, together with other records, right now.

He calmly said, no.

That same evening Dag Hammarskjold left the country on other U.N. business.

Under U.N. Staff Regulations, a staff member can be suspended only if a "charge of misconduct" is made against him.

On Wednesday, December 4, staff member Paul Bang-Jensen was summoned to the office of the Director of Personnel, J. A. C. Robertson. There, in the presence of Under Secretary Protitch, he was informed that, on instructions from the Secretary General, he had been suspended. He was given no reason either orally or in writing.

He was told to leave the premises at once and that he could only return as a visitor.

He was instructed not to tell anyone about his suspension. This included his colleagues, his superiors, his own staff, and the members of the Danish delegation who were to dine at his home the next evening.

When he again asked for the reason for his suspension, Robertson said he was not sure that Bang-Jensen could demand to know the reason. Only the U.N. guards would know that he had been suspended, to make sure that he did not come back into the building—except as a visitor.

Robertson did not bother to tell Bang-Jensen that two of these guards were waiting outside the door. With no little embarrassment, they escorted the now thoroughly angered diplomat to the U.N. gates.

Never in the history of the United Nations had such a method of suspension taken place. Robertson had his orders and carried them out in the presence of Protitch. Dag Hammarskjold was abroad. His Executive Assistant, Andrew Cordier, minding the store in his absence, later declared his own innocence.

J. A. C. Robertson was to leave the U.N. service and return to England less than two weeks later. Today, it is he who is blamed for the extraordinary and unnecessary expulsion of Paul Bang-Jensen from the premises of the United Nations.

Christian Winther has never said who gave him the news of Paul Bang-Jensen's suspension. But it was he who had the world exclusive on the matter. And, oddly enough, it was not until December 9, when the case broke on the Danish Government radio and was cabled back to New York, that Bang-Jensen learned the official reason for his eviction from the U.N. It was because "of noncompliance with instructions from his superiors." The same day the U.N. Information Office released a note to correspondents, explaining the Secretariat's position.

One key sentence in the note, Peter Marshall looked upon as being at complete variance with the facts: "In accordance with established practice, he [Bang-Jensen] was instructed *at the conclusion of his duties as a member of the Secretariat staff assigned to the Special Committee on the problem of Hungary to turn over to the Secretariat for safe custody under seal, official documents in his possession relating to the work of the Committee.*"[4]

One of J. A. C. Robertson's last official U.N. duties was to write a confidential letter to the man he literally had had thrown off the reservation two days before.

The letter heralded a new act in the drama; an act that would take a year to play out.

JACR/jmj

SRS/57   6 December 1957

CONFIDENTIAL

Dear Mr. Bang-Jensen,

In accordance with our conversation of 4 December, I write to inform you that the Secretary-General has appointed a group of three, consisting of Mr. Ernest Gross (as Chairman), Mr. Constantin Stavropoulos, and myself, to make a review of your conduct relating to your association with the Special Committee on Hungary.

The group is enjoined to begin its work forthwith and, after detailed study and evaluation of the matter, to convey to the Secretary-General on the basis thereof, such views, suggestions or recommendations for further action as it may deem appropriate.

Your suspension from duty, with pay, pending further investigation, which became effective 4 December 1957, is (in accordance with the provisions of Staff Rule 110.4), without prejudice to your rights as a staff member.

All pertinent documentation will be made available to the group, which may also interview such persons as it may consider likely to afford it helpful information. In this connexion, you are hereby instructed to hold yourself at the disposal of the group, and, in particular, to attend it at 3:00 P.M. on Tuesday, 10 December, in Room 3627A, bringing with you such documentation as you may consider relevant to help you in answering questions arising from the review.

Sincerely yours,

[signed] J. A. C. Robertson

Director of Personnel

Mr. Povl Bang-Jensen
18 Old Farm Road
Lake Success, N.Y.

cc: Mr. Ernest Gross
  Mr. C. A. Stravropoulos
  Mr. A. Cordier
  Mr. D. Protitch

CHAPTER 21

BEFORE SITTING DOWN with Ernest A. Gross, Peter Marshall gave himself a short briefing.

Gross was a lawyer with a respected career in the United States Government. He had served the Truman Administration as an Assistant Secretary of State and had been counsel to General George C. Marshall. Later, during the Korean War, he had been a deputy American delegate to the U.N.

In 1954, Gross had received a legal fee of $34,700 from the U.N.

That same year he was a panel Chairman of the "American Assembly," which issued a manifesto, two of whose signers were Andrew Cordier and Ralph Bunche. The manifesto deplored a tendency in the U.S. to adopt a rigid policy against the admission of Red China into the U.N.

In *Who's Who* for 1958, he listed himself as legal adviser to the Secretary General of the U.N.

Now the Secretary General, through Andrew Cordier,

had asked him to be Chairman of a group[1] of three to look into Paul Bang-Jensen's conduct.

The group, upon the issuance of its first press release on December 21, 1957, designated itself a "Committee of Investigation." In the course of its inquiry, it took testimony from only seven witnesses. It heard Bang-Jensen twice and his lawyer, Adolf A. Berle, Jr., once.

Its second press release was on January 15, 1958, and it recommended that the secret papers be destroyed. It also implied that Paul Bang-Jensen had been irresponsible.

On January 18, Ernest Gross conducted a press conference at the U.N. lasting an hour. Here, he openly attacked Bang-Jensen and referred to his "aberrant conduct." This conference was held despite Stavropoulos' assurance to Adolf Berle, who was leaving the same day for Puerto Rico, that nothing would be done until his return on January 22, except that the Secretary General would probably order the list destroyed.

On January 24 Paul Bang-Jensen, accompanied by Adolf Berle, was met by Dragoslav Protitch and Colonel Frank Begley, former Police Chief of Farmington, Conn., and now head of U.N. special police.

The four, bundled in overcoats, mounted to the windswept roof of the U.N.

There, Begley lit a fire in a wire basket, and Bang-Jensen dropped four sealed envelopes into the flames. In one of these he said were notes on the identities of the eighty-one refugees.

The method of destroying the evidence embarrassed Paul Bang-Jensen. He knew it would be implied that it was done in this way at his insistence. He was right, and Peter Marshall could not help but recall Andrew Cordier's words on the subject, "Well, it seemed as good a place as any to do the job."

The Gross group had been formed for the express purpose of advising the Secretary General. Hammarskjold's supposed desire to seek outside legal advice in the guise of Ernest Gross is illusion, at best. Gross's being "outside" the
U.N. applied only to a physical state, not an objective one.
But by the time the papers were finally disposed of, the
group had informed the world of its purpose, its recommendations, and its belief that Paul Bang-Jensen was not of
sound mind.

Shortly the group would issue its report to the Secretary
General, recommending Paul Bang-Jensen's dismissal from
the United Nations. The contents of this 195-page document would become known to many before it would become known to the man it was written about.

"Until this Hungarian Committee matter came up, Bang-
Jensen was a fine and devoted individual. I had known him
for some years, when I was a delegate and before, and this
manner had never been his."

Ernest A. Gross leaned back in his chair and told Peter
Marshall how Secretary General Dag Hammarskjold had, on
December 4, 1957, called him in as a private lawyer to review Bang-Jensen's conduct "relating to his association with
the Special Committee on the problem of Hungary." The
result was the "Gross Report," prepared by Gross, as chairman, with the assistance of two U.N. Under Secretaries,
Constantin Stavropoulos and Philippe de Seynes.

"Yes," Gross went on, "Bang-Jensen was an up-and-com-
ing young man. He had always done well. Never well
known, but he had done his work competently. . . ."

Gross had received Marshall courteously and they were
discussing the case. "You know," the lawyer said, "it's difficult to talk like this about a man who can't answer back."

Gross was behind a clean-top desk, only a manila folder

before him. Marshall sat in one of the several leather chairs. Outside the office windows, twenty-four stories above Wall Street, a light rain was falling.

"Mr. Gross, your report says that 'our function is investigative and advisory and does not in any way derogate from or prejudice Mr. Bang-Jensen's rights as a staff member.' You know, Bang-Jensen characterized your Committee as having prejudged his case."

Gross swung his swivel chair. "Well, how could that have been? I don't consider that he was prejudged. We were given a job and we carried it out, and later, his case was taken up by the Disciplinary Committee. . . .

"We have nothing to hide under a bushel. We did our job, Mr. Stavropoulos and Mr. de Seynes and myself, taking evidence from a number of people."

"What did you think about his mental state?"

"I think our report sums up our finding," Gross answered. "Don't forget, here was a man who had been accusing his colleagues for almost a year of willfully attempting to present an incorrect report. . . .

"This was not merely alleging errors, but was carried out by day-after-day allegations in memos, written charges of serious consequence. . . .

"This is a distressing thing. Supposing you or I were being accused in this manner, and yet we were doing our level best to carry on our work. No organization can carry on like that.

"I've been in government and I can tell some pretty hairy stories about personnel difficulties, so I know what a problem he was."

"What I'd like you to comment on is the criticism leveled at your Committee."

"What do you mean?"

"For instance, regarding the fact that the Gross Committee issued two interim announcements to the press during its investigation. You know Bang-Jensen was told the Committee was 'to convey its views, suggestions and recommendations to the Secretary General.' In his own words, Bang-Jensen 'took it for granted that the Group would report to the Secretary General privately and not in public.' He claimed that the release of the preliminary findings was 'prejudicial to his position.' "

Gross bristled. For an instant he glared speechless at Marshall. "Listen," he said. "I thought the entire report was going to be confidential from beginning to end. But you know Bang-Jensen launched an active campaign against us in the press. It was getting so that we, the Committee, were being tried. You can find it in the papers."

"Well, as a matter of fact, I've looked through back-issue files of New York papers for December, 1957, and haven't found a great deal—"

Gross shot another look at Marshall. "It wasn't necessarily all here in New York. Don't forget the foreign press."

"Then what about the second interim public announcement? This cited Bang-Jensen's 'aberrant conduct.' "

"The reason for that report was to settle the matter of the list. As far as I'm concerned, it was a separate matter from the general Committee study of Bang-Jensen's conduct. The January fifteen report recommended that Bang-Jensen be instructed to burn the list—the papers—in the presence of a U.N. Security Officer."

"How about your press conference three days later— what was the reason for that? Bang-Jensen said you told correspondents that you had checked in advance to make sure the term 'aberrant conduct' was not libelous. He claimed you made other slanderous allegations."

Gross paused and repeated himself. "The entire object of the press conference was to clarify the problem of the list, since many in the press were querying the U.N. about it. What was the list? I don't know. Bang-Jensen never explained what the documents or papers were that he had in his possession.

"It was foolish of him to keep them, whatever they were. He could have been blackmailed, or his family might have been threatened. Of course the matter caught the public's attention. We attempted to conclude this, and did so by having the papers burned.

"Hammarskjold didn't like the way it was carried out. It was a sort of Götterdämmerung affair. Hammarskjold believes the U.N. is an organization that settles matters in a procedural way. . . ."

Peter Marshall reflected. If Hammarskjold had not wanted the list disposed of in this manner, and if Bang-Jensen had not wanted it—who had ordered it?

"Mr. Gross, concerning the formation of your Committee, there's the fact that you have been a legal adviser to the U.N. in the past; as I understand it, Mr. Hammarskjold wanted *outside* advice. Could you comment on that?"

"I've served as a counsel for the U.N. for some years, specializing particularly in real estate matters or other problems that the regular U.N. legal staff might not be equipped to handle. Mr. Stavropoulos is the U.N. legal chief and a very good man, but he is not fully versed on some technical points of American law."

"What did you think about Bang-Jensen's contention of errors and omissions in the Hungarian report?" Marshall asked.

"Those!" Gross answered. "Why, Mick Shann went over and over the report with Alsing Andersen, trying to check them out. Even after the incident between Bang-Jensen and Shann in the Delegates' Lounge . . . and this was not the way the *Chicago Daily Tribune* presented it."

Gross reached in his desk and pulled out two newspaper clippings. One was an article on the U.N. by Alice Widener from the *Cincinnati Enquirer*. The other was by Chesly Manly in the *Chicago Daily Tribune*.

Gross pointed to the Manly story. "I know Ches, he's a friend of mine. He probably didn't mean to write it this way, or maybe he did. There wasn't any 'violent argument' between Bang-Jensen and Shann, as the *Tribune* puts it. That implies that Shann was on the enemy side. You see what I mean? How it's phrased there—the word 'violent.'

"The case was that Bang-Jensen came up to Shann claiming he had found further errors in the report. 'I've found errors and I want you to look them over.' So once again Shann had to argue with him about this. But it wasn't a violent discussion. And after all this, Shann went over all that Bang-Jensen had brought up."

(Shann's own report, Peter Marshall reflected, describes the encounter as "immoderate." Bang-Jensen was in "hysterical condition.")

Gross stopped briefly, then went on. "Shann was responsible for the report. He has felt terrible about all this. It was a good report, he did all he could to make it a good report. When I speak of how Shann felt, I know well. Don't forget, I am an old member of the club, a former delegate. I think you are being unfair to take these things up now.

"You know, this hits in many areas. It appeals to those who were frustrated in the outcome of the Hungarian situation. Don't forget, the U.N. did no more than the United States did . . . it takes a great deal of sophisticated thought to get the impact of this fact."

CHAPTER 22

FROM THE HOME of his friend, Henrik Kauffmann, in Washington, D.C., Paul Bang-Jensen sent a telegram dated December 9, 1957, to Ernest Gross. It said in part:

> ". . . the matters to be considered are obviously of a grave character, and I therefore respectfully request that the hearing be postponed for two weeks in order that I might make adequate preparation."

Ernest Gross replied the next day, putting the suspended diplomat's fears to rest. "This reveals some misunderstanding on your part. The group conducting the review is not holding formal hearings. It wishes to pursue, in the course of this review, questions arising from the body of material already in its possession. . . ."

It sounded like a fair enough invitation, Peter Marshall reflected, and Bang-Jensen must have thought so too, because on the thirteenth, he met the group of three on the thirty-sixth floor of the U.N. There, Ernest Gross further assured him:

"We were requested by the Secretary General, as I understand it, to discuss with you such matters as appear to us to be relevant, and we are not of course either a formal group or a committee in the sense of being guided by any rules or regulations of the Secretariat. *The only rules which I think we shall follow will be those of common sense, justice, and fairness.*"

Peter Marshall noted that Bang-Jensen had later referred to his two interviews with the Gross group as "unfortunate experiences," and after his second meeting on the sixteenth the Dane refused to attend further hearings without legal counsel. Marshall pondered the reason for this, and pondered too the replacement of one member of the three-man group.

J. A. C. Robertson, after serving Gross one week, left for England. His position was taken over by Philippe de Seynes, Under Secretary for Economic and Social Affairs. Stavropoulos remained.

Marshall never got a clear answer for the sudden switch. It had been known long before Robertson's appointment to the group that he was leaving.

As to Bang-Jensen's refusal to talk with these gentlemen again, Marshall got the answer from Bang-Jensen's own statement:

"I had taken it for granted that the group would report to the Secretary-General privately and not in public, and that the Gross group, if any report was to be published, would be careful to check that at least all factual statements were correct, and would also give me an opportunity to see the report before it was released to the press.

"I did not receive the transcript of the two hearings on 13th and 16th December until I had an attorney. It then proved that 231 of my answers were reported incorrectly in the transcript [which had been prepared by mechanical tape]. A considerable number of the answers are marked 'inaudible' and many of the answers as reported do not make sense; some state the opposite of what I actually said.

"I am not in possession of transcripts of testimony of any of the other witnesses before the Gross group.

"I have protested against the transcripts of the two 'interviews' and have been informed in writing that the members of the group accepted my protest but that they would rely on their memories, which unfortunately have proved to be weak, since quite a number of factual statements in the Gross report of 15 January [released to the press] regarding what I had told the group are indisputably incorrect. . . ."[1]

Ernest Gross had explained to Peter Marshall that the reason for the issuing of two public interim reports on the group's progress was to answer press attacks upon it and the U.N. In each of these public releases and the press conferences that accompanied them, not only was the U.N.'s position commended, but Bang-Jensen's actions were deplored.

Investigation on Peter Marshall's part revealed, as he had pointed out to Gross, that neither *The New York Times* nor the *New York Herald Tribune* had done anything but present the facts as they had come from the U.N.

The Danish press, though more vocal and detailed in its coverage of the strange affair, presented the case from all points of view. *Berlingske Tidende,* on December 11, did make the observation that neither the Danish Foreign Office nor Alsing Andersen, Chairman of the Hungarian Committee, had been informed by the U.N. of Bang-Jensen's suspension.

The London Times of the fourteenth stated that Bang-Jensen had taken the responsibility for the list in place of the U.N. It had the utmost concern for the safety of the refugees who had testified and it recommended the documents in question be destroyed.

Alsing Andersen had made this suggestion on November

1 in reply to Hammarskjold's letter of inquiry. Bang-Jensen was in favor of a similar course, and long had been. Now still other voices spoke out, saying, "Destroy the list!"

Finally, on January 15, 1958, the three gentlemen of "common sense" reached the same conclusion. Their reason, however, for recommending this course was somewhat different from the obvious. They stated in their written report that the former Deputy Secretary's method of concealing the secret list made it valueless. This was a piece of "common sense" that Peter Marshall puzzled over; he noticed that it had been happily applauded by the Communist bloc.[2]

During the period that Ernest Gross and his two Secretariat conferees were openly seeking a solution to what to do with the secret list, and privately investigating Paul Bang-Jensen's actions of the past year, considerable back-stage activity was taking place at the U.N.

Alsing Andersen returned from Denmark and sat down in a series of special meetings with the other four members of the Hungarian Committee. Before Christmas, the Committee overrode his suggestions and voted to have the papers turned over to the Secretary General. Following the holidays, it suddenly reversed itself and called for their destruction. Peter Marshall learned, although it did not appear in the press, that, at one of the emergency meetings, the Special Committee on Hungary voted to thank Paul Bang-Jensen for his contributions while serving it.

Through it all and up to the time that the documents were finally burned, neither Bang-Jensen nor his lawyer, Adolf A. Berle, Jr., was ever aware the investigation covered anything more than the charge of insubordination against the Dane for refusing to turn over the secret list.

Bang-Jensen was not asked to present witnesses in his own behalf, nor was his lawyer given the opportunity to cross-examine those who did testify. Of the seven witnesses who appeared before Gross, Stavropoulos, and de Seynes, four were openly hostile to Bang-Jensen.

And finally, Peter Marshall observed, Adolf Berle was never given the opportunity to file an answer to the charges against his client.

The final Gross Report was submitted to the Secretary General on February 7, 1958, and Peter Marshall decided that Bang-Jensen's own words pretty well summed up the proceedings based on "common sense, justice, and fairness":

"I did not receive the final report of the Gross group, dated 7 February, until 19 February at 2:45 P.M. I was instructed to keep the thirty-five-page report and its annex of 160 pages as confidential. The report, which recommends that I be summarily dismissed, contains dozens of obvious contradictions and statements contrary to documentary facts, numerous new accusations and allegations based on statements and material unknown to me, together with a great number of libelous statements impugning my mental health."[3]

To Peter Marshall, the Gross Report was the rack on which Paul Bang-Jensen was strung for the better part of a year. He did not think he could find any better description of it than the one made by J. Anthony Panuch, the international attorney, later to represent Bang-Jensen for a short period.

"In my long years of government service, in responsible positions of the United States Government," wrote Panuch, "I have never seen anything to approach the Gross Committee 'report' as a scurrilous and cowardly attack on one official of an international agency by his supposedly reputable colleagues, aided and abetted by an outsider, under the cover of the protection accorded them by the Privileges and Immunities Act."[4]

Peter Marshall found that the report and its annexes (se-
lected from a foot-and-a-half pile of documents), stripped
down to essentials, arrived at two basic conclusions: Paul
Bang-Jensen's behavior while he was serving the Special
Committee on Hungary showed a disordered judgment. All
Paul Bang-Jensen's charges were utterly groundless.

To reach these conclusions, the report made a number of
assumptions, ranging from derogatory to vicious.

1. *The position of Deputy Secretary to the Committee
entailed little responsibility, and what responsibility later
evolved came through Bang-Jensen's superiors.*

From the Hungarians who had been witnesses before
the Committee—from various Secretariat officers who had
served the Committee—and from a number of the annexes
attached to the tail of the Gross report, Peter Marshall had
found that the facts were diametrically opposite to the contention. Whether the job itself was supposed to be a responsible one might be debated, but certainly no one could debate that, through necessity and interest, Paul Bang-Jensen's
efforts had made it most responsible.

2. *Bang-Jensen was too sensitive and weak-stomached a
person for the work. "On occasion he became physically ill
during interviews."*

Peter Marshall knew that Bang-Jensen had only once dis-
played a strong sense of emotion. As K. had recounted, a
prospective witness, in showing how the Communists had
tortured him, had taken his false palate out of his mouth and
laid it on the table. Bang-Jensen had left the room for a moment. He did not become physically ill. In many other cases,
as Horvath has pointed out, the Deputy Secretary was criticized by the witnesses for his coolness.

3. *Bang-Jensen's allegations about "suppression" of a witness, "sabotage" in Vienna, and "security" in general are
without foundation.*

If William Jordan's refusal to inform the Committee

about the availability of the youthful witness who had been deported to Russia was not suppression, Peter Marshall wondered, what could it be termed?

As to "sabotage" in Vienna, Marshall observed that the report concentrated at length on the difficulties between Bang-Jensen and Jordan as to their disagreement concerning preliminary interviews. It said nothing about the known activities of Miklos Szabo, a Communist spy, who was able to take back to Budapest at least some of the names of the anonymous witnesses.

With regard to "security," Peter Marshall found that the report suggested Bang-Jensen had been lying about the lack of it. "Serious doubt exists concerning the actual occurrence of certain of these events."

Which events? Bang-Jensen's desk being searched several times in New York and Geneva? An anti-Tito Communist acting as a guard outside the Committee room in Geneva? A Communist photographer on a roof top in Vienna, allegedly, taking pictures of witnesses as they entered the building for interviews?

Or did the three writers of the report question that a Soviet citizen, reputed to be a Soviet intelligence officer, was assigned as a translator to the Committee in Geneva?

The gentlemen of the Committee did not say. They doubted seriously. They strongly implied that Paul Bang-Jensen was a liar and that his own methods of security left much to be desired. ". . . at one point during the Committee's work, Mr. Bang-Jensen sent from Europe to United Nations headquarters in New York a file of forty depositions containing the names of anonymous witnesses without raising any question as to the security of the witnesses."

Peter Marshall felt that Bang-Jensen's answer to this statement from the Gross Report deserved repeating:

"This is a complete fabrication without any basis whatsoever. The Gross Committee never asked me about it, and it was completely new to me when I read about it in the press. The Committee had been informed that this allegation has no basis in fact, but they have made no correction, although they have not even been willing to state on what alleged evidence they support this allegation.

"This is just one example of the numerous falsehoods with which the campaign against me is being conducted."

4. *Mr. Bang-Jensen's honesty was doubted on another level—the highest level of all; this had to do with the assurances he claimed to have given witnesses who wished to have their names kept secret.*

Here, Chairman Gross could have easily cleared away all doubt for himself, for Mr. Stavropoulos, and for Mr. de Seynes. All he would have had to do was to ask General Bela Kiraly, Sandor Kiss, or Janos Horvath. They could have told him. Janos Horvath had made the offer to testify, but it was not taken up.

5. *Bang-Jensen's concept of what constitutes a "fact," an "error," and an "omission" with regard to the writing of the Report is a matter of judgment. His judgment was bad, and his persistent cries of "sabotage" raised the question of his sanity.*

Yes, it was a matter of judgment, and in the examples listed by Paul Bang-Jensen publicly and from his drafts of Chapters II and VII, Peter Marshall believed the diplomat's judgment sound. "Sabotage" was in some instances a matter of definition, in others of exaggeration, and in still others, of strong possibility. Admitting that it was a serious charge to make, and that if unprovable it was ample ground for his dismissal from the U.N., it was never made because of mental instability. It was made from knowledge of Soviet methods and fear of their result. And behind both knowledge and fear, Paul Bang-Jensen was in possession of secret facts that justified to a large degree everything he said and did while serving the Committee.

These facts Peter Marshall would lay bare in due course, but for now he summed up in one sentence the substance of the Gross Report's description of Paul Bang-Jensen's character:

Paul Bang-Jensen, whose position as Deputy Secretary required little responsibility, was an oversensitive, highly emotional man, given to exaggeration and falsehood, who was driven out of his mind by cruel facts and overwork, and so turned on his superior, William Jordan, and accused him of evil-doing.

Let the reader decide.

CHAPTER 23

PETER MARSHALL thought that J. Anthony Panuch had the look of a politician, but unlike most politicians, the short, squarely built attorney was direct and open. There was nothing evasive in his words.

"I'd never heard of Bang-Jensen until Henrik Kauffmann and Just Lunning got hold of me. When Hammarskjold handed the Gross Report over to the U.N.'s Joint Disciplinary Committee in February, Kauffmann and Adolf Berle knew that Bang-Jensen needed a trial lawyer." Panuch paused to take a puff on his cigar. "So they got hold of me."

The two were seated at a small board table in the attorney's spacious downtown office. "Hammarskjold could have fired Bang-Jensen without going any farther, couldn't he?" Marshall asked.

Panuch touched off the ash of his cigar gently into his tray and nodded. "Of course. And the fact that Meurig Evans, Cordier's top assistant, was Chairman of the Disciplinary Committee, and the other two members subordinates of the signers of the Gross Report, is rather incredible in itself."

"That sort of thing couldn't happen in an American court."

"That sort of thing couldn't have happened in any court where the laws of justice are observed." Panuch nodded his head and raised his pale-blue eyes in emphasis.

"When I looked into the case, I thought this was a guy who was getting a real lousy deal. I went out to his house and I met his wife and those five kids. I saw those kids and I was hooked. Lord, they're wonderful!" The slightly gravelly-voiced lawyer in the conservative blue suit and the monogramed shirt wagged his head and had another puff on his cigar and then continued. "Bang-Jensen's trial before the Disciplinary Committee was a clear case of not giving a guy due process. He needed certain documents to prove the charges against him false. They wouldn't give him the documents."

"Well, even before the case went to the Disciplinary Committee, do you think bringing Gross into the affair was legal?"

Panuch gave a snort of derision. "It wouldn't be legal anywhere but over there. That's the way they set the whole thing up in the first place. But hell, bringing Ernie Gross in was to give people the idea the American Government was involved. The Gross Committee functioned as investigator, prosecutor, witness, judge, and publicist of its own actions. What could be more unfair?"

"Once you took the case, what happened then?"

"Well, I had a powwow with Kauffmann, Just Lunning, and Hesselund-Jensen, who was the Danish Ambassador to the U.N. I wanted to find out how the Danish Government felt about the whole thing. If the Danes were behind Bang-Jensen, it would be a big help."

"They were behind him, weren't they?"

"Yes, at the time. They wanted him off the hook. I warned Kauffmann though that he could be fired before we moved, so we had to move fast. The U.N. boys knew that if I handled this thing and hit them on the security angle, things would get rough."

"You mean the fact that their security is not as good as they tried to make it sound."

"Good Lord, how could it be?" Panuch gestured, disturbing the thin layer of smoke before him. "Anyhow, I had a talk with Bang-Jensen. He didn't trust anyone by that time. Soon as he'd talk to me, he'd call Berle and tell him what was going on. He was always cross checking.

"Well, I cross-examined him, and he said he had this paper which gave him the authority to keep the names. I thought, 'Brother, that's all you need, and we've got 'em,' but hell, when I asked to see the paper, he came up with something I couldn't really use."

"That was the memo from Cordier to the Controller's office."

"That was the one." Panuch waggled his cigar around in his mouth, his round, hard face looking well polished. "I gave this thing a lot of thought, and the only way out I could see was what they call an honorable disengagement . . . an exchange of letters, charges withdrawn, reception, pictures, you know, all the amenities.

"I checked with Kauffmann and his friends, and they were all for it. Bang-Jensen was being represented in the U.N. by a French lawyer at the time . . . Manfred Simon. He's a judge in Paris now. The Joint Disciplinary Committee had turned down my request to represent Bang-Jensen before it, so I went over to see Simon and told him what I had in mind.

"He thought it was a damn good idea. He was supposed to leave for Paris the next week, but he delayed his trip to try and help.

"Hell, an hour after I got back here he called me. Cordier had nearly flipped. Knowing me and how I felt about the case, he didn't expect anything but a tough fight. Now here I'd given the U.N. a way out, and he was all for it. . . ."

J. Anthony Panuch gently stubbed out his cigar. "You realize I was going way out on a limb on this? Cordier wanted to know if Bang-Jensen would go along with an arrangement like I'd suggested, and I had to say in my best judgment he would if the terms were right. Bang-Jensen had to get the top severance pay, whatever it was, and a clean bill of health. I also said they should try to use him in one of their overseas branches. Cordier thought that could be fixed too. So Simon put off his trip to work out the drafts.

"When I informed Kauffmann and the others about it, they couldn't have been happier. . . . It was all set to go. I called Bang-Jensen about four-thirty in the afternoon and told him about it. He seemed to like the idea at first . . . seemed quite excited."

Panuch sighed and leaned back in his chair. "A couple of hours later he called me and told me he wouldn't go through with it. I realize now that's where I made my mistake. He had a stubborn streak in him, and once he'd made up his mind to something—well, what I should have done was to have had him come in here. Then I could have told him what the arrangement was, and gotten him to sign the letter before he had second thoughts. I underestimated how bitterly and strongly he felt about the Gross Report."

"In other words, he had a chance to make a deal and he refused."

"It was the best deal he could ever have made," Panuch added, and then went on. "Well, I said, 'Look, Paul, you're tired. You come in and see me in the morning and we'll talk about it.' He came in about ten o'clock and we talked here until noon. Then I took him to the Uptown Club for lunch, and hell, we talked there until five. I couldn't budge him.

"I came back here and called Kauffmann in Washington. He was really shook up by the news. I told him I'd done everything I could. I said, 'Maybe my approach isn't the right one. He's your protégé; if he'll listen to anyone, he'll listen to you. Talk to him like a father, but you'd better talk to him fast because I've done all I can do.'

"Kauffmann came up from Washington that night, and Lunning and the Danish U.N. Ambassador, and I met him for breakfast at the Union Club. We tried to set up some kind of strategy for Kauffmann. We must have talked a couple of hours, and then we got out of there because we wanted Kauffmann to see Bang-Jensen alone." Panuch shook his head. "It didn't work."

"What do you suppose changed him, Mr. Panuch?"

"Well, I can only guess. I said he was stubborn, but I also believe he was confused.

"I've always felt there was the element of a classic Greek tragedy in the case. Bang-Jensen the heroic figure, not only ruthlessly persecuted for his honorable deeds, but doomed by forces within himself, unable to concede, unable to compromise." The lawyer laid his hand upon the table with a deft touch of punctuation.

"And that was the end of your part in the case, sir?" Peter Marshall asked.

Panuch's head came up. "No, not quite. I got a call from Simon and he wanted to know if I'd come over and talk to Cordier. I said, 'Look, I'll come over and talk, but it's very embarrassing and what good will it do? I don't have a client any more!' Hell," Panuch interrupted himself to explain, "if you represent someone and they don't take your advice, you're a damn fool to go on representing them. I'd spent a lot of time on this thing to get no results. . . . Well, I went over and made it clear that anything I had to say wouldn't help. Cordier is a practical guy, he was looking for some way to get out from under, but if Bang-Jensen wouldn't

play ball, there wasn't any way . . . and that was about it."
Panuch sighed with finality.

"What about his death? Do you have any doubts that he
killed himself?"

"No . . . What gets me most are those kids . . . those
five marvelous kids." The last was almost a groan.

"Just as much as a Greek tragedy, Mr. Panuch, I see it as
a tragedy of our time," Peter Marshall said.

"Yes, yes, of any time. He was a quixotic individual,
quixotic. His instincts were right, his intentions honorable.
He refused to give up the list of anonymous Hungarian witnesses to officials of the U.N. Secretariat, who took no security measures to safeguard the witnesses' identities. . . .
And in the end, he helped to hang himself."

CHAPTER 24

PETER MARSHALL was the first to arrive at the Petite Marmite on West 56th Street. He was sipping a Cinzano when Clifford Forster came in. Marshall hadn't seen the lawyer in some weeks.

"This is my favorite French restaurant," Forster said as they settled themselves at a table near the bar. "Now, how are things going?"

"I've followed Bang-Jensen's case," Marshall said, "into the muddy waters of the U.N. juridical set up—the Joint Disciplinary Committee, Joint Appeals Board and Administrative Tribunal—and frankly, I'm a bit lost."

Forster laughed. "Even a lawyer could get confused. Bang-Jensen's case was handled by those three bodies in Tinker to Evers to Chance fashion. You know, Paul never appeared before the Joint Disciplinary Committee, and when he couldn't get the eighty-seven documents he asked for—which he said would support his innocence—he took his case to the Appeals Board.

"The Appeals Board got rid of him like a hot potato, saying it was not competent to consider his request. You see, Paul waged and lost his battle on the issue of due process— the denial of papers, and other irregularities.[1]

"In the meantime, the Disciplinary Committee went on with its deliberations, which consisted of studying the Gross Report and hearing one additional witness. In June, it handed down its verdict that Paul be dismissed for misconduct. But before this happened, he made it known that he was going to carry his case to the U.N. Supreme Court, the Administrative Tribunal.

"On July third, Hammarskjold fired him on four charges. Three of them had nothing to do with the list. They concerned his conduct on the Hungarian Committee.

"Actually, Paul had two strikes on him before he ever went to the Tribunal. First, James Wadsworth of the American delegation had come out publicly and backed Hammarskjold's letter of dismissal."

"Yes, I know," Marshall said, "and Wadsworth's excuse was that he did it in answer to all the inquiries as to why the U.S. wasn't supporting Bang-Jensen. Frankly, I thought at the time it was one helluva note, and I think so even more now. Wadsworth apparently ignored Bang-Jensen's reply to Hammarskjold, and there hadn't been a final verdict on the case."

"Well, the second strike on Paul—and it was an even tougher one, really—was that Alsing Andersen had also agreed with Hammarskjold. Andersen had made a statement that he had gone over the entire report and that he had checked Bang-Jensen's charges of errors and found them groundless. Paul went back to Denmark because of this in October. He wanted Andersen to meet him face to face and admit that they had not checked over the Hungarian report together—only one chapter.

"Paul went straight to the Premier, Hansen, and asked him to intervene. Hansen refused and Andersen said he had no desire to talk to Paul. The long and the short of it was—and it's really remarkable—public opinion in Denmark became fully aroused on Paul's side. Finally Andersen admitted they'd only checked the one chapter together.[2] And then the government, which had been taking a hands-off attitude when Paul arrived in Copenhagen, turned around and put up what amounted to five thousand dollars for his defense. In about two weeks' time, Paul had nearly everyone in Denmark behind him, except the Communists. He had gotten rid of one strike anyway, and he was quite encouraged.

"I always felt he made a mistake to argue on due process, but that was the way he planned it. I became his lawyer then, and I would have preferred to fight the case on the reasons behind the dismissal. That would have forced a yes-or-no answer on whether he was guilty as charged.

"Well, you know the rest. The Tribunal dismissed his appeal on December fifth, 1958. It noted that he had denied himself the opportunity to have his defense considered on its merits."

"I'm not a lawyer, Clifford, but in reading over the verbatim record of Cordier's testimony before the Tribunal, it certainly seemed he was talking about his idea of the merits of the case."

"You're right. For forty minutes of that hour session, he blasted Paul, and I've never heard a more vicious or unwarranted attack on anyone. I'll never forget it . . . never . . . particularly Cordier's business about the bank."

This is what Cordier said:

"*As early as last November, the press of the world, under the inspiration of the continuous communication of the Applicant (Bang-Jensen) with the press, emphasized this same theme over and over and over again. We have four large volumes representing a partial list of world clippings in which there are hundreds and hundreds of clippings on this theme, demonstrating the complete lack, indicating, describing, alleging the complete lack of internal security measures and procedures of the United Nations, articles that could have only one inspiration, articles that could have only one source, articles that could not conceivably, by the wildest pitch of one's imagination, come from any other source.*

"Madame President [Suzanne Bastid], this was a body blow at the good name of the United Nations, a body blow at the integrity of the United Nations, a body blow at the capacity of the United Nations to perform its work effectively. And it came from one source, only from one source . . .

"Having said that as a background, if I might use an illustration, a parallel, would it not be most extraordinary if an employee of a bank would say: 'Well, I think that I am better equipped and I am more trusted to keep the money of the patrons of the bank, of the clients of the bank, than the bank itself,' and he does? He keeps the money of the patrons of the bank, then, as justification for it, he talks to the local press and says: 'Oh, you see, it's very simple, very simple indeed. The bank can't be trusted. That bank can't keep its money safely. If you put money in a bank, it'll leak out. It's not safe to keep it there.' Therefore, the Applicant writes his own rules, completely ignoring established practice, completely ignoring the question of the good name of the organization, completely ignoring the question of the integrity of the organization. He writes his own rules and insists that he is, for some reason, a better keeper of the money of the patrons of the bank than the bank itself.

"Well, one knows enough about public opinion to know what impact that kind of logic would have upon public opinion and, therefore, upon the good operation of the bank. The illustration, I think, is clear, simple and applica-

ble. It applies to the situation in which we find ourselves here." [3]

A lovely analogy, Peter Marshall reflected. The U.N. as a bank, and who had ever heard of a bank hiring robbers as its executives? He would make a list of some of the executives who had graced the U.N. bank in recent years; members of the Priesthood all:

VLADIMIR A. GRUSHA, former first secretary of the Soviet delegation to the U.N. He was accused of obtaining information from a Ceylonese U.N. officer, Dhanapala Samarasekara, on the investigation carried out by the Committee on Hungary. Grusha was ordered from the United States April 10, 1957. (Samarasekara, who was employed by the Secretariat Department of Economic and Social Affairs, was dismissed by the United Nations for his activities in December, 1957. The Ceylonese Government announced that it had changed its cipher codes as a precaution after this incident.)

VALENTIN GUBITCHEV, Soviet representative on the U.N. Secretariat, who on March 9, 1950, was given his choice in a New York Federal Court of serving fifteen years for espionage activities or going home. He returned to the Soviet Union on March 20.

VIKTOR IVANOVICH PETROV, Soviet citizen employed as a translator at the U.N. Secretariat. He hired an American aviation draftsman to do insignificant drafting work and later asked the draftsman to obtain information concerning United States military aircraft. He departed from the United States "by invitation" on August 23, 1956.

VADIM ALEKSANDROVICH KIRILYUK, a Soviet citizen employed as a political affairs officer in the U.N. Secretariat's Department of Trusteeship and Information for Non-Self-Governing Territories. He contacted an American citizen who had made inquiries concerning a scholarship in the Soviet Union. Kirilyuk, who was apprehended in Springfield, Mass., sought information from the American on the latter's experience with cryptographic machines while in the U. S. Army. He also left for home "by invitation" on January 10, 1960.

ALEKSANDR PETROVICH KOVALEV, who arrived in the United States as a second secretary to the Soviet U.N. delegation and was later a naval attaché at the Russian Washington Embassy. He recruited an agent and arranged to receive undeveloped microfilm containing material of intelligence significance. Declared persona non grata and left for home February 10, 1954.

COL. MAKSIM GRIGORIEVICH MARTYNOV, Soviet representative to the U.N. Military Staff Committee. After another Russian had approached a U. S. Army officer for military information, Martynov attempted to contact the officer. However, an F.B.I. agent, made up to resemble the American officer, met Martynov. At a second meeting with the F.B.I. agent, Martynov was accosted by several agents. He was expelled from the United States February 26, 1955.

CAPT. BORIS FEDOROVICH GLADKOV, naval adviser to the Soviet representation in the Military Staff Committee of the U.N. He paid $1,550 to a sales engineer for a New York marine engineering firm, asking the American to obtain information on power plants on naval craft. Expelled July 12, 1956.

ALEKSANDR K. GURYANOV, attached to Soviet U.N. delegation. Asked to leave the United States May 9, 1956.

ROSTISLAV E. SHAPOVALOV, a secretary to the Soviet U.N. delegation, expelled September 12, 1956.

KONSTANTIN P. EKIMOV, a Soviet delegation secretary. Left for home at United States request November 30, 1956.

KIRILL SERGEEVICH DORONKIN, former Film Editor, Radio and Visual Division of the Department of Public Information in the U.N. Secretariat. After a source recruited by the Soviets had obtained aerial photographs of the Chicago area, Doronkin met the person and took the photographs into his possession in a secret meeting (observed by F.B.I. agents) at the parking lot adjacent to the railway station at Scarsdale, N.Y. The United States Mission to the U.N. delivered a complaint to the Secretary General and Doronkin was not

re-employed when his U.N. contract terminated. He left the
United States March 11, 1959.

IGOR YAKOVLEVICH MELEKH, a Soviet who, when arrested as a spy
by the F.B.I. on October 27, 1960, was employed by the
U.N. Secretariat as Chief of the Russian Language Section,
Office of Conference Services. Named as a co-conspirator
with Doronkin, he had tried to obtain maps of Chicago's
military installations.

These are cases of Soviet U.N. employees and members
of the Soviet delegation to the United Nations who have
taken advantage of their positions in the U.N. bank to
pilfer the till. They are by no means the only cases of
Soviet bloc espionage conducted advantageously with the
U.N. as a front.

Other Communist officials employed at the U.N. have
been expelled. Lt. Col. Frantisek Tisler, the former military and air attaché at the Czechoslovak Embassy in Washington who defected to the West, in May, 1960, told the
House Committee on Un-American Activities the extent of
espionage conducted by the Czech delegation at the U.N. In
all, he estimated that 45 per cent of Czech Embassy and
Czech U.N. personnel "was engaged in some type of intelligence activity." [4]

Peter Marshall felt that this was the place to borrow a
line from Andrew Wellington Cordier, and in so doing,
sum up the entire case. As the Executive Assistant to the
Secretary General had so succinctly said: "The illustration,
I think, is clear, simple, and applicable. It applies to the
situation in which we find ourselves here."

Part Five: Execution

CHAPTER 25

"I KNEW Paul eleven years," Lew Johnson said. "I never admired him so much as in those months he fought his case at the U.N. He worked so hard for his ideals."

Peter Marshall had called on Johnson, a special representative of the national A.F.L.-C.I.O., at his office on 34th Street. He knew that the labor representative had been Bang-Jensen's most intimate friend. They had met as neighbors with mutual family interests.

Johnson, reserved and soft-spoken, shook his head. "Paul was torn between his allegiance to the U.N. as an institution and an idea, and the personalities high up in the organization who he felt were not living up to its conception.

"He was dedicated and determined to carry out his duties in the preparation of the report on Hungary. . . . The list of witnesses? In all good conscience, he told me he could never turn it over and hold his self-respect—'It would leak out and then murders would be on my hands.'"
Johnson lit his pipe. "Paul was willing to sacrifice his job and his career to protect those people. He was too good a

man for the era in which he lived. He didn't have the toughness to withstand all the barbs.

"But I remember him most vividly after his suspension. He had great faith in the appeals system. He believed in the written word, and there he made a very serious mistake—he was more of an idealist than a practical politician. He wanted the truth, and he got in trouble with those that didn't care."

"Didn't he feel that the odds were against him?"

"Not at all. He was always so energetic, so optimistic that he would win. We often visited him at his home, and at no time—during, before, or after his dismissal—did I ever find him anything but an exceptionally calm man. His behavior was one thing I can't praise enough.

"And I saw the way he worked to present his case. He literally did it single-handed. He was always rushing to the Flushing Post Office, sometimes even in town to Grand Central, to get off great bundles of mail.

"Helen said that the humiliation Paul underwent from the U.N. would have broken a smaller man—one who didn't have the weapons her husband had—'education, integrity, and yes, endurance.' And how he loved those children! And they him. Little Lars, he called the whole thing 'Father's argument.' One Father's Day, the children presented Paul with a big package of typing paper. I guess they saw him there, working all the time, and maybe one of them asked him . . .

"People only saw the public side of his battle. Few knew the inside story of the pressures brought against him to back down. The loaded hints: 'What does it matter; you can't beat the organization.' Or 'what are you trying to prove?' Or 'the harder you fight, the harder your future—and remember your responsibilities for your family.' Those kinds of things. Then there were the rumors—that he was insane and worse. That he was an alcoholic—" Johnson broke off, his voice low-pitched, the bitterness razor sharp. "So there he was . . ."

"And after his dismissal from the U.N.?" Marshall asked.

"That's the hard part to tell," Johnson said. "It wasn't easy, it didn't go easy for Paul. You'd think that a man with such a highly specialized background could get a job with a large firm or a foundation. He'd get so far and then someone would have a connection with the U.N., and that would queer it. Our Union tried to help, naturally. And I thought the A.A.U.N. (American Association for the U.N.) acted very cowardly, and it claims to be liberal.

"He was such a modest man . . . he needed the help of others. When he began sitting around with no developments, nothing to do, his attitude deteriorated.

"Then CARE came through in April, 1959. Dick Reuter, Executive Secretary at CARE, stuck his neck out to hire him as a consultant. At least that gave Paul an office where he had a desk, a phone, and a place where he could look for a permanent job."

"How did he make out?"

"Well, it was a very different environment from the U.N. It was hard for him. But as the months went by, he began to come back. His spirits were at their lowest ebb in March and April. From then on, he improved.

"While at CARE he took a management counseling test and scored an extremely high mark. It was recommended he look into the hotel management field . . . this never panned out. Later, just about two months before his death, there was some possibility he might get a post at the Danish Consulate in Chicago. It didn't come through either. It's rather sad and awful when you think of a man like Paul, with all he had to offer, not being able to get a good job."

"Have you any suspicions about his death?" Marshall asked.

"I accept ninety-five per cent of the suicide theory. But

I don't know . . . he never mentioned suicide to me. He never said he carried a gun—although of course it was his own. Sometimes I wonder about it. I still have some suspicion that it's possible he was directly forced to do it."

Peter Marshall nodded. "Had you been in touch with him near the end?" he asked.

"As a matter of fact," Johnson replied, "I talked to him that last Friday. We were going to have lunch together that following week—the week he died."

Johnson stopped and looked at his pipe. It was out. He put it aside.

CHAPTER 26

"ALL RIGHT," the editor said, "you raise a good many unanswered points all suggesting the probability that Bang-Jensen was murdered."

"Or that he was forced to commit suicide."

"Which is still murder. That's all very well, but to have murder, you have to have motivation. The list was burned. He was gone from the U.N. As that one man said, 'The Communists couldn't have cared less about him.' So where is your reason for murder?"

"If there is one," Peter Marshall said, "I think it's in the defector story."

"From time to time you mention that story—the Soviets who wanted to cross over—but what about it? You haven't answered that either."

"With luck on my part and patience on yours, that's what I'm going to uncover next. And if it comes out like I think it might, maybe we'll find motivation for murder."

"Is that what you think now, that he was murdered?"

"I don't know, Tom. Right now, it's six of one and half a dozen of the other."

The Elizabeth Carteret Hotel in Elizabeth, New Jersey, was a small, newly decorated hostelry on the city's main street. It reminded Peter Marshall of other small city hotels he'd stayed at. Clean, neat, with modest prices, modest food, modest accommodations, and the feeling of swift transience.

The Green Room was L-shaped and well populated with an animated throng. As he stood at the entrance peering somewhat self-consciously at the gathering, a very short man with a masterful nose and cauliflower ears bore down on him. In his lapel was a large campaign button with the name "Morris" on it. He seemed immediately aware that Marshall's lapel was naked.

"Hello there! Hello there! Welcome!"

Marshall's hand was momentarily imprisoned and crushed. "Hello," he said, smiling bravely.

"It looks like a good turn out." The little man nodded toward the assemblage, his voice coming from somewhere down around his knees.

"Yes, it looks fine," Marshall agreed, and then introduced himself, explaining he had arranged to meet the guest of the evening, Robert Morris, at the conclusion of the rally.

"Well, come in, come in!" The little man steered him into the room. "If you feel like a drink, have one," he waved toward a bar on the left, "or if you're hungry, the ladies have made sandwiches." A table loaded with sandwiches proved their diligence.

"I don't like to barge in," he said. "I can wait until Mr. Morris shows up."

"Nonsense! Nonsense! the little man boomed. "You may not be able to vote for Bob, but you can come in and support him!"

For the better part of the next hour, Peter Marshall supported the candidacy of Judge Robert E. Morris, conservative Republican, in his bid against New Jersey's incumbent Senator Clifford Case. He did this by explaining half a dozen times why he couldn't sign a petition for Morris, consuming several delicious sandwiches, one very strong rye, and observing with interest the wide cross-section of people present. It ranged from very young conservative Republicans to very old conservative Republicans, and it embodied differences in color and the extremes of wealth. The approximately one hundred supporters present had one thing in common, they were all for Bob Morris.

"Elizabeth is a Case stronghold, you know, but Bob's going to take it away from him. . . ."

The Paladin of the evening swept in unannounced and unheralded and was quickly surrounded by the captains of the rally. He was a tall, round-faced, smiling man, his straw-colored hair slightly mussed. There was almost a boyish look about him; he was full of energy, full of enthusiasm, confident.

In a telephone conversation, Robert Morris had told Peter Marshall he would have to see him on the run. His campaign was operating on a seven-day-a-week basis, and not much time for sleep.

From the looks of him, Peter Marshall thought, the candidate was showing no sign of weariness from his hard schedule. For so youthful appearing a man, Morris already had quite a background: Former Naval Intelligence Officer, former Chief Counsel of the Senate's Sub-committee on Internal Security, former judge of the Municipal Court of New York City, and now, a primary candidate for Senator of the United States.

It was not until late in the evening, when the speech

making was done, the questions answered, and the hand-shaking complete, that Robert Morris was able to sit down and talk to Peter Marshall.

They had the dimly lit bar of the hotel to themselves. "Take notes if you'd like to." By now Marshall knew that everything Morris said would be crisp and to the point.

"In November, 1956, I was Chief Counsel for the Sub-committee on Internal Security. We were the first to take testimony from Hungarian refugees. We put surgical masks on the witnesses and gave them false identities. On photographs, we blocked out the faces. The newspapers hooted at our precautions.

"We kept goading the U.N. and Lodge to set up their own investigation. . . .

"It wasn't until the summer of 1957 that I heard about Bang-Jensen. I never knew the man before that, but I heard about his difficulties and I called him up and introduced myself. I told him I commended him for his stand and asked if I could be of help. Bang-Jensen politely declined. He said he could not accept my assistance. 'I've got to be correct,' he told me. 'I'm an international civil servant, you a counsel for a United States Congressional Committee. It would not be proper to talk to you.' "

Morris took a long pull on his beer and went on. "It wasn't until the spring of nineteen fifty-eight that I finally met him. Admiral Walter Anderson and William Joyce, a lawyer, called on me to see if I could help Bang-Jensen. We all met at the New York Yacht Club, and there I got his story. I told him the best tactic would be to take a direct stand. This was an exploratory meeting to see if I could be of help, and as I say, I was for a direct stand. I told him the preparing of big briefs was a waste of time. The cards were stacked against him."

"But where does the defector story come into it?" Peter Marshall asked, wondering if it came in at all.

Morris set down his beer. "In the summer of 1958—you can check the date because it was the time of the shark scare off the Jersey coast—Bang-Jensen came down to visit me at my home in Point Pleasant. He brought his son Lars along, and they had a great time swimming, but I was worried about the sharks. Anyway, during that visit and two subsequent meetings, one at my home and one at the New York Yacht Club, he told me he had been singled out by Soviets wishing to defect to the West."

"That's plural?"

"Yes, potential defectors. There was one principal figure, a high-ranking Secretariat official. Bang-Jensen knew there were others, but he never knew how many."

"And he had his dealings with this one official?"

"Right."

"Do you know his name?"

"No. I didn't ask for names."

"Why did the Soviet come to Bang-Jensen?"

"He knew he was pro-American. He knew about Bang-Jensen's activities in Denmark in 1948 that helped to bring that country into NATO."

"The defector, representing other potential defectors, wanted asylum, is that it?"

"Yes. He wanted Bang-Jensen to contact the President. He told Paul the thirty-eighth floor of the U.N. was under Soviet control and that our own *quote* foreign intelligence was infiltrated, *unquote*. If Bang-Jensen was unable to make contact with the President, the defector suggested that he try Allen Dulles, head of C.I.A."

"How did Bang-Jensen go about trying to arrange a meeting?"

"His dealings were through James Barco of the U. S. Mission to the U.N. They had seven talks in all, running from November of 1956 to June of 1957. Nothing happened. The U.S. officials didn't make a move."

"What happened to the principal defector?"

"Bang-Jensen told me he was recalled, and he presumed they'd done away with him."

"Nice."

"I went to the U.N. and spoke to Barco. He admitted the talks. He said, 'All I'll tell you is that I made a full report to my superiors in the State Department. I did the right thing. It is what I thought I should do.' I told him what he had done was horrendous. When I reported back to Paul, he was crushed."

"The word from Barco went to the State Department and then somehow got back to the U.N.," Peter Marshall said, thinking about his talk with Andrew Cordier. He could hear the husky occupant of the U.N.'s thirty-eighth floor saying, "Why, in June we found out he'd been having meetings with one of the American delegates. It was against all regulations. If we'd known about it in November, he'd never have been appointed Deputy Secretary to the Committee."

And Peter Marshall could hear his own question to Cordier, "Do you know why he was having meetings of that sort?"

"It had something to do with trying to get the U.S. to take a stronger stand on Hungary."

Robert Morris brought him back to the present. "Yes, the word got to the Secretariat. As a matter of fact, Victor Lasky told Bang-Jensen that Cordier said to him, 'This guy is nuts. He tried to see the President.' Bang-Jensen's jaw dropped. He said, 'But that's true! I did try to see the President!'"

"They knew about the talks in June, 1957," Marshall repeated. He was wondering just how much this knowledge had to do with Bang-Jensen's being relieved of his duties as Deputy Secretary of the Committee after his return from

Denmark in August of that year. "Well, what happened then?"

"After that," Morris replied, frankly, "we had our differences. Bang-Jensen wanted to fight a paper war. He said he was reluctant to take more direct action because of the damage it might do the U.N. I told him that they would defeat him, crush him."

"Did you do anything about the story he told you concerning the potential defectors?"

"Yes. On August fifteenth, 1958, I wrote a memo on the entire matter. I sent copies to Paul, to Barco, and to the Senate Sub-committee on Internal Security."

"Did you see him after that?"

"I called him about six months later. He told me he appreciated and admired my fighting. The situation was affecting him very hard right then."

"And what about his death, do you accept it as suicide?"

"I believe he probably killed himself. What he said in the note decided me."

Peter Marshall could not help but be excited by what he had learned from Robert Morris. Since the beginning of his efforts, the story of defectors and their connection with Paul Bang-Jensen had tantalized and confused him. Now he hoped to get further clarification of this dramatic episode when he paid a call on James Barco, who had been, as Morris pointed out, Bang-Jensen's American contact. Little did Marshall know that, instead of clarification, he would run up against apparent contradictions which, for a time, would only confuse him further.

CHAPTER 27

PETER MARSHALL took an instant liking to James W.
Barco. He hadn't expected to, for the meeting had required
the surmounting of several road blocks. First, there had
been the policeman acting as receptionist in the outer foyer
of the offices of the U. S. Mission to the U.N. at 2 Park
Avenue. The policeman got "A" for effort, but Marshall
was sure the man never really understood the purpose of
his call and strongly suspected him of dangerous intent. A
brief conversation with a woman secretary and then a public-
information officer concluded the foray with the suggestion
that he write a letter. It was thought more propitious than
the direct approach.

He wrote a letter. He got a letter back from Mr. Wallace
Irwin, Jr., Director of Public Services, offering aid and
proposing he come in and talk.

He went in and talked and it was not altogether success-
ful, for discussing Paul Bang-Jensen made Mr. Irwin's
stomach churn. Irwin had never read Bang-Jensen's reply
to Hammarskjold's letter of dismissal. He knew nothing

about the Dane's past performance in the United States before joining the U.N. He thought James Wadsworth's statement was entirely justified because the man had a right to his opinion and the Mission was being swamped with critical letters.

Peter Marshall did not agree, but before they parted, he managed to state the purpose of his visit and he hoped he had convinced Mr. Wallace Irwin, Jr., that he was not out to bring criticism against any organ of the United States Government, so help him God!

Now, some weeks later, James Barco, small and very neatly dressed, affably ushered him into his office.

Wallace Irwin, Jr., was also present, and he and Marshall greeted each other like old school chums.

Barco had a quiet assurance, an aura of quick understanding. By the time they'd gotten seated, Marshall knew this was one American diplomat who had something on the ball.

"Well, where would you like to start?" he asked easily.

"As I understand it, you first knew Bang-Jensen when he was serving the Palestinian Conciliation Commission as its Secretary?"

"That's right. I've been Deputy Representative to the Commission since 1949. It had a Principal Secretary in those days and the purpose of the Commission was to try and iron out a real peace. Later the Principal Secretary became Acting Secretary and Bang-Jensen took over from Doctor Chai in that capacity. That's when I got to know him."

"You liked him?"

"Yes, I did. He was a man wanting to be of service, to do something to help. He attended all the General Assembly and Security Council meetings, not because he had to but, most of the time, because he didn't have anything to do. He wanted to keep himself informed. He wasn't the kind to sit around and be content just occupying office space."

"Was there anything about his character that worried you?"

"Not his character." Barco smiled and adjusted his glasses. "I think his greatest handicap was his accent. It was peculiar, and he was difficult to understand, often very difficult."

"That's right," agreed Wallace Irwin, Jr.; "I remember the one time I talked to him, I didn't understand half of what he said."

"Now, as I understand it," Marshall said, "Bang-Jensen came to you in November of 1956 on a confidential matter."

"Yes, our first meeting took place after the Security Council adjourned on the fourth. I met him by accident at the water cooler outside the General Assembly hall. We talked right there. It was quite informal, but of course it was confidential."

"You had other meetings. Did they take place here?"

"We talked several times up to March when he went abroad with the Committee. On his return, we talked again. Our meetings terminated in June when he went home, and he never renewed them. All our talks took place at the U.N. I knew I could always find him at the General Assembly meetings."

"Well, how did you arrange to meet? I mean, when one talk was over, would you plan for the next?"

"Once or twice I believe I said, 'Next time I come over I'll look you up.' "

"That informal?" Marshall said, puzzled.

"It was all very general. He didn't deal in specifics. Actually the content was such that another man might not have bothered to put it in a report, but I did."

"And it's classified?"

Barco smiled, "Mainly because most everything in this

business is classified. If you knew what the subject was, I don't think you'd find it particularly interesting."

"Not Soviet defectors?"

"Not Soviet defectors." The delegate shook his head.

"Nor Soviet domination of the Secretariat, top floor, nor the effort to get the U.S. to take a stronger stand in Hungary?"

"No, nothing like that either . . . nothing about espionage of any sort. On several occasions I suggested to Bang-Jensen that he talk to Ambassador Lodge, so that he could deal in specifics, but he didn't want to do that."

"Well, I guess we can't go on playing guessing games about the subject of the talks," Marshall said lightly, "but Robert Morris did come to see you, didn't he?"

"Yes, he did, and I told him we'd had the talks, that I'd written the report, and I wasn't at liberty to discuss it."

"Did Bang-Jensen ever ask you not to put his information in writing?"

"No, he did not. And if he had, I'd have had to refuse him. I have to follow certain regulations."

"Of course, Bang-Jensen was breaking regulations by talking to you in the first place."

"Yes, he was. It's not something I go around encouraging, but I'm there if anyone wants to see me."

Peter Marshall sighed. If Bang-Jensen hadn't spoken to Barco about defectors, what *had* he spoken to him about? "Look," he said, "do you think Bang-Jensen was the kind to go around telling lies?"

"Not in my estimation. He might exaggerate a bit to make a point. He wasn't the sort who lied . . . but he never spoke to me about Soviet defectors."

"Bang-Jensen came to us in the summer of '58," the F.B.I. man said. "We talked with him at length."

"Did you think he was mentally okay?"

"He was sane as you or I, a very solid citizen. He was careful and thorough in what he said. We were aware of some of it from other sources, but it wasn't anything we could act on because of our position."

Peter Marshall explained the dates from November to June and, at the time, made a wrong assumption, believing that if Bang-Jensen was having talks with Barco, he must be having them with the defector also.

"The dates are news to me," the F.B.I. man said, but then admitted, "there was a defector picture."

"Do you know his name? Did he represent other possible defectors?"

"No. That's as much as I can say."

"Well, it's good of you to say this much. Do you accept suicide?"

"Yes. What people don't realize is this: a man wears out physically; that, in turn, wears him out mentally. Someone in such a state doesn't think or act as a rational person would."

After the talk was over, Peter Marshall wondered if the F.B.I. man knew that Helen Bang-Jensen had said her husband was in good physical condition. Beyond that, up until his disappearance, he had been thinking and acting rationally.

It was only after some concentrated study of his notes that Peter Marshall got the answer to what Paul Bang-Jensen had discussed with James Barco, and in getting it, he found motivation for murder.

"Now let me get this straight." The editor raised his hand for quiet. "You say Bang-Jensen's talks with Barco all had to do with trying to make an appointment with the President or Allen Dulles?"

"That's what I say. Cordier even admitted to Lasky that

was what Bang-Jensen had tried to, and Cordier told me he knew Bang-Jensen had been having talks with Barco."

"Well, all that proves is that the Secretariat found out what he'd been doing."

"It also backs up Barco. Bang-Jensen never got specific with him, never mentioned Soviet defectors, spies, or dirty work on the thirty-eighth floor. All he asked for was a meeting. Naturally Barco and the State Department must have wondered if he was wacky. It was why Barco suggested Bang-Jensen talk with Lodge to get details. But Bang-Jensen wasn't talking with anyone but the top."

"Didn't you tell me that Henrik Kauffmann said Bang-Jensen met with Dulles in his home?"

"Yes, and that ties in too. It was right after Bang-Jensen had been suspended in December, '57. Kauffmann called him up and invited the whole family down for the week end. Bang-Jensen gave him the bad news and said maybe he'd like to retract the invitation. Kauffmann told him not to be foolish. He said Bang-Jensen had been wanting to see Allen Dulles . . . he'd be there too."

"Well, Paul drove down alone, and he and Allen Dulles sat on a couch for half an hour and made small talk. Dulles didn't seem to know anything about Bang-Jensen's earlier efforts to see him, and Bang-Jensen was dumbfounded. Of course, the thing was that Dulles probably never did know about Bang-Jensen's attempts. Someone down below didn't think it was important enough to pass it on or thought Bang-Jensen was crazy."

"All right, but I still don't see motivation for killing a guy just because the word gets back he's been trying to meet a top man in our government."

"Not then, my friend, but in the summer of '58 Bang-Jensen began to talk in specifics. He'd always been discreet to the nth degree. Now he'd been fired by Hammarskjold.

Now maybe his guard was down, and he talked. Not just to Morris and the F.B.I., but to others. And unfortunately, there aren't very many people on this earth who can keep their mouths shut. Something of what he knew leaked, got to ears that were hostile. It wouldn't have had to be much to make it dangerous for him."

"I'm listening."

"Who was the principal defector, whom did he represent? If I were the Russians, I'd want to know that. Bang-Jensen only assumed the principal defector had been found out. Maybe he hadn't been. . . . More directly, I'd want to know if Bang-Jensen had any proof of Soviet influence on the thirty-eighth floor, or infiltration of our foreign intelligence."

"On the basis of that, you'd kill him?"

"On the basis of two possible conclusions. Either the opposition knew that he had information they didn't have about one of their own and it was dangerous to them, or they weren't sure, and they picked him up to find out. After they'd found out, they couldn't let him go free. Apparent suicide, with enough doubt, would also be an object lesson to any militant anti-Communist in the U.N. I say the fact that he made the mistake of talking about potential defectors—people who had highly explosive information—put him in a dangerous spot. The Russians wouldn't know he'd gone to the F.B.I. They'd only know he was still a menace to them. They knew his character, knew he usually kept his mouth shut. . . . Only, someone he talked to didn't."

"He didn't die until November, '59. Why would they wait so long?"

"David Martin, the Senate Investigator, says they take their time. 'Perfect suicide' is one of their stocks in trade. It's happened to a lot of others. But I think they misjudged their timing. They should have gotten him when he was really in the dumps, not when he was back to almost his normal self."

"You really believe he was murdered?"

"You asked for motivation."

"All right, let's concede motivation. Now all you need is proof."

"Maybe I can't prove it, but I'll try."

CHAPTER **28**

"THE RECORD of the press in this country is a pretty sorry story with regard to Paul's case," Arthur McDowell said. "The *Brooklyn Tablet,* a Catholic paper, the *Indianapolis Star,* the *New Bedford Standard Times,* they backed him all the way, but aside from that, an occasional piece here and there and nothing else." The short, peppery Union official shook his head. "Of course, there were organizations like our own that did all they could: Brutus Coste and the Assembly of Captive European Nations, Baldwin and the International League for the Rights of Man. But I'm afraid we were small voices, very small."

"Didn't your Committee send out a petition in Bang-Jensen's behalf while his case was still before the Tribunal?"

The Executive Secretary-Treasurer of the Council Against Communist Aggression nodded and rubbed his hand down over the silver buttons of his greenish vest. With his ruddy complexion, blond eyebrows tufting, and pale blue eyes, his Scottish ancestry was boldly apparent.

"Yes, we sent a petition to John Foster Dulles. I'm

afraid there were a great many more people who would
not sign it than did. We had only forty-one signatures,
but they ranged from a Vice President of Dupont to
Roscoe Pound of Harvard. You know, twenty years ago
Paul came to this country to study, among other things,
Pound's writings on due process."

"Did you get any assistance from our Congress?"

Arthur McDowell smiled wryly. "Alvin Bentley of Michigan and Wayne Hays of Ohio, they were the only two
who signed. Kennedy would look into it and didn't. James
Roosevelt was too busy in his own district. Wayne Morse
was interested, as was Kenneth Keating—well, I could go
on. The National Education Association didn't have the
time or make the effort to investigate an issue on something that didn't concern teachers or classrooms."

"The stand, of course, was that it was an internal U.N.
affair, isn't that right?"

"Yes, that was the stand," McDowell said, "but it was
strengthened by a lot of U.N. information against Paul
circulated by Clark Eichelberger's American Association
for the U.N."

"After his turn down by the Tribunal in December,
you continued to try and help him," Peter Marshall said.

The Upholsterers' Union official sat down behind his
large, cluttered, convex desk. The light from the window
accentuated the high expanse of forehead. Marshall could
feel the inner force of the man. He supposed it was tem-
pered by the knowledge that Arthur McDowell had been in
the forefront of the battles against Communist infiltration
into the trade unions. He'd fought the Communists on
their own level, recognized their tactics, and outsmarted
them time and again. McDowell was proud of the High-
land blood in his veins, but Marshall detected in him a
quality he'd found in the Hungarians and in all those to
whom he had talked who had fought Communism. It

transcended nationalities, economics, and politics. It was a perception and an awareness of the enemy. It was a strength and a confidence. It was encouraging compared to the wishy-washy attitudes of others whom he had met, refusing to recognize the face of the Devil, welcoming their murderers with gutless sophistry and trying to convince everyone that the forces of darkness were indeed the purveyors of light.

"We few, we happy few, we band of brothers." Paul Bang-Jensen had been one of this small band made up of McDowells, of Horvaths, of Wideners.

"We tried to help him . . . all we could. His depression grew in the late winter months when nothing turned up. I think it reached its low point in the spring, early summer.

"Helen finally forced him to drive down and see us in April. He was going to work for CARE the next week. We tried to cheer him up so he'd shake off his depression. Actually he was objective about his own mood. He recognized the state he was in. He thought he had let Helen down and that she saw him as a weak man. He kept saying to me, 'If only I were a strong man, like you. But I'm a weak man; look what they've done to me! . . . He couldn't see how strong he really was."

"You mentioned Congressmen Bentley and Hays. Didn't they plan a Congressional investigation into his case?"

"In May, Congressman Bentley was ready to go ahead, but Paul said, no. He didn't think he would dare take the witness stand in his condition. He felt he might break down, and that would play right into the hands of all those who had been saying he was mentally unbalanced. So it was dropped."

"Until after he died."

"Yes, but I believe he might have been planning to take action at the time he died."

"I wish I could get proof of that."

"There doesn't seem to be any. Only Helen could answer the question." Peter Marshall didn't tell Arthur McDowell he had asked Helen Bang-Jensen this exact question in a letter, but she had never answered.

"So in May things were still bad," he said.

"I invited him to come to Washington on May eighth to attend a testimonial dinner for the Council Against Communist Aggression. There were over a hundred and twenty guests present. They included Admiral Arleigh Burke and twenty-six Congressmen from both sides of the aisle. Paul refused to sit on the rostrum, but I introduced him. One thing about it, he could have had all his expenses paid, but he wouldn't do that."

"You were in contact with him throughout the summer?"

"Yes, but did you know that for almost eight months Paul's application for a permanent visa to replace his diplomatic one was held up?"

"How come?"

"It got mysteriously mislaid somewhere between Immigration and State. No one seemed to know where it was or why it was being held up. Congressman Bentley helped us there too. But you can imagine the awful worry it caused Paul."

"To add to all his other worries."

"In August our two families had a get-together at his home. One night Paul and I sat talking on his patio into the small hours. The wives and children had long gone to bed. He said we Americans have no conception of how the Secretariat operates and is staffed. We have no desire to accept the truth. He wondered if we could ever develop the maturity to recognize duplicity and strike back.

" 'You're so full of optimism and good fellowship,' he said, 'you don't want to think ill of anyone. Because I confided in one of your security agencies, a man is dead now. What hope can you have of winning the battle when your own F.B.I. can't even cross First Avenue and expose the traitors amongst you? It's bureaucracy gone mad. I tell you I'm so discouraged about American methods of security that I would never trust another one of your security officers about anything.' "

McDowell paused as though listening, as though he could still hear the sound of his friend's voice on that August night.

"He felt responsible for the death of a man. I would assume he was referring to the potential defector whom he tried to help?"

"I would judge so."

"Was he sure he'd been sent home?"

"I didn't ask him, but I know that's how he felt. He also intimated to me that, when he was working with the Hungarian Committee, some of the witnesses were supplied to him by French and American intelligence people with the express understanding that only he would know their names."

Peter Marshall absorbed this new piece of information with surprise, and then asked, not very brightly, "He said that?"

"Yes, it was an 'explicit' agreement. You know, a lot of people have asked why he kept the list at all. Well, he wasn't sure at first, but later he became convinced that the U.N. was set up and operated for a definite pro-Soviet purpose. He knew one method of attack was to charge a person with financial irregularities, and this is why he kept such an accurate account of his expenses with regard to the witnesses."

"I can't get over this part about the intelligence agents."

"You must understand that Paul was extremely discreet until the last year of his life. He was opposed to publicity, but after he'd been fired, he recognized he should have spoken out. 'I should have had people like yourself to help me,' he said."

"I've read some of the releases your organization sent out on the two U.N. white papers that were circulated after his death."

"It's a disgraceful performance on the U.N.'s part. I have a ten-page letter to Eleanor Roosevelt, who attacked our stand on the matter. Perhaps you could use it.[1] You know, Mr. Marshall, one of the greatest tragedies of Paul's story is the fact that he was a good liberal, and he was completely deserted by so many others who consider themselves good liberals."

"And his death: you accept suicide, that he was worn out and could fight no longer?"

"When he was missing, I never considered suicide. In all the time I knew him, I never thought that. . . . I know also, Mr. Marshall, he had a devout belief in God."

CHAPTER 29

"THIS IS where Paul worked," Gordon Alderfer, a department head at CARE, said simply.

Peter Marshall saw a cubby-hole office, about six by six feet, enclosed by shoulder-high frosted glass. It was jammed between two other similar but somewhat larger office areas. On the glass beside the open entry was the number "13." Inside was a chair and a scratched desk . . . a coat rack. No window.

For a moment Marshall and Alderfer were silent. The contrast—from the waxed and carpeted corridors and the vista windows of the U.N. building three blocks up First Avenue to this! That had been Paul Bang-Jensen's fate.

"Will you come talk to Mr. Reuter?" asked Alderfer, a slightly built man with a characteristic of nervousness and intense eyes.

He led Marshall down a corridor to the Executive Director's office. Reuter welcomed them and they sat down at a long conference table. "Gordon told me of your project," Reuter said, nodding toward Alderfer. "I'm rushing to get off to Afghanistan on a six-week trip, but all of us will be glad to help you in any way we can.

"I think I should tell you how much we all liked Paul. He fitted in perfectly. He was the kind of man any organization can be proud of."

"What were the conditions of his employment?"

"We hired Paul for the contribution he could make. We had a need and we called on him to fill it. It was arranged that he would work for us six months as a consultant, and it was understood that he could look for another position that better fitted his abilities while he was here. Well, he came with us in April, and as you know, he hadn't come up with anything else by fall. We were pleased to renew his contract with us.

"Paul was in low spirits when he came here. But I think it's everybody's impression that he improved tremendously during the succeeding months. I personally think he made a great deal of progress. . . . Yes, I knew he went to a psychiatrist, but he never gave any hint that he was preparing to do away with himself. His work was appreciated. He got along fine with everybody. He was a real gentleman.

"At the weekly review meetings, Paul often had valuable comments to offer. You know, about ten days before his death he came to me with an idea for expediting certain CARE organizational matters. He suggested changes that were constructive and well thought out, and they were accepted."

Reuter touched his gold watch chain meditatively. "The one thing that impressed me was that, for a man that was going out to kill himself, he wasn't moping around. Here was a man who was active—at least in his business here—right up to the last week. As a matter of fact, the reason we know he didn't come in that Monday morning is because a secretary had left revisions of his plan on his desk for him to check over."

Reuter paused. "I'll just mention this because I thought it rather odd. Neither the police nor, as far as I know, any other similar agency ever came around to check into Paul's effects . . . papers and like that. It would have seemed normal to check here, that's all."

Later, Marshall went to lunch at Tudor City with Alderfer and two CARE associates, John Boland and Dr. Ralph Greenlaw. Boland, a soft-spoken man with a distinctly Irish face, had been Bang-Jensen's immediate superior and had the office to the right of the Dane's "13." Greenlaw, a tall, lanky former college professor, was Bang-Jensen's neighbor on the other side.

"We were all shocked at Paul's death," Alderfer said. "No one could believe it. As Dick Reuter said, when he came to CARE, he was pretty low. We had plans that he do some work that required compilation and headwork. He told us frankly that he wasn't up to it. I said: 'Take your time, get a look around here.' I know how it is to make adjustments in a new place. I knew he had the ability. Over the period he was here, I would say he showed a general upward curve . . . a rising curve with dips and climbs on the way."

"How did he get along with everyone?"

"Very well. Everyone was on a first-name basis with him," Boland said. "We all lunched around together at the restaurants in the airline terminal building, at Ferdi's, places like that. U.N. friends used to come over and shake hands with him there."

"I can give you an idea of his personality," said Greenlaw. "I came to CARE after Paul, and he made it a point to invite me out to lunch, get acquainted, make me feel at home."

"Of course," Boland said, "he wasn't any social butterfly. He didn't go to CARE functions of that nature. He was a home-body type. I knew he loved his family above all. On Monday mornings he would talk about his weekend, the way people do. Sometimes he'd have blisters on his hands and would tell me about the work he had been doing in his garden."

"His last week at CARE, was there anything unusual?" Marshall asked.

"It was noticed that Paul was out of the office quite a bit of the time," Alderfer answered. "He had carte blanche to come and go as he wanted. This was so that he could have every opportunity to look around for another job. No one thought anything about his being away, but I remembered it afterward. No one knew where he went."

"Did he leave anything in his office?"

"There was a plastic raincoat and a hat in his office. He seldom wore a hat. The raincoat was there in case of bad weather."

Marshall looked around the table. "What are your feelings about his death? Suicide or not?"

Alderfer replied, "I told you. I was physically ill when I heard the news. As hard as it is for me to believe it, I think he might have killed himself. But I don't know."

"He shouldn't have, he needn't have . . . but I can understand it," Greenlaw said. "He was psychologically the type who might commit suicide."

Boland impatiently interrupted. "I'm convinced he did not do away with himself. If it wasn't hypnosis, or brain washing, I think that somehow he was forced to kill himself."

"How?"

"Through his family, perhaps. Through a threat that was made against his family's safety."

Back at CARE, Boland asked Peter Marshall to come into his office. "I just wanted to show you this," he said.

"This will give you some idea of how well Paul was functioning at the end."

Boland handed a stapled typewritten report to Marshall. "This is an example of the work that Paul was able to handle in the fall. It's a report dealing with a CARE project in Libya. There are a lot of figures in it, it took quite a bit of research. It's very clear. Paul did a fine job."

"Isn't this the sort of work he was originally supposed to do?"

"Exactly," Boland said, "it makes it obvious that Paul was a pretty normal citizen. I remember, when he first came here, he was so low that sometimes he wouldn't come back to work after lunch. I went over to the airline terminal to get him one afternoon. I found him sitting on a bench, staring at nothing. It was like going out to bring your father home from the pub. 'Hello, Paul,' I said. 'Hello, John,' he answered. . . . 'Would you like to come back with me?' I asked him. 'Yes, John.' And we came back together.

"But toward the last weeks he was here, he was taking his job so seriously that once I had to calm him down when he became concerned about a CARE program he thought wasteful.

"As a matter of fact, in the end, he was trying to help me on a personal problem of my own—a religious problem I have. Figure that out. Here was a man who came here in some despair, who needed our help, and in the run of things he could think of us. That gives you an idea of the measure of the man.

"He hadn't forgotten about Hungary either. About the list of witnesses, he told me: 'I did what I thought should be done, and I know that what I did was right.' And it weighed on his mind that the General Assembly was meeting again on Hungary on November twenty-third—that was the day he disappeared. He said to me about a week before: 'My God! They're going to bring it up all over again

. . . and nothing will come out of it. The truth won't come out.' "

Boland riffled through the report Bang-Jensen had prepared. "Yes, he was quite a person. Kept up with international events. Was doing good work here. He was anxious to go on. It was wise of CARE to keep his employment on a sort of temporary basis. I think that one thing that Paul feared was that he might become permanent here. And he wanted to do more."

CHAPTER 30

ON FRIDAY, August 25, 1959, Paul Bang-Jensen left the
CARE offices at noon to go to lunch. He left alone. On the
corner of 42nd Street and First Avenue he met a man whom
he had formerly known at the U.N. Bang-Jensen thought
the meeting was chance, but in view of what followed,
Peter Marshall believed it might have been planned.

Later, in relating the encounter to his wife and to Dr.
Friedenberg, Bang-Jensen did not divulge the name of the
man whom he met. He identified him only as an officer in
the Soviet bloc at the U.N.

Where the two went after their meeting, Peter Marshall
did not know. Whether the man was one of the original
potential defectors, he did not know. All he knew was the
important details of their conversation. From what he had
learned, it went like this:

*"Paul, I hate to say it, but you underestimated the forces
you were up against."*

*"No, I don't think I ever did that. I fully recognize them.
But why do you say so?"*

"You thought security was bad. Do you realize I have actually heard tape recordings of Hungarian witnesses testifying in Vienna . . . those people who did not want their identities known."

"You can't mean it! They had microphones planted and—"

"Yes, yes! I've even heard your voice taking preliminary testimony. Now do you see what I mean? Do you see how you underestimated them, even knowing as much as you do!"

"No, no, I'm not surprised, not surprised at anything. But listen to me, my friend!" And now he was excited. *"If you could get one of those tapes, just one of them, do you realize I could exonerate myself! Do you realize I could prove beyond all doubt that I was not crying wolf . . . that I was right!"*

"I don't know if it would be possible. You can understand my position."

"Of course, of course! But you must try. If there are these tapes, if—how soon would you be able to find out if there's any chance? Could you do it this afternoon!"

"I don't know, and I wouldn't dare call you."

"All right, then we'll meet again. Look, my wife and children are going to the Cape this weekend. I'll meet you here in town on Sunday, wherever you say!"

"Paul, I don't know if I can do anything."

"You must try! Say you'll meet me on Sunday!"

Paul Bang-Jensen was excited and elated by the startling news. If he could only get one of the tapes. On Sunday, August 27, he met the Soviet official again, and he was told it was no use. The man could not produce.

But, Peter Marshall mused, was this man a decoy? Someone to lead Paul Bang-Jensen on? Why give him such news, if he could not produce? Why tell him anything if he was a member of the Soviet bloc, loyal or disloyal? How did you just happen to bump into Paul Bang-Jensen at noon on the corner of 42nd Street to give him such information if it wasn't all planned? The second meeting ended with the door still open:

"If anything happens, Paul, if there's any chance, I'll contact you . . . but you realize how dangerous it is?"

There was substantial evidence that other meetings had followed. One indication came from Janos Horvath, who recalled that, in their final talk on September 25, Paul Bang-Jensen had made several remarks, the gist of them being: *"Don't count me out on Hungary. I'm getting new information. Not all the people I'm dealing with are friendly."*

About a month before his disappearance, Paul Bang-Jensen called his wife and said he'd be a little late, he wanted to go to the public library. He did not arrive home until one in the morning. He did not explain his lateness, and his wife did not ask. This was the first time in their seventeen years of marriage he had ever done such a thing. His thoughtfulness toward his wife and children was an unvarying characteristic to the very end, but now he said nothing.

From those close to Paul Bang-Jensen, Peter Marshall knew that, more than any other time since he had become discouraged in the winter months, the last week of the Dane's life was his best.

Twice in those final days Paul Bang-Jensen and his wife went out together. Once they went to a movie. On Friday, they attended a PTA meeting. Bang-Jensen took part. He spoke. He appeared in good spirits to those around him.

Saturday he took his oldest daughter, Karen, and some of her friends into the city for a treat.

Sunday, after going to church with his family, he spent a pleasant, restful day.

Monday, November 23, Paul Bang-Jensen rose, as was his

routine, to fix breakfast for the older children. Karen helped him. She noticed nothing unusual about her father's behavior, nor did his wife. All in the family were acutely aware of his moods, even Nina, the youngest. They detected nothing, suspected nothing, had no premonition.

He went to his wife, who would get up shortly to prepare breakfast for the youngsters. He kissed her. It was the last goodbye.

And then he left his home and walked down the familiar street to where William Wetzlar would offer him a ride.

And, all the time, in his pocket was a gun with a fully loaded clip of shells. It was a gun he had bought in the war years for protection.

Peter Marshall asked himself, did he carry it that morning not to take his own life . . . but to guard it?

The editor had asked for motivation, and Peter Marshall had discovered that motivation for murder did exist. But the larger question had always been—what would make Paul Bang-Jensen leave home with a gun in his pocket, if not for the reason that was so obvious to the police?

If he knew on that bleak November morning he was going not to his office at CARE but to meet someone, and if that someone had said, "I think I can take you to a person who can tell you how to get hold of the tapes . . . but it may be dangerous," then would not Paul Bang-Jensen have pocketed his gun?

Cloak-and-dagger stuff? There were elements in what Peter Marshall had learned, and undercurrents in what he suspected, that would make most fictionalized cloaks and daggers look pale.

From start to finish, there had only been one trait in the character of Paul Bang-Jensen that pointed toward the ultimate extreme of suicide. It was his discouragement and despondency over his economic future. And although the worry was still there at the time of his death, he had come to accept it and had, through his own strength of purpose, slowly and painfully climbed up from the pit of despair in which he had found himself in those earlier months.

Other than that, everything in this extraordinary man cried out against the senselessness of self-extermination. Could such a man leave the wife and children for whom he cared so much and, by his act, fill their lives with sadness and loss, irreparable? Could he torture them by his absence for over two and one half days . . . all those hours, those long, empty, silent hours? Could this man, who destroyed his career to protect the lives of others, premeditatedly throw his own life away for the lack of a better job?

Could then a man with so fine a character, so strong a spirit, so sure a faith, throw all away because his spirit had been broken and his faith destroyed?

He could, if spirit and faith were gone, but they were not gone in Paul Bang-Jensen when he had left home that last Monday morning.

More than belief, however, Peter Marshall knew that it would take evidence to prove his theory, and so bring the attention of the proper authorities back to the matter. Did he have that sort of evidence?

The day was cold and colorless, and there was no hint of spring in earth or sky. It would be winter forever. He walked the rutted, iron-hard bridle path, taking his time, knowing he would come to that resting place once more.

Bundled in his parka, he tried to bundle his thoughts against the lonely woodland scene; the leaves dead and matted, the trees bare and dismal, the scattered newspapers cluttering the underbrush, attesting the messy thoughtlessness of man.

Why had he come here, really? Did he think he would find an answer here in this pitiful bit of country? What answer was here? . . . It was only a resting place.

It seemed years ago that he had taken that flight from Chicago, years ago that he had set out to find the answers to three questions in a man's life. Now he knew two answers for sure.

Paul Bang-Jensen had been unjustly accused, unjustly tried, and unjustly fired from the United Nations. Five days after he had been fired, this last great hope for mankind had held a commemorative dinner to observe the tenth anniversary of its declaration of human rights.

Paul Bang-Jensen had, while serving the Special Committee on Hungary, attempted to help several Soviets wishing to join the West, bringing with them information of great importance. Having this knowledge himself, and knowing that it went directly to the heart of the Secretariat, would explain to the dullest his tremendous concern over the preparation of the Hungarian report.

Two questions answered, and the third . . . death.

Peter Marshall had said to his editor, "I agree the autopsy report needs explaining . . . Gun in the hand, gun not in the hand. Stains on both hands, mark on the thumb. No estimated time of death, no powder burns around the wound. The position as reported by those first to view the body, and then the position as reported by the police. It may all have a very simple explanation. I know it's important, but there are two other points that are far more important."

"The time of death?"

"Yes, it's much later than anyone has concluded."

"If you accept George Hageman's word."

"I have no reason not to. He passed the spot twice with his dog that Wednesday afternoon around four. And he and his wife heard a shot that night at eleven."

"Which might not have been a shot at all."

"Granted, so leave it at four o'clock Wednesday afternoon, and say that he died sometime after that. I think it would make a large difference in the minds of a lot of people."

"Maybe. What's the other point?"

"The note that was found in his pocket. There are things about it—to me, it almost seems as if he was doing his best to tell his wife, to tell his friends, what he had said in that memo two years ago. 'I would never commit suicide. Any note to the contrary would be a fake!'"

"But the death note, I thought you said, was a rather noble farewell."

"Never mind what I said once upon a time. First, the date at the top of the page says 'Nov. 59.' Bang-Jensen was a meticulous person. In all the letters he wrote which I've gotten hold of, he put the day of the month, the year in full, and in all but one instance wrote out the month in full."

"Well, didn't Clifford Forster say he thought he wrote the note sometime in November and carried it around with him?"

"I know what Clifford said. That's his theory, and this is mine. If he was going to put the date, he'd have put the whole date. It's just an incongruity of character."

"But a person out to shoot himself isn't rational."

"No, so why bother with a date? What's more important is one line, the key line in the note. *I underestimated the forces I was up against.* Don't you realize that was one thing he never had done—but once? His wife, his doctor, his friends, anyone who knew him knew that, above all things, he recognized the enemy. He recognized him fully and only regretted that more of us didn't. Now, to both his wife and Friedenberg, he repeated that same phrase spoken to him by the unknown man he had met on 42nd Street in August, the man who had given him hope.

"And this was his way of telling his wife that he'd been

trapped, and that for once he *had* underestimated the enemy.

"I don't think we could prove it in court, but there's one more thing to back it up. On the bottom of the right-hand page of that note, you may recall I said I noticed the scribbled number 6 with a small capital 'A.' I figured if it meant anything, it had to mean something very significant—a last chance to indicate this was not what it seemed—'the perfect suicide.' "

"Well, all right, what does it mean?"

"The address where the Committee took testimony from the Hungarians in Vienna was number '6A.' It's a big six with a smaller capital 'A.' That's exactly how Bang-Jensen scribbled it on the bottom of the note . . . so exactly that it doesn't seem that it could refer to anything else. The U.N. voted the day he disappeared to debate Hungary. Suppose he'd been able to show up with just one of those tapes the Russians got at '6A'? We don't know for sure, but he'd told his wife about the secret tapes. It could be that '6A' was hurriedly written on the bottom of the death note in a last desperate hope to tell her he'd been trapped in the attempt.

" '*I understimated the forces I was up against.*' He underestimated them once, and he wrote it to show he was not taking his own life . . . that it was being taken from him!"

Peter Marshall came down the path and passed the point where it spilled out onto 233rd Street and 67th Avenue. He'd only seen a few walkers, and he was glad not to see more. The light was fading and the deadness of the cold had grabbed his feet.

God, would it never grow warm again! Would these ugly trees ever take leaf? Would the ground soften and birds sing once more?

Four months ago Paul Bang-Jensen had walked this path. Had he come to it with the willingness to end his life, or had he come forced to it?

For all the digging, and supposing, and finding of contradictions on the part of Peter Marshall, it could have been suicide . . . it could have been. But if it was—if it was that indeed, then Peter Marshall would take a line from the Danes who said: "No matter who pulled the trigger, it was murder."

He came to the place where they had found the body of Paul Bang-Jensen. He looked down at the empty, unrevealing spot, and a gasp went out of him.

The dead leaves had been pushed away, and in the hard, brown earth, someone had scratched the sign of a cross.

Appendices

APPENDIX 1 BANG-JENSEN'S MEMO TO HIS WIFE

[Reprinted from *U.S.A.*, Jan. 28, 1960, by courtesy of Alice Widener.]

MEMORANDUM

"Friday afternoon, 22 November 1957, I [Povl Bang-Jensen] handed my memorandum of that day to Dr. Protitch [Dragoslav Protitch, Yugoslav, U.N. Under Secretary for Political and Security Council Affairs]. Monday morning, 25 November, I was asked to come to see Dr. Sze, the head of the [U.N.] Health Clinic, at 2:30 p.m., I supposed on account of my 'Asian flu' last month.

"Dr. Sze somewhat nervously and without any preliminaries, stated as soon as I sat down, that it was not an administrative matter when he had asked to see me and that I was under no obligation, but he had been told that I recently had been under a great nervous strain—'what we in the Health Service hardly can believe from what we know of you'—but that the Health

Service was available and also had psychiatric advisers if I would like their help.

"I could not help smiling, and told Dr. Sze that I hoped he would not think I actually was mad when I laughed at this charge against me. I had to some extent anticipated something like this. When somebody did something seriously wrong, it was often the most clever to do it in such a bold manner, that people in general would say that nobody would dare to do that, and then accuse persons who actually did find out, of being mad, unbalanced or imagining things. In my very first memorandum to the Secretary-General [Dag Hammarskjold], six months ago, I had stated that certain people, no doubt, since they had no other defense, would maintain that I was overworked. I had therefore, I said, inserted a paragraph in that memorandum to prevent such an allegation:

'Since the person in question probably will realize that he hardly can make many believe I am a liar, he will no doubt insist that I am imagining things on account of overwork. I think Lennart Finmark [at that time Swedish personal assistant to Secretary-General Hammarskjold], with whom I had lunch today will be able to reassure you, if necessary, that I, at least, have maintained my sense of humour. In fact, after having lacked sufficient work for years—I wonder if you realize *how* overstaffed the Secretariat is—I have enjoyed tremendously coming back to a brisk working pace. May I assure you, half facetiously, but truthfully, that I feel better, eat better and sleep better than I have done for years.'

"I quoted that paragraph according to memory to Dr. Sze, and told him that it still held true. I could get annoyed about my children's peccadillos, but the matter in which I had taken action was much too serious and big to be excited or upset about it, the only way to take it was philosophically and, in spite of its sadness and seriousness, with a certain amount of humour. I could therefore assure him that I had not lost one hour of sleep on account of this matter. I said that I fall asleep five minutes after I put my head on the pillow, I sleep like a baby, and usually wake up exactly five minutes before the alarm clock is set to go off, so I can stop it in advance in order that it does not wake up my wife.

"Dr. Sze told me smilingly that I apparently was doing better than most, and that he was glad to see that I had maintained my sense of humour; this was indeed important in this kind of situation. I answered that I had had it refreshed during my recent 'flu', during which time I had re-read the classic Chinese philosophers, who know so much about human character.

"When I told him that the amount of work with the Hungarian Committee was not more than I had been accustomed to as an attorney, and during the war as Counselor of the Danish Embassy to Washington, it turned out that Dr. Sze [son of the former Chinese Ambassador to Washington] was a friend of Henrik Kauffman [former Danish Ambassador to Washington], and I suggested that he might ask Kauffman about me." * * *

(Note: The next sixty-five words have been deleted from Bang-Jensen's memorandum. They are favorable to him, but have been omitted to protect the person and position of an employee of the United Nations. They have been made known by me to proper authorities of the U.S. Government.)

"I also suggested that he might speak to .... [a U.N. official well known to Dr. Sze]. Nobody in the Political Department knew the full story, but I thought that those who knew some of it, rather than worrying about my nerves, were surprised that I could take everything so calmly; in fact, several had told me so. I intended to maintain the same detached and patient attitude, and I was sure I should be able to do so on account of the seriousness of the matter; I hoped one day I should become wise enough also to take small matters, as children's misbehaviour, quite as philosophically.

"Dr. Sze laughed and thanked me for coming; he repeated that it had sounded quite unlikely to him, that I would succumb to a nervous strain. He then pressed my hand firmly saying good-bye and added: 'And good luck to you.'

"The conversation lasted 5 to 10 minutes.

"My wife, who has been a calm, courageous and clear-minded advisor and who, like me, first was greatly amused about the call from Dr. Sze, has later begun to worry about this story which she connects with certain other facts. She fears, now that it is clear that I will not retreat, that the circles outside the Secretariat, *ultimately* responsible for the sabotage, might have decided that it is necessary to risk having me disappear out the window, or similarly, in 'a fit of depression.'

"I do not think so myself, because I believe that those circles will realize that I have taken safeguards to assure in that case that the proper authorities would receive documentary proof about what has been going on in the Secretariat.

"My wife has, nevertheless, insisted that I should inform a few of my friends, that under no circumstances would I commit suicide. I have done so, though reluctantly, since I fear my friends might think I am getting a little dramatic.

"My wife has also asked me to write this memorandum to her, and to make it clear also in this, that under no circumstances whatsoever would I ever commit suicide. This would be completely contrary to my whole nature and to my religious convictions. If any note was found to the opposite effect in my handwriting, it would be a fake.

(signed) Povl Bang-Jensen
Lake Success, 30 November 1957."

APPENDIX 2 LETTER OF RECOMMENDATION FROM NIELS BOHR

January 14, 1959

GL. CARLSBERG
COPENHAGEN

To Whom It May Concern!

First time I met Povl Bang-Jensen was on a journey to U.S.A. in 1939 when, after having completed his studies at the University of Copenhagen and started practicing law there, he was going to pursue researches in international law at the University of Chicago. I had already heard about the great esteem with which he was held in University circles and among his colleagues, and in our talks on the journey I was myself greatly impressed by his intelligence and the width of his knowledge and interests.

When during the war, in 1943, I returned to U.S.A. as member of a British scientific mission, Povl Bang-Jensen had joined the staff of the Danish Embassy in Washington under Ambassador Henrik Kauffmann who with such courage and wisdom worked for his country in its precarious situation. The loyalty and efficiency with which Bang-Jensen participated in these endeavours were admired by us all, and I know that Ambassador Kauffmann himself in a separate statement has expressed his high appreciation of Bang-Jensen's assistance in the many difficult problems with which the embassy in those years was confronted.

Since that time, I have kept in contact with Povl Bang-Jensen both on my journeys to U.S.A. and on his visits to Denmark. Always I found him a most faithful friend with whom it was a great benefit to discuss general outlooks for mankind and in particular the urgent problems connected with atomic energy developments involving such unique promises as well as unprecedented dangers for our whole civilization. Indeed, I feel greatly indebted to Bang-Jensen for advice and assistance which he on many occasions has given me in these matters.

After Povl Bang-Jensen in 1949 left the Danish Embassy in Washington to join the Secretariat of the United Nations Organization in New York, I also had opportunity on several occasions to learn about his devotion to the cause of this organization with which he worked for ten years. Due, however, to divergency of viewpoints in connection with his service with the U.N. Committee reporting about the tragic events in Hungary, this work has recently been terminated and he is therefore looking for another position where he can find proper opportunity to make fruitful his talents and wide experience.

On the background of my long acquaintance and friendship with Povl Bang-Jensen I take pleasure in recommending him most warmly as a man of high human ideals and of power of devoting himself with great zeal and effect to constructive endeavours.

(Signed) Niels Bohr

APPENDIX 3 MEMO: ALLEGED DUTIES OF THE DEPUTY SECRETARY

[Date of this note, "Mid-January 1957," appears to have been typed in at some later time.]

COPY

ANNEX A
NOTE BY MR. JORDAN, APPROVED BY DR. PROTITCH, MID-JANUARY 1957

*Special Committee on
the Problem of Hungary*

DUTIES OF THE DEPUTY SECRETARY

Liaison with Conference Section regarding physical arrangements for meetings, Conference Room, Interpreters, Precis Writers, etc. Insertion of notice in daily "Journal". Drafting of agenda when necessary.

Informing and keeping in touch with Chairman and Delegates regarding calling of meetings and cancellation of meetings.

Questions regarding technical aspects of documentation and translation.

Handling of practical arrangements for appearance of witnesses.

Drafting of official correspondence relating to working of the Special Committee.

APPENDIX 4 Memo Naming Bang-Jensen Keeper of Secret Register

Annex V No. 2

8 February 1957

Mr. B. R. Turner,
Controller.

Mr. A. Cordier,
Executive Assistant to the Secretary-General.

Payments to Hungarian refugees who testify at UN headquarters before the Committee on the Problems of Hungarian Refugees.

Certain Hungarian refugees, who wish to remain anonymous, will testify before the Committee on the Problem of Hungary now meeting at headquarters. The Secretary-General has approved the following arrangements concerning re-imbursement of expenses which the refugees will incur by appearing before the Committee.

1. Each refugee witness will be entitled to re-imbursement for the cost of round trip transportation between his home and UN headquarters, and in addition will be entitled to $10 for each day or fraction thereof that he testifies before the Committee. This per diem is paid in lieu of reimbursement of actual expenses for meals, lodging, taxes, and all incidental expenses.

2. You are authorized to make the payment set forth in paragraph (1) on petty cash vouchers made payable to "Refugee 1", "Refugee 2", etc., without further identification. The cash payable against vouchers will be picked up by the Assistant Secretary of the Committee, Mr. P. Bang-Jensen, who will sign for receipt of the funds and be responsible for turning them over to the entitled witnesses.

3. Mr. Bang-Jensen will be responsible for maintaining a secret register showing the names of the witnesses identified by number only on the petty cash vouchers. *This register will not be available to the Controller's staff,* but when the Committee has

completed taking testimony at headquarters the Under-Secretary for the Department of Political and Security Council affairs will notify the Controller of the total number of refugee witnesses who have appeared before the Committee.

cc: Mr. Muckell
Mr. Correa
Mr. Kien
Mr. Lloyd-Herman
Mr. Bang-Jensen
Mr. D. Stewart
Mr. V. Mills

APPENDIX 5 Telegram Sent to Prospective Witnesses

COPY
28 FEB. 1957

Office of the   3528   **PSCA**
Under-Secretary   3391

No distribution

DR. _____

COULD YOU APPEAR AS A WITNESS BEFORE COMMITTEE, IF DESIRED ANONYMOUSLY, IN GENEVA MONDAY ELEVEN MARCH AT THREE PM STOP TRAVELING EXPENSES BEING REIMBURSED STOP CABLE COLLECT

POVL BANGJENSEN
SPECIAL COMMITTEE ON PROBLEM OF HUNGARY
UNITED NATIONS

Dr. Protitch, Under Secretary, Dept. of
Political and Security Council Affairs

APPENDIX 6 — MEMO FROM WILLIAM JORDAN TO BANG-JENSEN

Annex II No. 2B

31 May 1957

I am as Secretary of Committee, and after consulting Mr. Narayanan, as Head of the Department, giving you this instruction:

My instruction is that you spend this afternoon in the study of Chapter XVI of the Report and that you abstain from attendance at the Committee.

APPENDIX 7 — BANG-JENSEN'S LETTER TO HIS SUPERIOR

Annex II No. 1

CONFIDENTIAL

4 June 1957

TO: Mr. T.G. Narayanan
Officer in Charge of the
Department of Political and Security
Council Affairs

FROM: Povl Bang-Jensen
Deputy Secretary, UN Special Committee

SUBJECT: *Report of the UN Special Committee on Hungary*

The Special Committee on Hungary today preliminarily adopted its draft report. The final meeting is scheduled for Friday, 7 June, at 3 p.m.

The members of the Committee and its Rapporteur, Ambassador Shann, are unaware that the report, as adopted, contains several dozens of errors of fact, which the Secretary of the Committee, in spite of my insistence, has refused to call to the Rapporteur's attention. With regard to questions of form and presentation, I have felt that I, as Deputy Secretary, should leave these and other questions of judgment to Mr. Jordan and the Rapporteur. I have felt, however, that it was my duty to call indisputable errors of fact to Mr. Jordan's attention, and that it, in my opinion, was his duty, as I have repeatedly stated to him, to let me show him the record, if there is any doubt in his mind, and then call the errors to the Rapporteur's attention.

None of the many factual errors in the report are of any significance for the main conclusions reached by the Committee. On the contrary, many of the correct facts further support the conclusions. However, some of the errors are of such a nature that they, if they are found out, would shake the general confidence in the reliability of the report and in some cases embarrass the members of the Committee. Statements in one Chapter might for instance contradict the statements in another; quotations might be attributed to the wrong source; incorrect hearsay evidence has been utilized instead of available testimony by eye-witnesses; the provisions of the Constitution of Hungary are incorrectly reported, etc.

The public will hardly be able to understand, that it has been absolutely impossible for the members themselves personally to check the correctness of the thousands of facts which are contained in the report. The members had largely to limit themselves to be certain with regard to the facts which are essential for the conclusions. Otherwise they have had to rely on the Secretariat, which, therefore, as the Chairman has pointed out several times during the meetings, in this respect has a particularly heavy responsibility.

There are 2,000 pages of testimony, and this is only a part of the material available to the Committee, which has to be checked. Hungarian newspapers, broadcasts, public addresses, legislation, numerous memoranda and much more has to be studied. Nobody needs to be ashamed because he does not find the many errors of fact in the drafts; nor should anybody in the staff be blamed because his first, and even what he considers his final draft, on close examination, by many pairs of eyes, little by little proves to contain several unexpected errors of facts. So did my own drafts, although I perhaps have had a better opportunity than anybody else, to become acquainted with and memorize the evidence, because I handled the witnesses outside the meetings. It so happens that I as a lawyer have participated in, what members of the Supreme Court of Denmark have described as the two most involved cases in Danish legal history. I can truthfully say, that they were not more difficult to prepare than this report. Nobody has, therefore, reason to feel embarrassed.

Nevertheless, when the errors first have been found, it is not too difficult to check whether they are correct or not, although in some cases it might be necessary to read and compare testimony from several witnesses and other evidence. In many cases it might also be essential that the person who finds the error has the opportunity to call attention to the evidence he has found, which has been overlooked or misunderstood—sometimes because the English verbatim record of the testimony has not been rechecked with the Hungarian record. Still, it is a relatively simple matter, and there is no good reason why the erroneous facts, once they were pointed out, have not been corrected before the drafts went to the Rapporteur for his approval; if not then, then at least before they went to translation, or at the very latest, before the drafts were discussed and preliminarily approved by the Committee. The whole report could in fact have been ready at least a week ago if this had been done.

Considering the delicacy of the matter, and in order not to stir up more heat than necessary until the urgently needed action to rectify the errors of fact in the draft-report has been taken, I shall prefer, unless requested of me, not to go into details beyond saying that the Secretary repeatedly has refused to call errors of fact, well known to him, to the Rapporteur's attention and that he has ordered me not to speak to the Chairman and the Rapporteur about the report, even in his presence.

Serious as the errors are, the whole draft could be made in perfect order—including translations—in 24 hours, provided normal cooperation can be expected. Only a very few pages would have to be rewritten and drafts for these are already prepared. The Rapporteur would be able to state in good conscience that no fundamental change had been made in the draft report, but that the suggestions of the members of the Committee had been incorporated, certain factual errors, which had been found by rechecking, corrected, and a few essential facts, which had been left out by oversight in the haste, been added. He could in a couple of minutes call any changes which possibly could interest them to the members attention.

From a personal point of view, I should much prefer to be relieved of my duties as Deputy Secretary. I fear, however, that this, as conditions are in this building, would shortly be known by the press, thus causing embarrassment to the United Nations and undermining the work of the Committee on Hungary. Besides, the errors of fact have to be explained at least to the Rapporteur and corrected, before the final meeting of the Committee on Friday afternoon.

I take it that you urgently will bring this memorandum to the attention of the Secretary-General or Mr. Cordier, and that you will also inform Dr. Protitch. Until tonight, I had hoped that my many warnings to Mr. Jordan during the past four months and my appeals to him as a friend would have been sufficient to straighten out everything so that I would not have had to raise this delicate and sad matter.

APPENDIX 8 REPORT ON BANG-JENSEN FROM JORDAN TO ANDREW CORDIER

Annex II No. 2

5 June 1957

TO: Mr. Andrew W. Cordier,
          Executive Assistant to the Secretary-General

THROUGH: Mr. T. G. Narayanan, Officer in Charge,
          Political and Security Council Affairs

FROM: W. M. Jordan, Secretary,
          Special Committee on the Problem of Hungary
          and Acting Director of Political Affairs Division

I informed you last night that Mr. Bang-Jensen had indicated to me his intention to speak to the Secretary-General regarding his objections to the Report of the Special Committee on the Problem of Hungary. In these circumstances, I felt compelled to bring the matter forthwith to your attention.

It had been my intention to raise the matter of Mr. Bang-Jensens' conduct in accordance with normal administrative procedure immediately upon the completion of the report. Taking the circumstances as a whole into account, I have no doubt that such was the wisest course in the interests of the work of the Committee. In this view the Rapporteur fully concurred.

I now therefore transmit (a) the memorandum of 30 May 1957, handed to me by the Rapporteur; (b) the terms of my communication to Mr. Bang-Jensen on 31 May 1957 directing him to abstain from attendance at the Committee. This communication was made by telephone; (c) a memorandum (unsigned) handed to me by Mr. Bang-Jensen on Friday night, 31 May; (d) a memorandum by myself on the problem, drawn up on Saturday last, 1 June 1957.

In view of Mr. Bang-Jensen's refusal to accept and abide by instructions, I would deem it appropriate that he be relieved of any further responsibilities arising from his position as Deputy Secretary of the Committee. In view of his general conduct in matters relating to the work of the Committee, I consider that he should be required forthwith to take sick leave, since I have no doubt that Mr. Bang-Jensen is a very sick man.

APPENDIX 9 MEMO TO CORDIER FROM T. G. NARAYANAN, WHO PASSES

Annex II No. 3

5 June 1957

TO: Mr. Andrew W. Cordier
       Executive Assistant to the Secretary-General

FROM: T. G. Narayanan, Officer in charge

of the Department of Political and Security Council
Affairs

SUBJECT: *Secretariat of the Special Committee on the Problem
of Hungary*

1. I am transmitting to you a memorandum, together with attachments, from Mr. W.M. Jordan as well as a memorandum from Mr. P. Bang-Jensen.

2. In view of my total lack of knowledge of and responsibility for either the substantive or administrative aspects of the work of the Committee or its Secretariat, since such had never officially come within my purview as Officer-in-charge of the Department or otherwise, I am unable to comment on any of the allegations in the memoranda. Since noon of 29 May, both Mr. Jordan and Mr. Bang-Jensen have spoken to me separately on some aspects of their mutual difficulties. My advice to both of them since then has generally been that, pending a resolution by higher authority of the issues involved, they should both endeavour to compose their difficulties and to make every effort to see that such difficulties did not affect the work of the Committee or the Secretariat's relations with it. Today they have both presented memoranda to me to be conveyed to you. I am at your disposal to assist you in this matter in any way you may wish to indicate.

APPENDIX 10 MEMOS: BANG-JENSEN APPEALS TO CORDIER AND DAG HAMMARSKJOLD

ANNEX II No. 5

URGENT CONFIDENTIAL

11 June 1957

TO: Mr. Andrew W. Cordier
Executive Assistant to the Secretary-General

FROM: Povl Bang-Jensen
Deputy Secretary
U. N. Special Committee on Hungary

SUBJECT: *Report on Hungary*

In continuation of our conversation of 6 June, I should appreciate if if you would inform the Secretary-General that I did not have an opportunity to see the final draft of the Report before it was distributed and subsequently adopted at the Committee's meeting Friday afternoon, 7 June, when the Secretary-General was present. I received no copy at that time, and since then, in spite of all efforts, I have been unable to borrow a copy even for a few hours. Mr. Jordan pretends that all available copies are being used by other members of the staff; he has given no explanation why sufficient copies were not rolled off.

I have asked to see the old master copy from which the final draft was produced; this also has been refused, nor has Mr. Jordan been willing to give any reason for this refusal.

From what I am told by other officers, it appears that the Report still contains all or most of the many serious errors of fact, which, as I have pointed out, can hardly be found by the members themselves, but will undermine general confidence in the Report and perhaps even make the Commission look ridiculous. I am, as you will understand, unable to tell whether perhaps new errors of fact have been introduced in the final draft and further essential facts omitted.

I am told by other officers that Mr. Jordan expects today to receive the final approval by cable from the representative of Ceylon, after which he intends to send the Report for printing. Whether Professor Fabregat, who has made reservations has finally approved the Report, I do not know.

As previously, I have again advised Mr. Jordan that I consider it my duty to send the Secretary-General this memorandum.

cc: Mr. T. G. Narayanan
     Officer in Charge
     Department of Political and
       Security Council Affairs

ANNEX II No. 6

PERSONAL AND CONFIDENTIAL

17 June 1957

TO: Mr. Dag Hammarskjold, Secretary-General

FROM: Povl Bang-Jensen, Deputy Secretary
U. N. Special Committee on Hungary

Since I have not had the opportunity to hear your views in connection with the problems dealt with in my memoranda of 4th, 6th and 11th June, there is now a practical question on which I need your advice.

I am leaving on home leave tomorrow, and during my stay in Denmark I shall, of course, see Alsing Andersen, as I usually do when I am in Denmark. He has, in fact, asked me to telephone him as soon as I arrive. We have known each other for more than a quarter of a century, so it has, therefore, been somewhat disturbing to him that Mr. Jordan ordered me not to speak to him about the Report.

As I leave now, I have not even seen the draft of the Report, which was distributed and adopted in the meeting at which you were present. I only know that, at least, most of the serious errors of fact have not been corrected.

At one time Alsing Andersen pointed out to Mr. Jordan, in writing, a number of errors of fact and omission. Mr. Jordan arranged a meeting at which I, contrary to the wishes of Alsing Andersen, was not allowed to be present. Alsing Andersen certainly realized, though perhaps not to the full extent, that he was given a run-around at that meeting. He afterwards expressed the view to me that it was not for him to argue with Mr. Jordan, but that he could expect that proper administrative measures would be taken inside the Secretariat to straighten out the draft. It was the Secretariat which, in his view, had the chief responsibility for the accuracy of the facts in the Report. My impression was that he felt reassured that, with the presence of you and Mr. Cordier at the final meeting on Friday, 7 June, any needed measures would be taken.

I do not quite know how to explain to him that the dozens of serious errors of fact have not yet been pointed out to the Rapporteur, except vaguely in a few cases. And in these cases the Rapporteur was not given the reference to the places in the huge volume of evidence and other material (of which each of us can only know a part), which proves why the facts as stated are indisputably incorrect.

Nor do I know how to explain to him, if he asks, why nobody in the Secretariat yet has spent just one hour to find out what the errors are, whether they are in conflict with the record, and how serious they are.

In a cable from Budapest, as reported in today's *New York Times,* it is stated that the Kadar Government is doubtful about arranging a trial of Mr. Imre Nagy, because Mr. Kadar himself was involved in the decisions of the Nagy Government. It is interesting to note that the most essential facts indicating the extent of Mr. Kadar's agreement with the decisions of the Nagy Government are omitted or incorrectly stated in the Report.

Apart from short visits to Oslo and Stockholm, I shall be in Denmark from 29 June to 7 August. My address will be:

> c/o Mrs. Ahnfelt-Rønne
> Kirsebaervej 2
> Espergaerde.

APPENDIX 11 BANG-JENSEN REPORTS SABOTAGE TO HAMMARSKJOLD

Annex II No. 14

STRICTLY CONFIDENTIAL

16 September 1957

TO: Mr. Dag Hammarskjold
          Secretary-General

THROUGH: Mr. Dragoslav Protitch
          Under-Secretary

FROM: Mr. Povl Bang-Jensen

More than three months have passed since I sent you my first memorandum, informing you of the various kinds of sabotage which had been and were being carried out against the Special Committee on Hungary.

In your note of appreciation of 7 June, you indicated you wished to see me about the matter. However, you never did so. Neither have you asked to see the evidence I offered you, although it appeared that preventive action against further sabotage was needed and it was alleged that the sabotage was carried out on your instructions.

Personally, I have been placed in an awkward position. While the Hungarian question was being discussed in the General Assembly, I have felt obliged to be discreet about my dismissal as Deputy Secretary—for which I still have received no explanation —and have remained silent in this connection although some might have concluded from this that it was I who had done something wrong. Sooner or later, however, it will be necessary for me to ask to have my record rectified.

In the meantime, I am in serious doubt about my duties as an international official. Sabotage has been carried out, allegedly on your instructions. You have failed to consider my evidence. Am I now expected to forget this matter? If not, to whom am I to turn?

[Hand written note:]

Dr. Bunche
Please give the necessary explanations
under your general mandate to handle
these allegations on my behalf.

a) *What* is the sabotage?
b) By whom has it been carried out?
c) What is the evidence for a) and b) that he has.
    It should be given to you, else I must regard it
    as non-existent.

H.D.

Exchange of Memos Between Bang-Jensen and Ralph Bunche

Annex II No. 15

[to:] Mr. Paul Bang-Jensen

17 September 1957

[from:] Ralph J. Bunche
        Under Secretary

1. This is to confirm the understanding reached in our talk late yesterday afternoon about your memorandum of 16 September 1957 addressed to the Secretary-General through Mr. Protitch.

2. You agreed to undertake to reduce to specific terms the general allegations of "sabotage" which you have made, by

(a) listing and describing the specific acts of "sabotage" alleged,

(b) identifying precisely in each instance the person or persons alleged to be responsible for the act, and

(c) indicating the actual evidence which in your view can be brought to bear in support of your allegations.

3. You accepted my offer to make Miss Paula Boynton of my office staff available to you for the above purpose, and it is understood that in a day or so you will dictate to her the information described in paragraph 2.

4. May I ask you also to provide, at the same time, a clarification of the sentences concerning sabotage in the last paragraph of your memo of 16 September. I pointed out to you yesterday that it reads as though it were preferring a charge against the Secretary-General, but you denied that there was any such intent. Will you, therefore, explain very clearly the meaning of these sentences.

It would be appreciated if you would confirm this understanding, either by initialing this memorandum or by a separate note to me.

Annex II No. 16

STRICTLY
CONFIDENTIAL

18 September 1957

TO: Mr. Ralph J. Bunche,
        Under-Secretary

FROM: Povl Bang-Jensen

I regret that I have to take exception to the phrase in your memorandum of 17 September: "You agreed to undertake to reduce to specific terms the general allegations of 'sabotage' that you have made." Your memorandum leaves the impression that I have made loose charges, neither specifying the acts of sabotage, nor identifying any of those involved, nor giving any indication of the evidence. I should not have felt constrained to make these remarks, if it had not been for our first unpleasant conversation of 28 August. Apart from telling me that I was "not coming with a halo around my head; we know enough about you", you accused me of making "wild allegations", while at the same time you refused to look at the evidence I offered: "It would be ridiculous to spend even five minutes to look at it".

You also continued to insist to the very end of that meeting that the only charge of sabotage I had made in my memoranda, which you maintained you had read carefully, was with regard to the errors of facts in the Report, a charge you alleged had been repudiated by the Chairman and the Rapporteur. It was in vain that I pointed out that this was not so, and that even the very memorandum of 27 August, which was the occasion for our meeting, specified other acts of sabotage. Insofar as these last charges are concerned, there was not even any reason to ask me for further evidence. You could have just lifted the telephone and asked Mr. Jordan if it was true that none of the material which had been received during the last three months had been circulated to the members in spite of the agreement reached at the last meeting of the Committee, during which the Chairman stated that he wanted to make it clear what the duties of the Secretariat were, so that there should be no misunderstanding.

I shall be pleased, as agreed, to furnish you with specific examples, which will be easy to investigate, of the chief category of sabotage against the Committee, with indications of the responsible persons, but I should appreciate it if you would confirm that you feel free to investigate them objectively and thoroughly whatever facts might appear regarding the Secretary-General.

On 9 September, I gave you, at your request, details about the important message—I know now it was a cable—to the Hungarian Committee, regarding Minister of Defense, General Maleter's bodyguard, which at least had not been communicated to the Chairman. You gave me clear indication that you were going to get to the bottom of this—which in my opinion should be very simple.

It was surprising to learn from you during our meeting yesterday, more than a week later, that I was "all wrong" in this charge. Apparently you had seen no reason to inform me of this earlier and ask me for more information.

(a) You had found out that there was an "explicit letter" from the Rapporteur, stating that he did not want any supplementary report or more hearings. I failed to see why this should permit the Secretariat to suppress an important cable to the Committee regarding an unusual, prospective witness. Even if all members had agreed with the Rapporteur, such a decision would, of course, not mean that the members did not want to have the opportunity to revise it, if something unusual happened. Even the Rapporteur might have liked to hear him or at least have an informal statement from him. Besides, at least the Chairman for one, as you know, wanted to have a supplementary report prepared. Mr. Hammarskjold, by the way, according to Mr. Andersen, tried to influence him against this idea.

(b) You stated further, that, anyhow, I only knew and had only charged that the cable had not been sent to the Chairman. It seemed to me that it was unlikely that it had been sent to the other members if not to the Chairman. You did not feel, you said, that one could assume that. However, you had apparently found no reason to ask Mr. Jordan if the cable actually had been sent to anybody.

(c) Nothing had been withheld from the members, you maintained, because the cable had been listed in the routine list of documents circulated to the Committee. Leaving aside the question of the adequacy of this, I asked whether it was not true that this list had only been sent to the member after I had raised the issue. You asserted that you had not noticed the date.

I should have thought that the fact, that this message had not been sent out, would have made you curious to know whether any material at all had been sent to the members as agreed in the last meeting of the Committee. Just one question to Mr. Jordan would have sufficed to clear up this point. You might then also have asked Mr. Jordan whether it is correct that he maintains that he has held the cable and the other material back from the members of the Committee on instructions from the Secretary-General.

I take it that you will ask him this question, and that after our conversation yesterday, you will take up the matter again and inform me of the result of your further investigations. Would you kindly let me know if this assumption is not correct.

With regard to the last paragraph of my memorandum of 16 September, which you asked me to clarify, I can only state that it means exactly what it says, no more and no less. It contains a brief statement of facts and two questions which I hope the Secretary-General will answer. They are not rhetorical and it seems to me that they are increasingly pertinent.

Annex II No. 17

19 September 1957
2932

[to:] Mr. Paul Bang-Jensen

[from:] Ralph J. Bunche
      Under Secretary

In your memorandum of 18 September you indulge freely in allegations which are supported only by distortion of fact. You now take exception to something which you readily agreed to do in our discussion of 16 September, without question and without any reference to our first conversation of 28 August. With regard to this latter conversation, you are fully aware that it was only after it had gone in circles for a considerable time, with you rejecting every suggestion from me that there could be a valid difference of opinion about your charges and insisting that your view was the only possible right one that I said to you that "there is no halo over your head which makes your personal opinions sacrosanct." At no time did I make the statement you now falsely attribute to me, namely, "we know enough about you." You know also, that my reference to "wild allegations" in our first discussion was a reflection of my incredulousness when you indicated that the allegations you were making and the investigation you were seeking had as a major purpose to establish that the Chairman and Rapporteur of the Special Committee were being "duped" by the Secretariat. In our talk you used the word "duped," which you changed to "deceived" in the written summary of the talk. Nor did I give to you as you assert, "clear indication" in any form that I was "going to get to the bottom" of your allegations concerning the message from General Maleter's bodyguard. The rest of your memorandum is a polemical presentation of your views, requiring no response from me.

I have consistently informed you that I am not conducting an investigation of your allegations; that in the memoranda you have submitted and the oral statements made to me these allegations are in my opinion general and unsupported; and that it is for you to support your allegations by setting them forth precisely and in detail and by presenting supporting evidence in each instance. This you agreed and promised to do in our meeting of 16 September. I await your fulfilment of that promise. Miss Boynton continues available to you for this purpose.

Annex II No. 20

STRICTLY
CONFIDENTIAL

20 September 1957

TO: Mr. Ralph J. Bunche,
        Under-Secretary

FROM: Mr. Povl Bang-Jensen

It appears from your memorandum of 19 September that you and I have very different recollections about what took place at our first conversation on 28 August. I can tell you that I went straight to my office and made copious notes about our conversation. However, in order not to deflect attention from more important matters, I shall not, at this stage, make my corrections to the statements in your memorandum, nor shall I ennumerate the other ways in which you tried to intimidate me, nor begin a discussion of your extraordinary views regarding the duties of the Secretariat, which, unfortunately, you were not willing to give me in writing.

It is, however, rather remarkable that you can write that I insisted that my view was the only possible right one, since I again and again pointed out that with regard to the errors of fact in the report there was no question of one man's view against another's view, but a question of facts which anybody could check with the record.

At our next meeting, you were extremely cordial and charming, without giving any explanation for the change. It was a very pleasant meeting. It is a pity that it now appears that we do not agree about what happened at that meeting either.

You tell me now that "I have consistently informed you that I am not conducting an investigation of your allegations". This is surprising since you told me two or three times during that meeting that Mr. Hammarskjold had not given you any explicit permission to investigate the Maleter matter, but since, in a handwritten notation on my memorandum of 9 September, he had left it to you to use your own discretion in dealing with it, you felt that you were entitled to look into it. I assured you that I shared your interpretation of Mr. Hammarskjold's terms and that in fact I should think that most would feel that it was your duty to do so. You have apparently forgotten this. Perhaps you do not recall either that you even asked for my advice about how to proceed.

I have taken no exception in my memorandum of 18 September to what we agreed about in our discussion. On the contrary, my memorandum explicitly state that I will furnish you with specific examples of sabotage, as agreed. I am still willing to do so, although I fail to see that there is much point in doing it any longer, since you now tell me in advance that you will not investigate them.

Annex II No. 21

[to:] Mr. Povl Bang-Jensen

23 September 1957
2932

[from:] Ralph J. Bunche
Under Secretary

Your memorandum of 20 September is acknowledged. I note that in it you set forth, in your words, "one example from each of three main categories" of your allegations of sabotage. I assume from your description and your choice of them that these are prime examples of your allegations and the evidence you adduce in support of them.

As for the rest of your memorandum, I do not attempt to reply since it is not my way to descend to an exchange of insinuation, causticism and reproach. For my part, the bare facts are enough.

Only to keep the record straight, however, I deny categorically that I "tried to intimidate" you in any way. It may be pointed out, also for the record, that what you describe as my "extraordinary views regarding the duties of the Secretariat" were that the report was the responsibility of the Committee's officers and members and *not* of its Secretariat, that the Secretariat was to serve and not to direct the Committee, and that it was preposterous to contend, as you did, that the Secretary-General should institute an investigation to establish that the Chairman and Rapporteur were being "duped" by the Secretariat of the Committee. I have never informed you that I was "investigating" the Maleter or any other allegations made by you and I most certainly did not ask your "advice about how to proceed" in any investigation. On the other hand, I was willing to hear what you had to say and did hear you out on the Maleter matter.

As for your reference to the possibility that I might recom-

mend that you be dismissed, again the record is entitled to
accuracy in context. Near the end of our first talk I said to you
that in all frankness, considering your admitted and continuing
disregard for authority, regulations and procedures which you
justified on the grounds that having seen something which you
regarded as a wrong you had a duty to expose and correct it;
your going over the head of the Committee Secretary to the
Chairman and Rapporteur and over the acting head of your
Department directly to the Secretary-General; your defiance of
instructions from the Secretary concerning attendance at meetings; the shameful scene which you created in the Delegate's
Lounge in your near violent attempt to press your views on the
Committee Rapporteur; your approach to the Secretary-General,
in one of your memoranda to him, on the grounds that you were
of the same social set in Scandinavia;—in view of such attitudes
and actions on your part I observed that *if my advice should be
asked* I would have to take the position that you had forfeited
your further entitlement to the responsible post and level you
enjoy through a gross lack of judgement and sense of propriety.

APPENDIX   13   Hammarskjold Appeals to Alsing
Andersen

ANNEX II No. 27

18 October 1957

Mr. Alsing Andersen
Permanent Mission of Denmark to
  the United Nations
Hotel Beaux Arts, Room 1708 N
307 E. 44th Street
New York 17, N.Y.

PERSONAL AND CONFIDENTIAL

Dear Mr. Andersen,

I wish to bring the following matter to your attention.

Last week Dr. Protitch discovered that Mr. Bang-Jensen, who

as you know was relieved sometime ago of his duties as Deputy Secretary of the Special Committee on the Problem of Hungary, was holding in his custody, outside United Nations Headquarters, the list of witnesses who appeared anonymously before your Committee together with some relevant correspondence.

The normal procedure is, as a matter of course, that confidential files, which may have been in the possession of an individual officer while connected with the work or needed by him during the activities of an organ he is serving, are returned immediately to the custody of the United Nations Archives or—in a case like the present one—put in a safe under special care in view of their confidential nature. Dr. Protitch therefore requested Mr. Bang-Jensen to bring in the list and relevant correspondence and hand it to him. Mr. Bang-Jensen refused to comply with Dr. Protitch's request which was repeated on three separate occasions.

After receiving a report from Dr. Protitch on this matter, I requested Mr. Bang-Jensen to explain his refusal to obey the order from the Head of his Department. Mr. Bang-Jensen, in a memorandum to Dr. Protitch of which a copy is attached, repeated what he had already told him orally, characterizing himself as a "trustee" for the anonymous witnesses.

I understand that Mr. Bang-Jensen was charged, with your and the Rapporteur's agreement, to deal particularly with witnesses applying to be heard by your Committee. This, I take for granted, was not in his individual capacity, but as an officer and member of the Secretariat attached to the Committee. For the convenience of the work, and to protect the anonymous witnesses, he kept a list and dealt directly with those individuals. The list was, nevertheless—if I am correctly informed—at your disposal, and the witnesses who appeared either under their own names or anonymously before the Committee were selected after reference to you. After the end of the hearings, and when that part of the work of the Special Committee was over, it would seem that this list and the relevant correspondence constitute a part, although confidential, of the record relating to the report of your Committee.

In the light of these developments I would appreciate to receive your observations on the question of substance involved;

    Mr. Bang-Jensen's procedure in giving firm commitments not to reveal the names of the witnesses to anybody; and

    the consequences of such a promise, if given, for the status of the name lists as part of the Committee documentation to be under the custody of the United Nations.

The questions are of considerable importance, not only as a matter of principle, but also for practical purposes.

    I would appreciate having your views as soon as convenient on this serious problem.

Yours sincerely,
Dag Hammarskjold

APPENDIX 14 MEMO: DRAGOSLAV PROTITCH ORDERS
BANG-JENSEN TO SURRENDER THE LIST

Annex II No. 31

29 November 1957

To Mr. Poul Bang-Jensen

    By order of the Secretary-General, you are instructed to deliver to me, immediately, the list of witnesses who corresponded with or appeared before the Special Committee on Hungary, together with all other records or correspondence pertaining to the work of the Committee and now within your control or possession. For your information, in pursuance of the recommendation of the Chairman and Rapporteur of the Committee, and in accordance with the established practice for the safekeeping of important documents in the Secretariat, all of these materials will be put by me under seal and in safe custody.

D. Protitch,
Under-Secretary for Political and
Security Council Affairs

APPENDIX 15 LETTER APPOINTING INVESTIGATING GROUP

ANNEX I

TO: Mr. Ernest Gross *   4 December 1957

In view of his refusal to comply with an important order conveyed to him by the head of his Department at my request, Mr. Povl Bang-Jensen of the Department of Political and Security Council Affairs has been suspended, pending further investigation.

Before any other personnel action affecting him is taken, I wish a thorough review to be made of Mr. Bang-Jensen's conduct relating to his association with the Special Committee on Hungary, by a group of three consisting of yourself, Mr. J.A.C. Robertson and Mr. Constantin Stavropoulos, with you as Chairman. All pertinent documentation will be made available to this group, which may also interview such persons as it may consider likely to afford it helpful information.

I request this group, after detailed study and evaluation of the matter, to convey to me on the basis thereof, such views, suggestions or recommendations for further action as it may deem appropriate.

By order of the Secretary-General

Andrew W. Cordier, Executive
Assistant to the Secretary-General

* Identical letters *mutatis mutandis* were sent to Mr. C. Stavropoulos, Mr. J. A. C. Robertson and later to Mr. Philippe de Seynes.

APPENDIX 16 BANG-JENSEN'S LETTER TO TRIBUNAL SEC-
RETARY

October, 18, 1958

Mr. Mani Sanasen
Executive Secretary,
U.N. Administrative Tribunal
New York.

Dear Mr. Sanasen,

. . . The Administration still refuses—in fact, if not in words—to make the requested documents and testimony available, and even fails to give any clear reason for this. The brief of the Respondent completely ignores the legitimate and essential questions in the end of my application, that is that the Administration, for each of the 87 items listed in my request for documents (Ap. 11), separately answer the following questions: :

(1) Does the document exist?
(2) Does the Administration consider the document so "secret" that it cannot be made available due to "the necessary protection of secret material"?
(3) Does the Administration maintain that the document is not relevant to the case, and if so, why?

The specific and separate reply to these questions are of paramount importance, because the answers in themselves will prove that I have not received due process,—that the Administration has suppressed some of the most essential documents in the case, and that the Administration has supported its charges by referring to documents which do not exist.

Besides without the Administration's prompt reply to these questions in advance of the oral proceedings, these obviously will become extremely involved and time-consuming. . . .

Very sincerely yours
Povl Bang-Jensen

APPENDIX **17** COMMENTS IN DANISH PRESS

Front-page editorial, *Information* (independent), Copenhagen, Oct. 10, 1958

After One Hour and Fifteen Minutes.

The article INFORMATION printed yesterday regarding Member of Parliament Alsing-Andersen's inadmissible stand in the Bang-Jensen case has made a deep impression. This, of course, was to be expected, since it forcefully demonstrated that Alsing-Andersen as Chairman of the U.N. Committee on Hungary had given an inaccurate explanation to Secretary-General Hammarskjold, maintaining that he had undertaken a satisfactory investigation of the allegations, which were the chief basis for Bang-Jensen's dismissal from the United Nations.

The reaction to INFORMATION's article has so far been a reply from Alsing-Andersen and numerous communications to us which, referring to the article, point out that the stand of Denmark in this case is not expressed by Alsing-Andersen's behaviour.

Alsing-Andersen's answer is to be found in "Social-Demokraten" today and we reprint it in full on page 3. It fully confirms INFORMATION's report that the satisfactory investigation, which Alsing-Andersen testified to Hammarskjold about, was limited to a conversation of an hour and fifteen minutes with the U.N. officials whom Bang-Jensen accused. However, Alsing-Andersen still maintains that this can be called an "investigation." How unreasonable this assertion is, is evident from the fact that Alsing-Andersen confirms that the complaints involved 30-40 points just in one chapter of the Hungarian report. Obviously, it would have been physically impossible to investigate all these points in one hour and fifteen minutes. Just to present an accused with an accusation and then uncritically to accept his denial, is not an investigation. Besides, there were many other chapters in the report about which many other points have been raised.

While it thus has been established that Alsing-Andersen's statement to Hammarskjold necessarily is incorrect, the question remains, how Denmark can indicate its true position in the case, which is not the one represented by Alsing-Andersen. There is, however, serious danger that this will be presumed in New York, unless something is done.

INFORMATION has received proposals for a collection to a Bang-Jensen fund. While we do not reject the idea as a sign of sympathy, we do feel both for reasons of principle and considering the financial aspect, that it is for the Government to undertake Denmark's effective support.

The Government can hardly take sides in this case, but in supporting Bang-Jensen's appeal efforts, it would act in accordance with the views expressed in the leading newspapers of all the political parties that the case should be investigated properly. This action should be taken through diplomatic channels, but wholeheartedly and not as hitherto by interventions which perhaps are formally correct but ineffective. Furthermore, the Government ought to finance the future conduct of the case.

Bang-Jensen is now asking to see Foreign Minister Krag, who will act wisely in consulting the heads of the political parties and by listening to public opinion—if his own feeling of justice does not suffice.

Politiken, Copenhagen (Liberal Party), second largest daily in Denmark, carried on Oct. 22, 1958, an article by Mr. Erling Foss, Danish Civil-Engineer and businessman, who was one of the leaders of the Danish Underground during the Nazi occupation of Denmark. Excerpts follow in translation:

"Good nerves—Good conscience."

A small circle, convened by the League for Tolerance, Monday night, had an unusual experience, when they heard Bang-Jensen's explanatory account regarding his dismissal from the United Nations Secretariat. He has been described as a man "whose nerves *failed*", by which his attackers are hinting at something much worse. Actually his dismissal was due to the fact that he himself did not *fail* to keep his word to the unfortunate suppressed Hungarians.

It is not permitted to report the closed meeting as such,—however, it must nevertheless be the duty of those present to give Bang-Jensen the appropriate testimonial.

Never can a man have stood on a Danish rostrum who appeared wiser and more restrained and who presented a large and complex case more excellently, clearly and well-balanced.

One has never heard a man, who has suffered so much injustice, speak with more assurance and composure—without bitterness—, confident of the great mission of the United Nations.

At the same time, although he has been abroad for many years, he could speak with a Danish sense of humour and a quiet smile, forgiving the weaknesses of other people.

This was a man, involved in a large case of principles and of far reaching importance, who spoke with firm and calm conviction, as only a man with a good conscience can do.

. . . .
. . . .

He is entitled to receive all possible support from his own country and its Government.

ERLING FOSS.

APPENDIX 18 ARTHUR McDOWELL REPLIES TO ELEANOR
ROOSEVELT

March 4, 1960

Dear Mr. McDowell:

I have read the letter you wrote on the Bang-Jensen case and I am not at all in agreement with you.

The UN documents in the Bang-Jensen case are informative and convincing and what you write is nonsense and rather wicked.

Very sincerely yours,
/s/Eleanor Roosevelt

March 28, 1960

Mrs. Franklin D. Roosevelt
55 East 74th Street
New Yorkk 21, N. Y.

Dear Mrs. Roosevelt:

In your March 17 note of acknowledgment of my rather strong response of March 15 to your earlier comment on my strictures on U.N. officers and their apologetics and apologists in the Bang-Jensen tragedy you express doubt as to whether I have read the U.N. account of the Bang-Jensen case and recommend that I do so.

Let me assure you that I have read carefully every document issued on the Bang-Jensen case for public consumption by the United Nations and the U. S. State Department and the U. S. delegation to the United Nations since Mr. Bang-Jensen was finally dismissed in July of 1958 by U.N. Secretary General Hammarskjold.

At that time Mr. Wadsworth of the U. S. delegation played Pontius Pilate to Mr. Hammarskjold's Caiaphas (see Luke 22:71) by approving the U.N. Secretary's action in a premature and gratuitous statement, anticipating even the result of still further pending appeal to and review by U.N.'s own Administrative Tribunal. I, therefore, have also acquired and followed carefully the equally equivocal State Department papers as issued.

I have read the moving and terribly clear brief submitted by Bang-Jensen to the Administrative Tribunal of U.N. at end of 1958, in which the Tribunal evaded the issues he raised, as had all other bodies, U.N. and U.S., and stultified itself in many respects, but who at least sternly reproved and repudiated the improprieties of the incredible and illegal special Gross Investigating Committee.

I am virtually certain, from your response, that you have not yet read these particular and important documents or the several documents prepared for our Council from August 1958 forward, based on lengthy firsthand interviews with Mr. Bang-Jensen and a carefully developed acquaintance with the man and his career, which I strongly recommend, in turn, that you now study.

It is not without significance that Mr. Alsing Andersen, of Denmark, relied upon by U.N. officialdom and its apologists to discredit Bang-Jensen by supplying supporting statements and accusations, turned on like a spigot at Secretariat request, even when younger, was a home body who as Defense Minister at time of Hitler's invasion of Denmark failed to furnish even token opposition to that invasion, and stayed in office as an amenable collaborator with the Nazis.

In significant contrast, Bang-Jensen, along with Danish Ambassador to U. S. Kauffman, was indicted for treason by the captive Danish parliament at Nazi demand, for negotiating for U.S. essential legal access to Danish Greenland for our defense. This was a risky service to us and cause of freedom, which your late husband must certainly have known and appreciated and which, if you are not aware of it, you can get well briefed upon by Adolph Berle who handled our part of the negotiations and knows the debt which the U.S. owes to Bang-Jensen for which its diplomatic representatives at the U.N. repaid in a treacherous counterfeit coinage indeed, twenty years later at the U.N.

I assume, however, that your tentatively posed question as to my acquaintance with the U.N.'s stated case in the Bang-Jensen matter refers to the U.N.'s official releases, issued successively on December 22, 1959, a month after discovery of the body of the gallant and magnificent Danish friend of the U.S. and of freedom, and the further explanation for the earlier explanation and apology, issued under date of January 1, 1960, and which, I believe, the Association for the United Nations has undertaken to circulate and therefore takes responsibility for and underwrites. These documents, it is true, did not reach my attention immediately due to the fact that from a week after Bang-Jensen's tragic death in November until mid-January I was not in my office but in either hospital in Virginia and Philadelphia or convalescent center in Florida.

Although my files on the Bang-Jensen matter are very voluminous indeed and have been heavily drawn upon by investigators for Senator Dodd's investigations for his subcommittee of Judiciary, no one sent me copy voluntarily. One of the editors of *The Saturday Evening Post* and an editorial writer for The Philadelphia *Evening Bulletin* then called my attention to them and their pitiable internal self contradictions, and on January 26 I wrote Colenel Katzin for them, and received them in full in a letter from Wilder Foote, dated January 29, 1960. Although I was already familiar with them and then proposed to issue one of our documents in analysis of them, another illness and convalescence in my Union's Salhaven center in Florida intervened and this analysis was not prepared, and I assumed, incorrectly, as it now seems, that the weakness of these official U.N. statements was in any case internally self-evident.

The presumably final U.N. document, entitled "A List of Facts About the United Nations and the Case of Mr. Bang-Jensen," was issued January 1, 1960, nearly a month and a half after Bang-Jensen's death and the sensational publicity, including that in magazines and newspapers that had in some cases deliberately refused space to the case in interest of protection of present U. S. Administration and U.N. Secretariat, in late 1958 when final appeal was going to Tribunal. By it the U.N. Secretariat case and that of those outside it who attempt the defense of its procedure in the Bang-Jensen matter must stand or fall.

Here is the record as I read it in this final U.N. Secretariat document of defense of its course.

In Paragraph First it is asserted that Bang-Jensen was never the sole custodian of the names of the 81 witnesses who demanded anonymity.

The fact is that this statement is meaningless and misleading and seeks to cover up the only fact that Bang-Jensen asserted, which was that he was custodian of the *sole complete list* since, as the U.N.'s own statement in ninth paragraph of same document states, that to Bang-Jensen was assigned the task of paying all these witnesses "their costs of travel and per diem" and that he had *sole authorization* to sign such receipts himself "which were not to be made available to the Controller's staff for the usual auditing procedures." The U.N.'s statement on page 4 of its January 1, 1960, and page 10 of its December 22, 1960, admits that when an individual claimed to have been such a witness, the U.N. when requested could only check the man's recollection of testimony for verisimilitude with recorded testimony for confirmation, as no other person or record in the U.N. could confirm the name, in spite of U.N. documents' claims that many others screened and knew witnesses.

Paragraph Second—The U.N. statement that Bang-Jensen "was not dismissed for refusing to divulge the names of these witnesses" is completely contradicted and proven false by the statements on page 7 and 8 of the U.N.'s own earlier Bang-Jensen explanation of December 22, 1959, which describes the steps leading directly from October 9, 1957, "discovery" that only Bang-Jensen had the list of witnesses, through the orders to deliver his list to others in Secretariat and his suspension for this precise "insubordination," on December 4, 1957, and appointment on same date by Secretary-General Hammarskjold of the illegal Gross investigating committee which for many weeks concerned itself only with the list and its ultimate disposal by destruction, which did not take place until January 24, 1958. Only after this did the Gross committee take up the additional charges which the committee now developed and which the U.N.'s own Administrative Tribunal found were improperly processed and outrageously handled in terms of the use and abuse of one-sided publicity by this improper committee which had no justification or legal basis under U.N. rules or machinery. Even a child reading the record must realize that if Bang-Jensen had surrendered his list and taken a rebuke in silence, he would be alive today and employed in good standing at his high ranking and well paid post in the U.N.

Paragraph Third—The statement that Mr. Bang-Jensen was not a member of the Committee on Hungary is meaningless and misleading. Every such committee in general, and particularly in international affairs such as the U.N., has the real work done by the professional staff, and the U.N.'s own earlier statement even in trying to downgrade Bang-Jensen's importance states that in addition to disbursing, as trusted officer, all expenses to witnesses on his own sole discretion, he worked on "formal introductory chapter, the first of the seventeen chapters of the Report," took an interest in the drafts of several other chapters, and criticized "serious errors of omission or commission in the parts drafted by others which the chief of staff and then the chairman and secretary of the committee went over with him point by point and rejected almost all," but admittedly, even antagonistic as they were, *not all* of Bang-Jensen's criticism of "entire range of report."

Paragraph Fourth—The U.N. statement says that "Mr. Bang-Jensen was not summarily dismissed." This technical denial fails to cover up the fact that he was most summarily suspended with the extraordinary and disgraceful circumstances that the Secretariat suddenly sent two U.N. policemen to bar him from his desk and physically escort him from the premises, an indignity never inflicted on the lowliest dismissed clerk, an action of invidious, prejudicial and disgracefully summary character, which even the Gross Committee, headed by a man who could see no conflict of interest in acting as chairman of an extra legal committee to review and approve the action of the Secretary General bringing charges, for whom he was at same time and previously personal legal counsel, even this committee did not find justification for such procedures. No merit whatsoever adheres to the meretricious claim that dismissal was not summary. The elaborate and extraordinary procedure, the first part (the Gross Committee) completely outside prescribed or allowable U.N. procedures, according to its own Administrative Tribunal, was part of a prolonged process required to let public opinion forget and become confused as to original issue which would have convulsed American and free world public opinion about present U.N. and its Secretariat.

In Paragraph Fifth, and falsely, it is asserted that he was finally dismissed in July 1958 for grave misconduct (not insubordination). This is clearly refuted by the Secretary's own statement in suspension action and the clear fact that the so-called misconduct charges were developed by the extra legal Gross Committee after the explosive issue of the list of witnesses had been disposed of by Bang-Jensen's public destruction of the list and a totally new series of extra legal hearings had been started by the Gross Committee.

Paragraph Sixth—The U.N. statement declares that "the responsibility for protecting their (the Hungarian witnesses) identity rested with the United Nations . . . , governmental members, the Secretariat staff and ultimately the Secretary-General himself." This is an extraordinary claim indeed since neither the Secretary-General, the Secretariat staff or the governmental members, except Bang-Jensen, as indicated by the complete silence of U.N. statement and common knowledge, not one of these took the single, most obvious minimum step to guard the security of the committee which was the object of the most intense hostility of the Soviet Union, wracked with the internal strains of its mass murder of 25,000 Hungarians and its own consequent civilian and military defections against the obvious desire of the communist rulers to show that this Soviet Union disposes in western Europe and beyond, a vast, ruthless, skilled, secret and conspiratorial apparatus which has been proven able to reach out and murder its leaders, most prominent opponents, such as Trotsky in far off Mexico City even while under official protection of the government of that country; yet not one step was taken by any of those cited above as responsible, to even appoint a security officer as the Hungarian investigating committee proceeded from city to city on the periphery of the communist bloc where communist intrigue and espionage operation is both commonplace and notorious. By own admission the Secretary-General, et al, did not even know, from January to October of 1957, that Bang-Jensen had kept secret a list of witnesses or that anyone had such a list.

Paragraph Seventh—On list of points of U.N. statement is the meaningless one that among staff others than Bang-Jensen knew a few names of witnesses, as could have the members as well as the chairman and secretary of the U.N. Committee on Hungary. None of these, however, it is obvious from U.N.'s own statement had to deal with all witnesses administratively, so that their incidental knowledge of a few names each is irrelevant to fact that when it came to a witness list of the 81 who asked for anonymity, the names had to be and were belatedly demanded by U.N. Secretariat of Bang-Jensen.

Paragraph Eighth—On list of U.N. second press release apology on the Bang-Jensen case is the statement that "Mr. Bang-Jensen was never authorized to assure any witnesses that he alone would know their names." Here is nub of dispute between U.N. Secretariat and Bang-Jensen. B-J asserted that his instructions allowed him to give such assurance, and asked for access to a list of documents and memorandum which would prove it, which, under a variety of bureaucratic pretexts, were never furnished. Beyond that, he asserted the principle of law, never challenged, that as an authorized agent, his pledge, once extended, was binding on his principal, the U.N., whether they agreed he had such instructions, or not.

The U.N.'s own statement in point "ninth" of the January 1, 1960, issue states clearly that "Mr. Bang-Jensen was authorized to pay such witnesses and to sign the receipts himself, which were not to be made available to the controller's staff for the usual auditing procedures" (of the U.N.). The admitted fact that Bang-Jensen only was in charge of this operation and exercised this authority and was never asked for any resulting list of such payments until many long months after the Hungarian Report was adopted and a related controversy involving the Secretary-

General and his closest associates had sprung up, leaves the public only this one certain fact admitted and public, and that
supports Bang-Jensen and not the U.N. claims.

I could go on through ten and eleven, but why pile up words.
The claim that the U.N. Secretariat has a security system, when
it never even thought to appoint a security officer for the Hungarian Committee and the futile attempt to compare equally
earlier cases with the heat and pressure of the Hungarian events
which were putting the whole Soviet empire to test, are self-
refuting. I have not only read the U.N.'s latest statements, but
without reference to many facts that months of correspondence
and questions have developed for me, I have found clear contradiction of the U.N.'s own case against Bang-Jensen in the
U.N.'s own imprinted release, indelible and undeniable. Yes, I
have read the U.N. releases on the Bang-Jensen case and they
make me sick of heart and stomach.

I do not resent your question as to whether I had read the U.N.'s
intended defensive and self-serving releases which I have bitterly
criticized and which criticism led to your first letter of March 4.
The complete surrender of rational standards or process in political controversy by many, if not most, in our day is both sad and
true. Sad and true is also the fact that our liberal spokesmen, and
not least the university trained and even placed personnel are
some of first to surrender their claim to intellectual processes
and procedures when their strongest political or personal senti-
ments are involved. One of the first and, to me, most dismaying
results of Senator Joe McCarthy's cheapening of the currency of
political controversy in the U. S. was the evidence that his liberal
opponents quickly exchanged vices with their opposition and
paid him the most delicate of compliments by imitating his
methods, from pulpit to press.

When Rebecca West, who happens to disagree with you and most
of American liberals on the historical role and usefulness of the
American Congressional Investigating Committees, wrote a series
of articles for *The Times* of London, in 1953, explaining and

reporting, in her incomparable fashion, on them to the English audience, who have no background in their government for such, and perhaps for this reason had their Burgess and Maclean get away, while our Hiss was caught, and even laid their Allan Nunn Mays and Klaus Fuchs by heels only with Canadian and American aid; Rebecca West received a flood of abusive and atrocious American mail, all from reputed American liberals who call themselves intellectual.

A Harvard history professor we both know wrote her a note insolently denying her right to have an opinion on the investigating committee question different from his own. When she wrote him a biting note of rejoinder he sent the correspondence to the editor of the *New Yorker* with suggestion that he might want to reconsider continuing such a co-editor and correspondent. She wrote me indignantly of receiving scores of letters from self-styled American liberal intellectuals whose letters bore unmistakable internal evidence that they had clearly not read the articles they complained of and abused, and which challenged her very right to write the articles. Then there came a subsequent series of other letters from other members of same group who obviously had also not read the articles they abused, but equally certainly had read copies of the Harvard professor material and the other early denouncers' correspondence, also still without reading the material discussed. The Sunday before I received her letter I went to church in Philadelphia and heard Leslie Pennington of the First Unitarian Church of Chicago preach a sermon, also denouncing the Rebecca West articles. As an old friend, I bearded him afterwards and asked if he had read the articles he denounced in his sermon. An honest man, he flushed scarlet and admitted that he had not but said spiritedly that he had read and spoke on the basis of a secondhand account in a denunciatory article on the articles in the *New Republic* by another respected liberal church leader. The Rebecca West intuition about her American critics was proven to the hilt.

On the Bang-Jensen matter I, too, feel strongly. The day his body was found in that Queens park and I got a glimpse of that

agonized face of a man I had come to like and respect enor-
mously, I sat in the New York train, on my way to a speaking
engagement up in New England, and wept openly and publicly,
something I cannot remember doing before in all my adult life,
even in times of family loss. However, my feelings are no substitute for facts, however intense the feelings. The facts though
are there. I looked into them and then on basis of those facts I
asked for justice for Bang-Jensen in late summer of 1958, as I
had asked for justice for Sacco and Vanzetti in 1927, and lost my
job for my urgency and the men died anyway. I protested the
injustice to a man by a great institution, as I had the Mooney-
Billings case in 1929 and got pitched out of my university for my
pains, though later belated justice was perhaps done there. In
1943 I passionately denounced the Soviet ally for the cynical
murder and libelling, after death, of the Polish Jewish Socialist
leaders Alter and Ehrlich, personal acquaintances to me this
time, by Stalin and his hangmen and was mocked by the failure
of high and low in U. S. politics to even take warning. The new
liberal light Wendell Willkie, who had a few months before
asked for their release in Moscow on behalf of Presidents Murray
and Green for all American labor and had been mocked by
Stalin's cynical promise to investigate fate of two men he had already then had secretly executed, ducked the labor protest meeting at Mecca Temple that fateful 1943 winter, and I took a new
measure of the new and old liberals when allied tyranny and
crime was now involved.

In summer of 1958 I found the injustice to Bang-Jensen com-
pounding the felony of all our cowardice, weakness and double
thinking and talking on the Hungarian issue. I raised the banner of protest against injustice again, but tragically the liberals,
who had been strong even in cause of Sacco-Vanzetti thirty years
before, of Mooney and Billings, even of Alter and Ehrlich, were
now tragically, shamefully silent. It was not a conservative
Massachusetts Governor and system of justice, or a California
utility company frameup, or even the direct action of a Soviet
dictator, but the good liberal personal symbols of the good
liberal cause of the U.N. who were now in the dock morally. It

was our liberals, warm friends and acquaintances Bunche, Gross, Lodge and perhaps even Hammarskjold who were accused of deep wrong to a brave man in freedom's cause and denial of human rights, not far away, but right in the U.N.'s own halls. In the end the tragic death of Bang-Jensen illuminated the ineradicable blot on the escutcheon of not only the U.N. Secretariat and its institution, but on that of many liberals as lovers of justice.

There were a few who spoke up still for Bang-Jensen from the old company: Morris L. Cook here in Philadelphia; Edgar Ansel Mowrer whose "Germany Sets the Clock Back" rang the alarm on the Nazis in 1932 when many who in London today march in protest over mere echoes in swastika painting of the dead Nazi day were advocating disarmament and even thought you could do profitable business with Hitler; there was Eugene Lyons who had helped assemble the Sacco-Vanzetti letters, but he was long since assigned to conservative side; there was a tiny telephone booth guard of labor, but the big names gave much private sympathy but no public support. The main support for a simple cry for justice now came from a politically conservative side. Congressman Wayne Hays of Ohio, signing on my thin list of protestants, was balanced by conservative Bentley of Michigan. There was Roscoe Pound of Harvard, but not one name of those liberal law schools' deans, who dote on unpopular legal causes celebre if the alleged victim is a sympathizer with tyranny, stood up for the proven friend and fighter for liberty, Bang-Jensen. They didn't argue or disagree with us, they simply ducked and were silent.

I say to you frankly that to me, from long perspective and experience, this was a real test and one most all liberals and labor flunked, and I must include you. A small portent perhaps, no large than a man's hand placing a pistol at his head, a liberal in every sense and, by every test, betrayed by liberals, with few exceptions, and most of those exceptions private, not public. It is a twilight period for political liberals and in the gloom they may have lost their way again, as so many did in early days of the Soviet tyranny's illusion of hope in the late twenties and thirties, as a good number plus many deluded churchmen did in case of bloody China in the forties. Only this time, in the Bang-Jensen case, it was not the illusion of the far off and foreign. It was here, at home, and there was a shamefaced conscious turning of the head away from the unpleasant facts and all their implications for themselves and their beliefs.

Perhaps I am wrong. I hope I am for the young people's sake, and I still have a housefull of them. Young Arthur, my oldest son was thrilled to act as your extra voice and ear at the Liberal Religious Youth area conference at Freeport, Long Island, a week ago, at the final seminar. He is Middle Atlantic treasurer of that Liberal Religious Youth Federation. My daughter, a second year Temple University student, hopefully reports real stirring from their lethargy and alleged conformism among students in universities on this civil rights issue, picked up at last by southern Negro students and a few of their white contemporaries. I hope it is real, but my children and the Bang-Jensen children have met and know one another, as they met and knew the man who is dead. They cannot and will not, I feel, long lift any banner or break any lance on behalf of a cause whose long listed spokesmen, when the going gets rough, and it is our friends and favored institutions who are shaking the balances of justice, act like the old deacon at the prayer meeting called to pray for rain, who denounced the little girl who came and brought an umbrella. You will remember that the little girl said, "Oh, I see, faith is believing in what everyone knows ain't so."

If modern youth catches that tired accent they will furnish few and poor quality recruits for the good causes of 1960 and beyond.

Sincerely yours,

[signed] Arthur G. McDowell, Executive
Secretary-Treasurer

P. S. In September 1958, when we still hoped that the Administrative Tribunal would redeem the U.N. name and procedures when it met in November, I received through the mail, as corresponding secretary of the Philadelphia Lincoln-Civil War Society, the item below, and sent it on as a counsel of courage and determination, in a personal letter to Povl Bang-Jensen up at Lake Success.

Then our appeal fell on deaf ears and it became clear that the great liberal community and the American partisans of the United Nations could not reach the level and stature of the old slave holders of Charleston, South Carolina, and Bang-Jensen was denied even the historical analogy of that epitaph, for apparently dismay overcame him and he surrendered the Christian hope in death. He never regretted his stand, but he often complained of his own weakness in feeling crushed. The men and women of our day shrink more than a little against these words:

James Lewis Pettigru, during the years preceding the Civil War, and until his death in 1862, opposed slavery and secession. In spite of his opposition to the Southern cause, his fellow-citizens of Charleston, S. C., placed the following inscription on his grave:

UNAWED BY OPINION
UNSEDUCED BY FLATTERY,
UNDISMAYED BY DISASTER
HE CONFRONTED LIFE WITH ANTIQUE
COURAGE:
AND DEATH WITH CHRISTIAN HOPE.
IN THE GREAT CIVIL WAR
HE WITHSTOOD HIS PEOPLE FOR HIS
COUNTRY:
BUT HIS PEOPLE DID HOMAGE
TO THE MAN
WHO HELD HIS CONSCIENCE HIGHER
THAN THEIR PRAISE:
AND HIS COUNTRY
HEAPED HER HONOURS ON THE
GRAVE OF THE PATRIOT

TO WHOM, LIVING
HIS OWN RIGHTEOUS SELF-RESPECT
SUFFICED
ALIKE FOR MOTIVE AND REWARD.
(Courtesy—Trooper Bethel)

AGMcD:mb
oeiu-14

[Mrs. Roosevelt did not reply to this letter.—The authors]

Notes

CHAPTER 3

1. Mrs. Bang-Jensen and her children have been awarded, by an act of the Danish Parliament, an annual pension of approximately $2,000 (*New York Herald Tribune*, July 14, 1960). Also a scholarship fund for the Bang-Jensen children has been set up under the auspices of The Council Against Communist Aggression.
2. U.N. white paper: "A Chronological Record of Facts . . . ," Dec. 22, 1959; U.N. white paper: "A List of Facts About the United Nations and the Case of Mr. Bang-Jensen," Jan. 1, 1960.

CHAPTER 7

1. See Appendix 1, reprinted by courtesy of Alice Widener.

CHAPTER 9

1. See Appendix 2.
2. Foregoing historical data supplied in conversations with Adolf A. Berle, Jr., and Henrik Kauffmann.

CHAPTER 10

1. *Facts About Hungary*, compiled by Imre Kovacs, Hungarian Committee, 1958.
2. Krishna Menon was the only non-Communist U.N. delegate to vote against withdrawal of Soviet troops from Hungary.

3. *Facts About Hungary*, p. 130.
4. Excerpts from U.N. debates, quoted from *The Hungarian Revolution*, ed. by Melvin J. Lasky, New York, Frederick A. Praeger, 1957, p. 208.
5. Associated Press Report, *ibid*, p. 230.
6. Bang-Jensen expressed the foregoing opinions in conversations with Janos Horvath, Bela Kiraly, Laszlo Varga, Arthur McDowell, and John Boland.

CHAPTER 11

1. Told to the psychiatrist F. S. Friedenberg by Bang-Jensen.

CHAPTER 12

1. See Appendix 3.
2. From Bang-Jensen's reply to Dag Hammarskjold, released July 20, 1958, p. 3. For the memorandum of Feb. 8 from Andrew Cordier, see Appendix 4.

CHAPTER 13

1. Paraphrased from testimony given to Special Committee on Hungary by Hungarian deportee witness.
2. See Appendix 5.
3. This statement is based on reliable but unconfirmed hearsay.
4. All factual statements made by K. are corroborated by the Annexes of the Final Report of the Committee Investigating the Bang-Jensen Case (commonly known as the Gross Report).

CHAPTER 14

1. The foregoing statements are from the Annexes of the Gross Report.
2. Corroborated by Bang-Jensen's reply to Dag Hammarskjold, released July 20, 1958, p. 14.
3. The foregoing statements are from the Annexes of the Gross Report.
4. Bang-Jensen's example from his reply to Dag Hammarskjold, p. 15.
5. Messinesi's statement is from the Annexes of the Gross Report.
6. *Ibid.*
7. Hungarian refugee sources now claim to have evidence that Kadar's broadcast of Nov. 4 was made from Uzgorod, in the Soviet Ukraine. All factual statements and paraphrased conversations through the balance of this chapter (excepting the comment on pp. 157, 158 by unnamed U.N. official) are based on the Annexes of the Gross Report.

CHAPTER 15

1. Conversation based on the Annexes of the Gross Report.
2. See Appendix 6.
3. Annexes of the Gross Report.
4. Bang-Jensen's reply to Dag Hammarskjold, p. 19.
5. Bang-Jensen's list of omissions from Chapter VII, given to Alsing Andersen, K. C. O. Shann, and William Jordan.
6. From Bang-Jensen's reply to Dag Hammarskjold, p. 20. All factual statements through the balance of this chapter are based on the Annexes of the Gross Report.

CHAPTER 17

1. See Appendix 7.
2. See Appendix 8.
3. See Appendix 9.
4. See Appendix 10.

CHAPTER 19

1. See also Appendix 11, Bang-Jensen's memorandum to Dag Hammarskjold, Sept. 16, 1957; Appendix 12, exchange of memoranda between Bang-Jensen and Ralph Bunche, Sept. 17-23, 1957.

CHAPTER 20

1. From memorandum from Dragoslav Protitch to Dag Hammarskjold, Oct. 11, 1957.
2. See Appendix 13.
3. See Appendix 14.
4. Bang-Jensen was relieved of his assignment to the Special Committee on Hungary on Aug. 24, 1957, and was not asked to turn over the secret list and relevant documents until Oct. 10, 1957.

CHAPTER 21

1. See Appendix 15.

CHAPTER 22

1. From "Irregularities in the Handling of the Bang-Jensen Case," prepared by Bang-Jensen.
2. *Pravda*, Jan. 24, 1958 (via Tass); *Nepszabadsag*, Jan. 21, 1958.
3. From "Irregularities in the Handling of the Bang-Jensen Case."
4. From letter from J. Anthony Panuch to Manfred Simon, Mar. 27, 1958.

CHAPTER 24

1. See Appendix 16.
2. See Appendix 17.
3. From testimony given by Andrew Cordier before Administrative Tribunal, Nov. 26, 1958.
4. From information furnished by Associated Press, United Press International, and letter from Henry Cabot Lodge to Dag Hammarskjold, May 24, 1960.

CHAPTER 28

1. See Appendix 18.

Index

A.F.L.-C.I.O., 237
AVH, 80, 81, 82, 103, 131
  dissolving of, 82
Administrative Tribunal,
  U.N., 174
"American Assembly," 207
American Association for the
  U.N., 239, 257
Anderson, Walter, 244
American resolution, 94-95
Andersen, Alsing, 116, 122,
  124, 129, 147, 154, 175,
  190, 199, 212, 216, 217,
  230
Andropov, Yuri V., 83, 110,
  163-164
Annexes, 174
Arkadev, Georgy Petrovich,
  199
Arm, Walter, 43-47
Assembly of Captive Euro-
  pean Nations, 256

Associated Press,
  eyewitness account of Russian attack, 93-94
Autopsy report, 49-50

Bang-Jensen, Helen, 18, 19-20,
  80, 115-117, 253, 259, 262
Barco, James W., 246, 248-251,
  253
Bastid, Suzanne, 232
Begley, Frank, 209
Belaunde, Victor Andres, 87
Bennett, Glenn, 14, 16, 17
Bentley, Alvin, 257, 258, 259
Berle, Adolf, Jr., 9, 11, 20, 69,
  71, 208, 217
Berlingske-Tidende, 216
Bohr, Niels, 70
  letter of recommendation,
  280-282
Boland, John, 264-267
Brooklyn Tablet, 256

Bruce, Donald, 42, 43
Bunche, Ralph, 181, 193-194, 208
Burke, Arleigh, 259

C.I.A., 8, 245
Carahalios, Mrs., 40, 41
CARE, 5, 9, 239, 262-267
Case, Clifford, 243
Cassandra Club, 85, 87
Chai, Doctor, 249
Chicago Daily Tribune, 213
Chicago Enquirer, 213
Christian, King, 71
Church World Service, 15-16
Cohen, Abraham, 26, 27, 28, 30-32
"Committee of Investigation," 208
Committee to Defend America by Aiding the Allies, 70
Cook, Morris L., 320
Cordier, Andrew, 14, 118, 119, 120, 121, 128, 147, 176, 178, 181-182, 183-187, 199, 204, 207, 225, 235, 246
attack on Bang-Jensen, 231-233
Cornehlsen, John H., 50
Coste, Brutus, 256
Council Against Communist Aggression, 256, 259
Csepel Arms Factory, 103
Csepel Youth, 103

Danish press,
comments in, 307-309

Danish underground, 66
Declaration of Neutrality, 83
Dixon, Sir Pierson, 91
Dobi, Istvan, 151, 159
Dobrynin, Anatoly F., 199
Doronkin, Kirill Sergeevich, 234
Duckworth-Barker, V., 123, 133, 136, 146, 147, 165
Dulles, Allen, 8, 245, 252
Dulles, John Foster,
quoted on Hungarian problem, 87-88
Duties of the Deputy Secretary of the U.N. Special Committee on Hungary, 282

"Easter Crisis," 73
Eichelberger, Clark, 257
Ekimov, Konstantin P., 234
Evans, Meurig, 223

Federal Bureau of Investigation, 20, 251, 254, 259
Ferdinand, Yale, 128
Ferdi's Sidewalk Cafe, 128
Finmark, Lennart, 178
Forster, Clifford, 6, 7-11, 20, 229, 274
Free Europe Committee, 100
Freedom Fighters, 80, 81, 82, 92, 104
Freeman (magazine), 57
Friedenberg, F. S., 39, 51-53

Galka, Joseph, 26, 28-30
Gallo, Larry, 42-43
Germany Sets the Clock Back (Mowrer), 320

Gero, Erno, 81, 102
Girardin, Paul E., 49
Gladkov, Boris F., 234
Greg, Jan, quoted, 80
Greenland, 71
Greenlaw, Ralph, 264
Grimes, Richard E., 48, 49-50
Gross, Ernest, 206, 207, 214
Gross Committee, 207-213, 214-222
Gross Report, 10, 59, 173-174, 176, 218-220, 222, 223, 230
    criticism of, 218-219
    inconsistencies in, 215-217
Grusha, Vladimir A., 233
Gubitchev, Valentin, 233
Guiringaud, Louis de, 91
Gunwardene, R. S. S., 123, 126
Guryanov, Aleksandr K., 234

Hageman, George, 32, 33, 273
Hammarskjold, Dag, 83, 84, 85, 86, 96, 118, 128, 138, 142, 147, 175, 176, 179, 204, 212, 217, 230, 253
Hansen, Premier, 230
Haskins, Reverend, 11, 12-18
Hays, Wayne, 257, 258
Hedervary, Miss de, 130
Hegedus, Andras, 81
Heltai, Gyorgy, 189
Hesselund-Jensen, 224
Hiss, Alger, 181
Horvath, Janos, 79, 106-109, 112, 124-127, 134, 135, 145, 175, 188-189, 219, 221
House Committee on Un-American Activities, 235

Hungary,
    negotiations with Russia, 111-112
    1956 revolt, 79-113
    Soviet troops enter (1956), 80, 81, 82, 83
    State Security Police, 80, 81
    U.N. Special Committee on, 100

Indianapolis Star, 256
Information, 307-308
International League for the Rights of Man, 256
Irwin, Wallace, Jr., 248

Johnson, Lew, 237-240
Jordan, William, 119, 123, 124, 129, 136, 142, 143, 145, 146, 158, 159-160, 162, 165, 168-172, 177, 179, 180, 190, 191, 219
    disagreements with Bang-Jensen, 119, 120-122, 130, 134-136, 145-146, 147-167
Joyce, William, 244

Kadar, Janos, 82, 146, 148, 149, 163-164, 178
Kauffmann, Henrik, 9, 11, 66, 68, 69, 71, 72-75, 214, 223, 224, 252, 253
Kavago, Jozsef, 124
Keating, Kenneth, 257
Kennedy, John, 257
Kernstein, Arthur, 47, 50
Kernstein, Stanley, 47, 50
Kethly, Anna, 79, 96, 97, 124, 125, 134, 163

Khrushchev, Nikita, 189
Kiraly, Bela, 79, 109-114, 124, 125, 134, 221
  quoted, story of Revolt, 95, 109-113
Kirilyuk, Vadim Aleksandrovich, 233
Kiss, Sandor, 79, 100-107, 112, 125, 221
  quoted on story of Revolt, 101-106
Konductorov, Leo, 82
Kos, Peter, 82
Kossuth Foundation, 107
Kovacs, Imre,
  quoted on Hammarskjold's handling of Nagy's letters, 85
Kovalev, Aleksandr Petrovich, 234
Kubiack, Allison, 32, 38-39

Lasky, Victor, 246
League for the International Rights of Man, 7
Leggett, Chief of Detectives, 45
Leistikow, Gunnar, 68, 69
Letters,
  appointing investigating group, 305
  Arthur McDowell replies to Eleanor Roosevelt, 309-323
  Bang-Jensen's to Tribunal Secretary, 306
  Bang-Jensen's to his superior, 285-288

Nagy's appeals to U.N., 83, 84, 89-90
  of recommendation from Niels Bohr, 280-282
Life (magazine), 98
Lodge, Henry Cabot, 88, 90, 91, 92, 93, 98, 249
London Times, The, 216, 317
Lunning, Just, 223, 224
Lyons, Eugene, 320

Maack-Petersen, Alfred, 69
Magyars, 96
Maleter, Pal, 111, 112, 188-189, 195
Manly, Chesly, 213
Marshall, George C., 208
Martin, David, 10, 254-255
Martynov, Maksim Grigorievich, 234
McCarthy, Joseph, 317
McDowell, Arthur, 256-261
McNally, Joseph, 46
Memoranda,
  alleged duties of the Deputy Secretary of the U.N. Special Committee on Hungary, 282
  Bang-Jensen and Bunche exchange of, 295-302
  Bang-Jensen to his wife, 277
  Bang-Jensen appeals to Cordier and Hammarskjold, 290-293
  Bunche and Hammarskjold exchange, 194, 199-202
  exchange of Bang-Jensen and Hammarskjold, 177-

179, 180, 199
Hammarskjold appeals to Andersen, 302-304
William Jordan to Bang-Jensen, 285
naming Bang-Jensen keeper of secret register, 283-284
Narayanan, to Cordier, 289-290
Protitch orders Bang-Jensen to surrender list, 304
report on Bang-Jensen from Jordan to Cordier, 288-289
J.A.C. Robertson to Bang-Jensen, 205-206
sabotage reported to Hammarskjold, 293
Menon, V. K. Krishna, 87
Messinesi, Philip, 123, 143, 144, 147, 148-149, 152, 153, 158, 169-172
Middle East (Suez) Crisis, 80, 81, 83, 85, 86, 88, 90, 92
Mooney-Billings case, 319
Morris, Robert, 242-247
Morse, Wayne, 257
Mowrer, Edgar Ansel, 320
Mulholland, Andrew, 40

Nagy, Ferenc, 146
Nagy, Imre, 80-99, 106, 108, 109, 127, 146, 175, 189
November 1, 1956 message to U.N., quoted, 83
November 2, 1956 message to U.N., quoted 84, 89-90
Narayanan, T. G., 162, 176

National Education Association, 257
NATO, 74, 245
New Bedford Standard Times, 256
New Republic, 318
New York Herald Tribune, 45, 216
New York Times, The, 28, 89-90, 191, 216
New Yorker, 318
Newsweek (magazine), 8, 20
Nuñez-Portuondo, Emilio, 85

Palestine Conciliation Commission, 186, 249
Panuch, Joseph, 20, 218, 223-227
Pasztor, Thomas, 135
Petrov, Viktor Ivanovich, 233
Pettigru, James Lewis, 322
Philadelphia Lincoln-Civil War Society, 322
Political and Security Council Affairs, 119
Politiken, 308-309
Poullain, 144
Pound, Roscoe, 257
Pratt, James, 197
Pressman, Gabe, 32
Protitch, Dragoslav, 90, 119, 142, 176, 197-198, 204

Report of the Special Committee on Hungary, 81-82
adoption of, by the U.N., 195
drafting of, 140-172

Representatives of the Hungarians in Exile, 126
Reuter, Richard, 239, 262-267
Revolutionary Council, 109
Robertson, J. A. C., 185, 204-206, 215
Rodriguez Fabregat, Enrique, 123
Roosevelt, James, 257
Russia,
  negotiations with Hungary, 111-112
  policies towards Hungarian Revolt, 85
  troops enter Hungary (1956), 80, 81, 82, 83
  vetoes American proposal for Council censure of military attack on Hungary, 93

Sacco-Vanzetti Case, 319
Saturday Evening Post (magazine), 15-16
Schager, John, J., 45
Schreiber, Marc, 123, 133, 136
Senate, U.S., 10
Senate Sub-Committee on Internal Security, 57
Serov, 189
Seynes, Philippe de, 118, 215, 221
Shann, Keith C. O., 122, 136, 142, 144, 147, 150, 153-157, 161, 177, 180, 199, 212
Shapovalov, Rostislav E., 234
Sik, Endre, 95

Simon, Manfred, 225
Sixteen points of Hungarian students, 101-102
Slim, Mongi, 123
Smallholders Party, 107
Sobolev, Arkady A., 90, 91, 93
Soletsky, Doctor, 48
Spies in U.N., list, 233-235
Stalin, Joseph, 80
Stavropoulos, 176, 221
State Department, 246
State Security Police, Hungary, 80, 81
Strauss, Lawrence, 50
Subcommittee on Internal Security, 244
Szabo, Janos, 79, 84, 90, 91, 96
Szabo, Karoly, 197
Szabo, Miklos, 219
Szabo, Thomas, 88, 91, 95
Sze, Dr., 56, 203
Szentadorjany, Doctor, 78

Telegram sent to prospective witnesses, 284
Tildy, Zoltan, 107, 188
Tilghman, John, 32
Tisler, Frantisek, 235

U.N. Charter, quoted, 99
U.N. Joint Appeals Board and Administrative Tribunal, 229-230
U.N. Joint Disciplinary Committee, 223, 225, 229
U.N. Special Committee on Hungary, 59, 100, 114,

118-172, 189, 273
dissension in, 119, 120-122,
  130, 134-136, 142-167
duties of the Deputy Secretary, 282
European hearings, 132-139
members, list, 122-123
security problems of, 119-
  121, 136, 175
U.S.A. (Widener), 56, 58-62
U.S. Mission to the U.N., 248

Varga, Bela, 76-79, 134
Varga, Laszlo, 76-79, 95, 96

Varnai, Zseni, poem, quoted,
  103-104
Vaughan, David, 14
Vitetti, Leonardo, 87

Wadsworth, James, 230
Walker, Ronald, 92
Warsaw Treaty, 83, 89
West, Rebecca, 317
Wetzlar, William, 53-54, 271
Widener, Alice, 56, 58-62, 174,
  212-213
Willkie, Wendell, 319
Winther, Christian, 180, 204

118-124, 180-193
discussion of, 170-174, 191,
190-192, 196 (n 2f)
duties of the Deputy Secretary, 28
European ministers, 197-199
members, the meeting,
security problems of, 190-
191, 194-195
U.N.A. (Widener), 305-306
U.S. Mission to the U.N., 295

Verga, ..., 290, 291
Verge, Leslie, 73, 85, 86

Varani, Zanni, poem, quoted,
103-104
Vaughan, David, 14
Vitru, Leonardo, 87

Wadsworth, James, 220
Walter, Ronald, 92
Wanning, Terry, 91-92
West, Rebecca, 97
Weston, William, 52-54, 277
Wharton, Allen, 50, 52-55, 174,
272-273
Willkie, Wendell, 319
Wisdom, Christian, 180, 303

40992